T0097773

From the
Jewish Heartland

From the Jewish Heartland

Two Centuries of Midwest Foodways

ELLEN F. STEINBERG

JACK H. PROST

UNIVERSITY OF
ILLINOIS PRESS
Urbana, Chicago,
and Springfield

Library of Congress Cataloging-in-Publication Data
Steinberg, Ellen FitzSimmons, 1948–
From the Jewish heartland : two centuries of Midwest foodways /
Ellen F. Steinberg, Jack H. Prost.
p.   cm. — (Heartland foodways)
Includes bibliographical references and index.
ISBN 978-0-252-03620-0 (cloth : alk. paper)
1. Jewish cooking.
2. Jews—Food—Middle West.
3. Jews—Middle West—Social life and customs.
I. Prost, Jack. II. Title.
TX724.S735   2011
641.5'676—dc22   2011008193

To
all the Großmutters,
Bubbes,
and Nonas
who took the time to pass along
their traditions

Contents

Acknowledgments

When we began this project, we never expected to meet so many people who were so willing to help us gather the data we needed. They invited us into their homes, businesses, and archives; they freely shared stories and treasured recipes. Our lives, and this book, have certainly been greatly enriched because of them.

We are hugely indebted to our longtime friend Jane Polan for sending us a copy of the film, *Gefilte Fish*, which helped us understand how this quintessential Jewish dish has been prepared through three generations of one family. Diane Everman, archivist of the St. Louis Jewish Archives, enthusiastically helped us identify the author of one of our manuscript cookbooks, Ruth Ginsburg Dunie. She also went beyond every reasonable expectation to secure corroborating materials; we truly appreciate those efforts. Heartfelt thanks also go to Carol Christian, Ruth's granddaughter, without whom we never would have "known" Ruth, a woman whose recipes form such a huge part of this book.

Thanks are also due to Susan Hoffman, archivist of the Upper Midwest Jewish Archives, for allowing us to rummage through the rich data sets housed in Minneapolis and for facilitating contact with Linda Schloff, director of the Jewish Historical Society of the Upper Midwest, Eltheldoris Grais, and Herbert Schechter. Linda pulled boxes of material germane to our research, thereby saving us untold hours of work. Etheldoris, probably one of the most charming women we have ever met, spent hour upon hour talking about her life in the Iron Range and her culinary expeditions around the world, and sharing her special recipes with us. We cannot adequately express our appreciation of and to this marvelous woman. Thanks are also due to Herbert Schechter, who shared such vivid stories about his grandmother, Esther, that we felt as if we had known her personally, and wished we had.

Bakeries and delicatessens are so central to Jewish foodways in the Midwest, it is hard to imagine life before them, or without them, yet finding owner-operated ones can be challenging. Many thanks, therefore, are owed to Brian Miller of Jake's Deli in Milwaukee, Wisconsin, and to Bette and Judy Dworkin of Kaufman's Bakery and Delicatessen in Skokie, Illinois, for still "being there." Brian enthusiastically provided us what he calls a "360 degree experience": hand-carved corned beef, pastrami and *matzo*-ball soup served up in a real 1950s atmosphere, while Judy and Bette eagerly shared information about their business history and recipes, along with family stories, as we munched our way through fabulous samples of their specialties. Ronnie and Elaine Pratzel of St. Louis are also owed sincere thanks for carving out time from running their busy bakery business to relate the history of the St. Louis Jewish community, of Pratzel's Bakery, and of their famous *Tzizel* cornmeal-covered bread and bagels, which we devoured with great gusto.

Thanks are due, also, to Marc Schulman, president of Eli's Cheesecake Company, and to Debbie Littmann Marchok, vice president of Marketing for that firm, for archival photos of the founder, Eli Schulman, and for providing us with his famous Chopped Liver recipe, along with ones that are "almost-but-not-quite" the ones for Eli's famous cheesecakes, plus permission to publish them; to Stacey Schwartz of "Cooking for Fun" who spoke with us at length about why and how she conducts culinary classes for children; and to Aharon Morgan of the Good Morgan Fish Market, who spent quite a while discussing the "trends" he sees in Jewish foodways, and for teaching us how to recognize really fresh fish.

One reads so many admonitions these days cautioning people to be wary of "unsolicited" Internet contacts. We are very happy that Joseph Israel decided to ignore that advice and respond to our e-mailed pleas for assistance in finding a Sephardic Jew who would be willing to talk "food." He and his wife, Matilde Cohen Israel, corresponded with us at length about the Sephardim, in general, as well as about traditional recipes that they have adapted using locally available and Midwestern-grown ingredients. When we finally met, it was as if we were old friends. Thanks are also due to Simone Munson at the Wisconsin State Historical Society for pulling material we needed for this project, then having it shipped from Milwaukee to Madison so we could study it all in one place; to Aimee Ergas, director of the Jewish Historical Society of Michigan, for permission to reproduce Annabel Cohen's tasty recipe for *Borekas*; and to John Monaghan, head of the Department of Anthropology, University of Illinois at Chicago, for his unswerving support of our research.

From the
Jewish Heartland

Introduction

There was no "Midwest" until the 1900s. Until then that large, open stretch between the continent's coasts, the "inter-ocean," if you will, was simply "out West" on the "fringes of the prairies." It was "the Heartland"—except nobody called it that yet, much less the folk who wandered through en route to somewhere else. However, those who settled along its plentiful waterways, around its numerous freshwater lakes, amidst the rich, fertile farmlands, in its nascent towns, or in burgeoning urban centers during the nineteenth century mostly called it "home."

Ultimately, this region became, and continues to be, the nation's grain belt; the country's breadbasket; birthplace of the most "American" of Americans. Here, "comfort foods" reflect not only the area's diverse heritages, but also incorporate regional products from the states that make up the Midwest's core: Illinois, Indiana, Iowa, Michigan, Minnesota, Missouri, Ohio, and Wisconsin.

Here one finds an amalgam of ethnicities and creeds, each of which has contributed to the cultural and culinary flavor that is Middle America. When asked, Midwesterners often identify themselves by both ethnic and religious descent—but not always. Walter Ehrlich, author of *Zion in the Valley*, explains the single exception:

> When they came to America, then, [the] Jews brought [their] multifaceted heritage with them—just as all other immigrants brought *their* heritages with them. But those other heritages which they were justly proud of and whose cultures they retained within the parameters of their new American way of life—were fundamentally *nationality*-based, whether Italian or Polish or Norwegian or German. Even German-Jews maintained their *German* cultural ties long after coming to America. For most Jews who came from eastern Europe,

however, no such national ties existed. They had never been considered national citizens as Jews in Western Europe had been. . . . [Eastern European] Jews had been viewed as outsiders, virtual aliens, and not as "Russians" or "Poles" or "Austrians." Their *nationality*, according to many official records, was *Jew* or *Hebrew*. . . . The heritage brought to America by eastern European Jews was, accordingly, a cultural heritage tied singularly to their *religion*, not to a nationality.[1]

If Ehrlich is correct, part of this cultural heritage included what many today define as "Jewish food." Yes, the dishes these immigrants from Eastern Europe prepared and ate were the ones that bound them to their faith, enforcing and strengthening their relationship with the Almighty and each other, and were an expression of *Volksgeist* (group spirit). Indeed, their foodways were tied up with traditions, anchored to a ritual calendar, and governed by rules and regulations.[2] However, as we will show, their foodstuffs comprise only one part of the rich and varied cuisine that can rightfully be called "Jewish."

Recipes for traditional Jewish dishes were oftentimes carried to the United States embedded only in women's memories, inscribed in their work-worn hands, or, less frequently, in treasured, well-thumbed cookbooks. But after these immigrants arrived in America, their recipes did not necessarily remain the same as they had been in the Old Country. The foods were "tastes of home," yes, but ones that changed and evolved in response to a variety of factors, and continue to do so down the generations. In fact, although they maintained their "Jewishness," they often developed a distinctive Midwestern flavor.

Where but here would you find so many innovative "Jewish" taste treats whose ingredients include regional crops and products? We count *Tzizel* bagels and rye breads coated in Midwest cornmeal; *baklava* studded with locally grown cranberries; dark Pumpernickel bread sprinkled with almonds and crunchy Iowa sunflower seeds; tangy catsup concocted from Michigan's wild sour grapes; Sephardic *borekas* (turnovers) made with that state's sweet cherries; rich Chicago cheesecakes; native huckleberry pie from St. Paul, Minnesota; and savory *gefilte* fish from Minnesota northern pike, all mentioned in this book, among those incomparable gustatory delights. The reader can also sample some of those flavors, by cooking the reworked recipes found in the appendix.

Too, we track geographically based culinary recipes and changes made to them through time by presenting and analyzing ones from Midwestern Jewish sources, both kosher and non-kosher. We discovered some of these recipes in anonymous Midwestern Jewish homemakers' handwritten manuscripts, scribbled in the backs of Jewish commercial or fundraising cookbooks, or published in journals and newspaper columns. We also gathered a number of them during interviews focused on orally transmitted legacy recipes, and during discussions with Jewish bakers and delicatessen owners. And, finally, a few were given to us by people who had inherited them from their grandmothers and mothers.

One large group of recipes had been written into a composition notebook by a woman we initially called "Mrs. L. F. D." from our reading of the partial label on its cover. We purchased this collection on the Internet, knowing nothing about the author or time period covered by the recipes. The book was in tatters, but the recipes were unmistakably "Jewish." Based on a couple of recipes, we figured the cookbook dated from around the 1910s or so. We despaired of ever finding the author, though. How do you search for a woman whose last name is unknown? With great good fortune, coupled with hours spent poring through archival, census, immigration, birth, death, and cemetery records, we managed to identify her as Ruth Ginsburg Dunie, a 1903 Lithuanian immigrant to the United States, who lived most of her life in St. Louis, Missouri. The story of who she was and how we located her appears in chapter 3 of this book.

The majority of the handwritten recipes we collected were German-Jewish "by descent," although Ruth Dunie's were a conglomerate. They were "German," Eastern European, and, perhaps even Sephardic (certainly Italian or Greek). They, therefore, reflected both her Lithuanian birthplace and the cosmopolitan environment in which she lived. The orally transmitted recipes we amassed were primarily Eastern European in origin. When we explored the reasons behind this, more than one person informed us that Eastern European "*Bubbes* [Yiddish term for grandmothers] never wrote anything down. You had to stand there and take dictation and watch." However, to our surprise, in addition to Ruth's, we did discover a group of those kinds of manuscript recipes in the Upper Midwest Jewish Archives. These were compiled at some point, most likely during the 1960s, by Esther Schechter, an Eastern European Jewess, apparently at the behest of one of her daughters. Initially, we thought the recipes were in Yiddish. However, as it turned out, they were not really written in that language, but in phonetically spelled English using Yiddish letters.[3]

We labeled our handwritten cookbooks as "Jewish" when they included recipes calling for that quintessential Jewish food, *matzo*, the unleavened bread used during *Pesach* (Passover), or when they designated recipes for specific Jewish holidays. We considered the recipes scrawled in the back of commercial cookbooks as having "Jewish authorship-origins" if those books had been written by Jewish authors, *and* also had checkmarks or notations next to Jewish holiday and/or High Holy Day recipes, or when they were produced by identifiably Jewish institutions, such as temple sisterhoods. Admittedly, this is not a foolproof system, but it was the best method we could devise.

We are aware of only one instance in which we were misled. We purchased a copy of *The Sentinel Jewish Cook Book* (1936) from a used bookshop. Someone had neatly written "Rabbi John Shambarger, Redkey, Indiana, 1937" on the first free end page. From this, we surmised that Rabbi Shambarger was most likely the book's original owner. A fancy, gold-printed label for "Shambarger's: Catering To Your Epicurean Tastes, Muncie, Indiana" affixed beneath the inscription seemed to reinforce this supposition. We also assumed that the dog-eared pages of *The Sentinel* identified some of the recipes, like the almond dumplings called *Mandel Kloese*, a *Macedoine* Salad of Fresh Vegetables, Chicken Fricassee, and Plum *Küchen* (cake), which this rabbi had used when he catered Jewish events.

However, a bit of sleuthing disavowed us of these notions. It appears from Mr. Shambarger's October 20, 1984 obituary in *The Muncie* (Indiana) *Star* that he was neither Jewish nor a rabbi. Further, we could find nothing in newspaper advertisements for his catering service to suggest it ever served the Jewish community. Too, although he did own and operate a restaurant in Redkey, a town not far from Muncie, we found no evidence in the book containing his renowned dishes, *The Mad Chef of Red Key: A Stirring Experience* (1988), that he ever served any of the foodstuffs he had tagged in 1937 at his restaurant. Obviously, we have no way to ascertain whether he cooked any of *The Sentinel*'s recipes at home.

In the pages that follow, we also document the availability of fruits, vegetables, and other comestibles throughout the Midwest that impacted how and what Jews cooked. We consider, too, the effect of improved preservation and transportation on rural and urban Jewish foodways, as reported in contemporary newspapers, magazines, and published accounts. Then, we examine the impact on Jewish foodways—the cultural, social, and economic practices relating to the production and consumption of food—of large-scale immigration, relocation, and Americanization efforts during the nineteenth and early twentieth centuries, paying special attention to the attempts of social and culinary reformers to modify traditional Jewish food preparation and ingredients. In sum, we explore the state, shape, change, and evolution of Midwestern Jewish cuisine through time. Throughout the book, we reproduce sample recipes from our manuscript collection. The transcriptions retain the formatting of the originals; we present them as written—omissions, misspellings, and all. We use these as "ethnographic data," indicative of culinary and cultural habits, modified by local circumstances and economic situations. Hence, most of the recipes are contained "in-text." Only the ones we "taste-tested" and reworked for the modern cook appear in the appendix.

Most of the ingredients listed in the recipes by initials are easy to figure out. "B. P." stands for "Baking Powder," and "Y. P." for "Yeast Powder." Only a single ingredient designation was truly puzzling. Some of Ruth Dunie's recipes called for "I Potato," but did that stand for "Idaho," and, if so, what variety? Luckily, in one recipe, she spelled out "Irish Potato," so we concluded that her other shorthand notations of "I Potato" also referred to that creamy-white tuber. Ditto marks, frequently used by our cookbook authors, reference the measurements or word in the line above. Where we reproduce recipes given to us by people in written form, we have retained their formatting, along with any marginalia and side comments. We believe this presentation provides insight into how people think about and discuss the foods they make.

Further, Hebrew and Yiddish words are often transliterated into English with different spellings. In quoted passages, we have retained the original spellings out of consideration for the historical record, even when they differ from those used in the body of this work. We also kept the spellings and punctuation in the news articles and books we quoted to maintain their historical accuracy.

1

The Early Jewish Presence in the Middle West

A simple marker, erected by the Jewish Historical Society of Michigan, in Michilimackinac State Park, Mackinaw City, commemorates the first Jewish settler in that state: a German-Jew from Berlin named Ezekiel Solomon who landed at the northern tip of the Lower Peninsula in 1761.[1] The plaque tells little about Solomon except that he survived an Ojibwa massacre at Fort Michilimackinac in 1763, was a fur trader who ran a general store provisioning the British army, and was one of the founders of Canada's first (Sephardic rite) synagogue, Montreal's Shearith Israel.

Information about Solomon is somewhat scanty. It seems he arrived at Fort Michilimackinac via Detroit, through the Straits of Mackinac, the narrow stretch of water connecting Lake Huron to Lake Michigan and separating Michigan's Upper and Lower Peninsulas. Before the advent of railroads, that waterway served as one of the paths into the Midwest and Great Plains that immigrants followed.

What data are available reveal that he operated the Solomon-Levy Trading House at Fort Michilimackinac during the time it was a British military post. Most likely he exchanged guns, powder, and bullets for fur pelts.

The fort actually resembled a small community more than a military installation. Solomon even built a log house within the confines of the tall stockade fence, which, as it turned out, afforded scant protection during an Indian raid in 1763. He was captured by the Ojibwas, traded to the Ottawas, and then hauled up to Montreal, where he was finally ransomed.[2] However, this traumatic experience did not convince Solomon to take up a safer occupation. In 1779, he and a group of Montreal businessmen, possibly J. Levy, Richard McCarty, and one Mr. Grant, opened a general store at the same fort.[3] One report states there is reason to believe that Solomon also traveled down through Lake Michigan, then along the Illinois River as far south as Cahokia, Illinois, to trade.[4]

Barred since 1763 by Spanish decree from entering or settling in the Louisiana Territory, Jewish traders set up shop on the other side of the Mississippi in the boom-town of Cahokia. Without a doubt, Solomon would have conducted business with one of its most prominent, and infamous, citizens, Isaac Levy. Probably no relation to Solomon's business partner in Canada, Isaac had started out in Virginia, moved to Indiana, then down to Illinois. He became the town doctor, shopkeeper, money-lender, Indian trader, liquor dealer, and army supplier, rolled into one.

When Solomon lived in the territory that eventually became part of the state of Michigan, great glades of majestic hemlocks and pine stands fringed the territory on either side of the narrows. The clear lake waters abounded with fish. Its shoreline teemed with raucous loons, large Canada geese, hundreds of ducks, muskrats, and beavers. Woodpeckers, wild turkeys, white-tailed deer, black bear, raccoons, and porcupines made their homes in the mixed-wood forests. The French, and later, British, soldiers and traders kept a goodly supply of domesticated chickens, cattle, and pigs for food. They constructed outdoor brick and clay ovens for baking bread and other cooking chores. They also dug deep root cellars for provisions, such as corn, beans, squash, meats, and poultry. Wild cherries, grapes, and acorns were there for the harvesting. Solomon would have had little trouble, then, finding something to eat. Certainly his diet would have included fresh-caught lake perch, salmon, trout, and whitefish.[5] He might also have made stews from beans, wild onions, and, perhaps even, beef, kept warm in the dying embers of a brick oven. Occasionally, he may even have whipped up a nutritious and filling egg custard, a favorite German dessert.

History says that Solomon divided his time between the fort, even after its relocation to Mackinac Island in 1781, and Montreal, Canada, where his Catholic wife and children lived. Solomon, one of the first non-French fur traders to penetrate the Upper Great Lakes region, died in 1808 or 1809.

Across the Mississippi River from Cahokia, in a bustling village of 1,500 people called Saint Louis, Joseph Philipson, a German-Jew from Pennsylvania, saw a business opportunity in the newly acquired Louisiana Territory. Explorers, such as William Clark and Meriwether Lewis, travelers, and settlers were arriving in ever increasing numbers via land and river routes. So, in 1807, Philipson opened a general store, selling them provisions such as coffee, almonds, and butter. By 1808, he was advertising in the *Missouri Gazette*: "seasonal supply of dry goods, a general assortment of groceries, among which are . . . fresh teas, coffee, chocolate and sugar, shad, mackeral."[6]

At first, his two brothers, Simon and Jacob, stayed in Philadelphia. However, they visited frequently, probably carting along supplies for Joseph's store. Eventually, though, Jacob also moved to Missouri. He opened his own business, trading manufactured goods for fur pelts and lead ore coming out of the Missouri Territory from a combination mercantile store–residence in nearby Sainte Genevieve. The two brothers partnered in the St. Louis Brewing Association, joining other local beer-makers, such as John Coons and Jacques St. Vrain, in what ultimately became one of St. Louis's largest industries.[7] Simon finally joined his brothers in 1821. He bought a farm, where he raised poultry and sold eggs.

The city of Dubuque, Iowa, sits on a large, flat plain adjacent to the mighty Mississippi River. Still a key spot for traffic along that waterway, Dubuque was founded in 1833, the same year that Alexander Levi, a French-born Jew of Sephardic origin, landed there. Levi had come upriver from New Orleans to make his fortune in what had been part of the Louisiana Purchase.

The lush land on both the Illinois and Iowa sides of the river boasted mighty forests, lakes, brooks, undulating hills, shallow dales, native prairies, and rich seams of lead, called "Galena." Levi, who later became involved in the ore business himself, first opened a grocery and clothing store to serve the miners. The canned goods, sugar, tea, coffee, and other supplies he sold would have arrived by river from New Orleans and St. Louis, or, less frequently, overland from states to the east. Perhaps, like shopkeeper George L. Ward of Alton, Illinois, he, too, traded some of his inventory for "country produce."[8]

In 1847, Levi returned to France, where he married a distant cousin, Minette Levi. They returned to Dubuque, where they eventually had five children. Minette would have brought her French-Jewish recipes with her. More than likely, she made good use of river-caught bass, trout, and buffalo fish, along with fowl, locally raised beef, corn, wheat, vegetables, and potatoes in her savory everyday and holiday cuisine. Undoubtedly, she whisked goose, duck, and chicken eggs into fluffy *omelettes*. As a Frenchwoman, she would also have seasoned her dishes with kitchen-garden herbs, garnished them with sautéed Iowa-grown mushrooms, and created rich Gallic sauces.

Although we have no hard data about whether the Levis kept kosher, Simon Glazer, in *The Jews in Iowa: A Complete History*, states that "[Minette] was as faithful a Jewess as [Alexander] was a faithful Jew." We do know, however, that they helped establish Dubuque's first Jewish congregation in 1863, and donated land to the city for use in perpetuity as a cemetery for those of the "Jewish persuasion."[9]

Soon after Levi arrived, German-Jewish peddlers began crisscrossing Iowa with backpacks and wagons stuffed with goods and notions—anything and everything people might need or want. According to the *Fort Madison Courier*, the first were Nathan Louis and Solomon Fine. When they saw spots they liked, they settled down and opened retail stores: one in Keokuck, and the other in McGregor.[10] Iowa's Jewish population had begun to grow.

By the 1840s, more and more settlers were forging farther westward and northward. Steamboats carried passengers from New Orleans to St. Louis, then from there, farther upriver, with increasing regularity. Two of the passengers who made the trip in 1845 from Prairie du Chien to La Crosse, Wisconsin, were John M. Levy and his wife, Fredericka Augusta, both German-Jews who had met and married in St. Louis.

John harbored a vision of lucrative fur trading with the Winnebago Indians. The Levys traveled with a dog, two cats, one horse, a cow, "a whole family of hogs," a "box of chickens," and their son, Willie.[11] Once settled on the fertile coulees along the tall bluffs overlooking the Mississippi River, they built a story-and-a-half log cabin. After they moved in, Fredericka planted her garden. In memoirs translated from German by her ten-year-old grandchild, she recollected, "We raised tomatoes, cucumbers, and onions." She picked wild strawberries, dried native plums and acorns, and, in one instance, served potatoes and pork to the Indians, along with "a great dish-pan full of flour." One time even, the family feasted after hunters brought back a bag of what were probably either passenger pigeons or prairie chickens.[12]

The Levys lost their most lucrative trading partners a scant three years later when the Indians were forcibly removed westward to Long Prairie (Minnesota). However, John continued to sell tobacco, tea, coffee, and whiskey to the lumbermen who rafted down from Black River, contracted to deliver mail to St. Paul, Minnesota, and eventually opened a hotel and a bank.[13] The Levys were soon joined by twenty-two other adventuresome German-Jews fleeing the failed revolution(s) of 1848. Some had traveled to La Crosse "by canal all the way. When the Alleghany Mountains were reached, the canal boats were hauled up over the mountain grade with ropes. The passengers and freight were not transferred, but hauled bodily up and over the grade."[14] These intrepid adventurers went on to establish the first Jewish Reform congregation in that nascent city.

In 1851, the lure of fur trade riches drew Joseph Ullmann, originally from Pfafstadt, Alsace, to St. Paul, in what was then the Minnesota Territory. He traveled upriver from St. Louis on a sternwheeler, the route his wife, Amelia, and their small son would repeat a year later. Amelia's journey was made in May, shortly after winter's icy grip had released the northern waters of the Mississippi River. It brought her to "the end of the world."[15]

The small settlement of 1,200 people rising from the Mississippi flats where Amelia disembarked may have seemed far from everything familiar to such an urbane German-Jewess, yet it was really just a short distance from bustling Fort Snelling. Located at the confluence of the Minnesota and Mississippi rivers, this installation received supplies of salt, corn meal, pork, flour, whiskey, beans, peas, vinegar, and candles sent from St. Louis under military escort by water and land conveyance. Beef, on the hoof or in barrels, regularly arrived from Prairie du Chien. Plentiful as those supplies were for the soldiers, apparently they were not distributed to nonmilitary personnel.

Writing forty years after her journey from the river's edge over a "rough, unpaved country road," Amelia recalled that the family's stay in St. Paul's best "frontier hotel" was miserable, primarily because of the food. "The bill of fare of the first day's meals was with little variations that of succeeding days; bacon, potatoes, biscuits, tea for breakfast and supper, soup and a pie made from dried fruits were the additions that distinguished dinner, the midday meal, from the other two. Fresh meat, fruit, vegitables were too great luxuries."[16] She claimed her son was ill most of those first months due to poor nutrition, since fruits and vegetables brought from St. Louis had spoiled by the time they reached Minnesota. Finally, wearied of "bacon, potatoes and tea," she arranged with the owner "of the only cow in town" for weekly deliveries of milk and butter. Once Joseph built a wooden plank kitchen area attached to his fur trading room, life took a new turn for Amelia. She became more content with local conditions.[17]

As vocal as she had been about bad hotel food, Amelia was strangely silent about what she cooked once the family had settled into its real home. She did mention one Mr. Coulter as "killing cattle and packing away the beef in salt and sawdust for consumption during the winter," and later preserving a "quantity of buffalo meat."[18] We can assume her family purchased some of those provisions to tide them over the winter months when ice clogged the Mississippi and even dogsleds had difficulty making it through snowdrifts with supplies. She also noted that steamboats came up the river carrying provisions for the winter, including milled flour from Prairie du Chien, "crackers from St. Louis, bags of potatoes from the south, and butter in earthenware jars from Ohio," and that they had goodly amounts of beer.[19] However, we do not know whether she learned to cook Minnesota wild rice, added locally grown wild huckleberries, currants, or cranberries to any of her traditional German dishes, or prepared fish dishes using the northern pike, sunfish, bluegill, and crappie, caught in the lakes and rivers around St. Paul, which were staples for other settlers.

During the next ten years, the family grew apace with Joseph's fur business. Ultimately, in 1866, in pursuit of better schooling for their children and to further Joseph's career, they moved to Chicago, but not before helping to establish Mount Zion Hebrew Association, Minnesota's first Jewish congregation.[20]

Jews found their way to Ohio around 1803, but their numbers remained small until after the Civil War. In the years following, it was here that more than a few Jews gravitated after leaving the East Coast. Many started as itinerant peddlers, but stayed to open retail shops in some of the state's towns and cities.

Cincinnati eventually became a favored destination for Jewish craftsmen and retailers.[21] English-born Joseph Jonas, the first Jew to settle in Cincinnati, found that its strategic location on the Ohio River afforded numerous local and long-distance commercial opportunities, especially since farmers regularly brought their crops in from the countryside to sell or to ship down to New Orleans. The Jewish merchants' customer bases, then, would have included the local populace—ironworkers, meatpackers, textile factory hands, and artisan woodworkers alike, as well as down-river markets. The city thrived, both as a destination and as a gateway to open western lands. And the Jewish community, which in 1822 had lacked even *matzo* (unleavened bread used during Passover celebrations), soon boasted Orthodox and Reform synagogues.[22]

Farther west, on the sandy shores of Lake Michigan, at the confluence of the Chicago River, lies the city of Chicago. The first Jew to arrive there in 1838 was also a peddler, one J. Gottlieb. He stayed only long enough to have his presence noted, then pushed on to California.[23] Other Jewish peddlers and businessmen soon followed, but with the intention of putting down roots. By 1845, there were enough Jewish men living in Chicago for a *minyan* (a quorum of at least ten adult Jewish men). Two years later, the Jewish community was financially strong enough and numerically large enough to consider forming a congregation to serve their religious needs. This congregation became Kehlilath Anshe Ma'ariv (Congregation of People of the West).

Another reason behind the formation of K. A. M., as it became popularly known, was food-related. In 1846, the Bavarian-born Kohn brothers, prosperous owners of a clothing store, welcomed their three brothers, sister, and mother, Dilah, to Chicago. Over the course of the next year, Dilah became frail and sickly, not because of the city's fetid air or from some unnamed, wasting illness, but because she was slowly starving; she refused to touch any non-kosher meat or poultry. Consequently, along with a rabbi to serve their newly established congregation, the men of K. A. M. also hired a *shochet* (ritual slaughterer) so Dilah could eat.[24]

Once Dilah's meat protein requirements were met, supplementing her diet would have been relatively easy, especially since a Jewish farmer reportedly came into the city on a regular basis to sell his homegrown vegetables.[25] Perhaps this farmer was Henry Meyer, who, around 1842 with the backing of the Jewish

Colonization Society, had purchased acreage in the Schaumburg area north-west of Chicago for a farming community.[26] The flat, open fields, surrounded by extensive wilderness, were immanently suitable for growing corn, wheat, potatoes, and other vegetables. Further, free-ranging geese, ducks, quail, prairie chickens, pheasants, rabbits, and deer would have been rich food resources for those Jews who did not keep kosher. Nevertheless, Schaumburg's few Jewish colonists soon left—some to farm their own land, others for the city. Meyer, however, stayed on, at least for a while, convinced that "Chicago opens a vista into a large commercial future, and the land around it, which is flowing with milk and honey, is particularly adapted for tillers of the soil."[27]

Solomon Schoffner ran a stagecoach stop in Reedsburg, Ohio, during the mid-1840s to serve those who chose a land route to the west. Yet the Schoffner family did not stay there very long. Instead, they migrated to Chicago, perhaps seeking greater economic opportunity and/or a more developed Jewish com-munity life. Once in the city, their son, Richard, forsook the family business along with the traditional spelling of his surname. He eventually partnered with cousins in founding Hart, Schaffner & Marx clothiers.[28]

In Warrenton, Indiana, a German-Jewish entrepreneur named Meier Heiman saw dollar signs in the operation of the Noon Day Stage Coach Stop and Trad-ing Post. He took over the business in 1852, then proceeded to expand. With the help of his brothers, Leon, Jacob, and J. L., he added a log section from which he sold groceries, goods, and other services. The new space housed both a tavern and a dance hall, too, while a separate barn was reserved for mule sales.[29]

Overland travel by stagecoach in those days was a tedious venture, and one more often than not fraught with dangers. It took weeks to complete the bone-shattering, occasionally harrowing, journey from New York to Cincin-nati, and months to make it to Chicago. Typically, travel took place during the late spring through the early fall months. However, unseasonal blizzards, bit-ing sleet storms, torrential rains, blistering temperatures, washed-out roads, horse or mule breakdowns, or wolf attacks could all delay westward progress. Stagecoach companies often contracted with local businessmen to provide these hardy travelers with food and overnight accommodations along their routes.

A correspondent for the *New York Tribune* wrote that, by 1865, along the outer edges of the Midwest and farther into the frontier regions all the way to the Pacific Ocean, overland stagecoach "[s]tations average about 10 miles apart. [Horses or mules] toil wearily along from 12 to 22 miles per day. . . . [E]very 24 hours you stop half an hour for a meal—often a culinary marvel—of good coffee, sweet milk, fresh butter and eggs, caned fruits, ham and eggs."[30]

One can assume that earlier in time, similar way-stations dotted the landscape from the East Coast to the Middle West.

Stagecoach arrival times were often erratic, making it difficult for station cooks to keep food hot. Despite the uncertainties, it seems that filling dishes of beans, potatoes, soups, and bread frequently greeted weary travelers at whatever time they appeared. Sometimes, travelers were responsible for purchasing their own viands. Patrons might spend between a quarter and a half-dollar for a meal consisting of locally procured "meat and game entrees, seasonal vegetables, salads, and delicious desserts," or between six and ten cents for a piece of corned beef.[31]

The available stagecoach food reports make it sound as if travelers were served rich, nourishing foods whenever and wherever they stopped. It might be, though, that the information is skewed since journeys only took place during the best months of the year—periods when local produce would more than likely be available, when poultry was laying, and when cows were giving milk. Other times, however, because of poor local crop or hunting conditions, little was to be had.

Stouthearted folk who elected to travel westward in caravans had to wait until a sufficient number of wagons could be assembled before they could roll. Typically, that number was one hundred. In the spring of 1854, Fanny and Julius Brooks, German-Jews from Frankenstein, crammed themselves into a covered wagon along with eight other people. Their route to California from New York took them through the Midwest, with a layover in Galena, Illinois, fifteen miles east of Dubuque. At that time, Galena, located on the banks of the broad Fevre River that flowed into the Mississippi, was the busiest port between St. Paul and St. Louis and a common "pass-through" spot for those forging even farther westward.

Each of the ten California-bound travelers was allotted one hundred pounds of luggage, including bedding and clothes, to be stowed in the wagon bed. Every adult was supplied with 100 pounds of flour, 50 pounds each of sugar and bacon, 30 pounds of beans, 20 pounds each of dried apples and peaches, 5 pounds of tea, 1 gallon of vinegar, 10 bars of soap, and 25 pounds of salt.[32] Cattle typically accompanied these wagon trains, so along with the above supplies, milk from the cows, small game and bison killed on the prairies, and wild fruits picked en route, many of the migrants probably ate better food, and more of it, than they had in their native lands or back East. At the very least, if they did not run into trouble during the trek, the women could cook their native dishes within the limits of the foodstuffs they had been allotted. They undoubtedly also had time to watch while others in the caravan fixed their meals, and, perhaps, even to sample the results.

According to the Brooks's daughter, Eveline Auerbach, by journey's end, following a sojourn in Galena lasting until June 1855, Fanny had formed an opinion of Americans and their culinary skills. "The Yankees were lovely people but very wasteful and poor cooks. Their main forte was bread, pies and hotcakes, ham or bacon and eggs. Their vegetables were cooked without taste and their meats either done to death or raw."[33]

Like Fanny and Julius, Solomon Nunes Carvalho, a South Carolinian of Sephardic descent, an observant Orthodox Jew, and a member of one of the oldest Jewish families in the United States, only passed through the Midwest. He trekked westward and southward from New York to Missouri, through Kansas, on to Utah, and, finally to California, as a member of Colonel John Charles Frémont's expedition to find the best overland railroad route to connect St. Louis with the Pacific coast. His story reveals the physical, mental, and emotional ordeals often faced by early travelers, both Gentile and Jewish.

An artist and photographer, Carvalho started out in September 1853. In preparation for the trip, he had carefully packed "daguerreotype apparatus, painting materials, and half a dozen cases of Alden's preserved coffee, eggs, cocoa, cream, and milk, which [Alden] sent out for the purpose of testing their qualities. There was in them sufficient nourishment to have sustained twenty men for a month."[34]

The Illinois River was too low to navigate, so Carvalho took the stage to Alton, Illinois. From there, although burdened by heavy baggage, the rest of his trip south to St. Louis took only a few hours. The expedition's journey across the treeless prairies began the same day he arrived in River City. Frémont's route took them to the Shawnee Methodist Mission, then up the Kansas River as far as the Pottawatomie Baptist Mission. The men camped near the settlement, where "two or three stores with no assortment of goods, and about thirty shanties [made] up the town," until the end of September. During that layover, Carvalho wrote, "I went to every house in the place for a breakfast, but could not get anything to eat except some Boston crackers, ten pounds of which (the whole supply in the town) I bought."[35]

The men ran into trouble before long. Colonel Frémont became so ill he returned to St. Louis. Temporarily without its leader, the expedition nonetheless pushed onward, slowly making its way across open land until Frémont rejoined them. They stopped briefly at Fort Riley, then moved into buffalo country at the Smokey Hill River.

The weather turned freezing. The men still forged ahead, failing to kill any buffalo; failing to find much small game; failing to locate any natives with whom to trade. Eventually, though, in the Green River Valley at the mouth of the San Rafael River, the explorers procured a small supply of parched and toasted grass seed from Indian women. Carvalho commented that they tasted like roasted peanuts. His purchased quart amounted to three days' rations.

Once the expedition ran out of seeds, Carvalho's food-related problems became truly acute. He noted that "a large porcupine was killed and brought into camp to-day by our Delawares [the expedition's Indian scouts and guides], who placed it on a large fire burning off its quills, leaving a thick hard skin, very like that of a pig. The meat was white, but very fat, it looked very much like pork. My stomach revolted at it, and I sat hungry around our mess, looking at my comrades enjoying it."[36] Away from the Indian villages and any military garrison, and totally out of foodstuffs, the expedition was reduced to eating its horses and mules. Carvalho agonized, "I then partook of the strange and forbidden food with much hesitation, and only in small quantities. . . . [I]t serves to sustain life. . . . [W]e were, from our own imprudence, entirely without food, a Delaware killed a cayotte, brought it into camp, and divided it equally between our messes—my share remained untouched. I had fasted 24 hours, and preferred to remain as many hours longer rather than partake of it. The habits of the horse and mule are clean; their food consists of grass and grain; but I was satisfied that my body could receive no benefit from eating the flesh of an animal that lived on carrion." Rather smugly, he added, "Those who did partake of it were all taken with cramps and vomiting."[37]

Unbeknownst to anyone, however, Carvalho had secreted away a small store of supplies, which he brought out only when life looked particularly dire. He wrote that although his six dozen tins of Alden's foods had been "wantonly destroyed during our six weeks camp on Salt Creek . . . I had reserved with religious care, two boxes containing one pound each, of Alden's preserved eggs and milk.—(The yolks of the eggs were beaten to a thick paste with a pound of loaf sugar, the milk was also prepared with powdered sugar, and hermetically sealed in tin cans.) . . . A paper of arrow root . . . I had also reserved. These three comestibles, boiled in six gallons of water, made as fine a blanc mange as ever was *mangéd* on Mount Blanc. . . . Our dinner in honor of 'New Year's Day,' consisted, besides our usual 'horse soup,' of a delicious dish of horse steaks, fried in the remnants of our 'tallow candles.'"[38]

During the 1800s and even as late as the 1910s, Jews who kept kosher often had a difficult time during their overland journeys to or through the Midwest.[39]

They either had to carry food with them, like Carvalho, hoping their supplies would last until they reached their journeys' ends; subsist on purchased or bartered eggs, milk, nuts, and/or fruits, if they could find them; or eat at "kosher" hotels or boarding houses of which there were woefully few. In the latter case, there was another not-so-insignificant issue involved—the cost. An 1879 letter to the editor of the *Chicago Daily Tribune* suggested that Jews traveling to and through Chicago were being excluded from Gentile-run boarding houses and hotels, not because of prejudice, but because it was difficult and expensive to feed those who required "kosher" food.[40]

2

Midwest City Life

The Sephardim and the German-Jews

Sephardic Jews were never numerous in the United States, although they were the first to relocate to North America during the seventeenth century. Even after a larger second wave in the 1900s brought Sephardim to American shores as refugees from savage pogroms and bloody revolutions, their numbers remained few; in fact, fewer than 70,000 emigrated.

Their history reflects the wide sweep of Sephardic settlement—from Spain and Portugal, to Egypt, Turkey, Greece, Tunisia, Yemen, Yugoslavia, Lebanon, Italy, India, Iraq, Iran, Israel, Syria, South America, the Caribbean, and beyond. Yet, a mere scattering of them found their way to the Midwest, and then mostly to the larger cities, such as Indianapolis, Detroit, Chicago, and, more recently, Minneapolis-St. Paul.

Wherever the Sephardi settled in the Heartland, the local press often noted, and continues to remark upon, their presence and customs, because they were distinct enough from the more familiar Ashkenazi to warrant comment. They were multinational and multilingual by culture and practice. Instead of speaking German or Yiddish, as did most of the Ashkenazi of Europe, many Sephardic Jews spoke, wrote, and prayed in Ladino. This language evolved from medieval Castilian Spanish and Hebrew, with additional borrowed words from Turkish, Arabic, Greek, and French. Other Sephardi, however, spoke different languages, such as Neo-Aramaic, as did the Kurdish Jews, or Judeo-Arabic, as did the Syrian Jews. Sadly, these ancient languages, along with Yiddish, as means of everyday communication rather than solely for ritual purposes, seem to be dying out with the passing of the older generations.

In 1899, the *Milwaukee Sentinel*, quoting *Popular Science Monthly*, defined the difference between the two major Jewish groups for the general public, under the category of "News." It reported:

> Tradition has long divided the Jewish people into two distinct branches: the Sephardim, or southern, and the Ashkenazim or North European. . . . The Sephardim are mainly the remnants of the former Spanish and Portuguese Jews ousted from their homelands [in 1492]. They constitute in their own eyes an aristocracy of the nation. They are found primarily to-day in Africa; in the Balkan states, where they are known as Spagnuoli; less purely in France and Italy. A small colony in London and Amsterdam still holds itself aloof from all communication and intercourse with its brethren. . . . The Ashkenazim branch is numerically far more important, for the German, Russian, and Polish Jews comprise over nine-tenths of the people.[1]

The press may have understood some of the differences between the two groups, but, at the core, the Ashkenazi initially had difficulty accepting the exotic Sephardi as "Jews." Many kept to themselves and had different *minhags* (traditions). Gloria Asher, perhaps tongue-in-cheek, summed up the dissimilarities in terms of language and food: "People who spoke something like Spanish instead of Yiddish and ate grape leaves instead of gefilte fish (poached fish balls) were simply not Jews!"[2]

True, the Sephardic Jews spoke differently, and their cuisines reflected foodstuffs and recipes adopted and adapted from their non-Jewish neighbors, but the differences are much deeper and more complex than Asher claims. Sephardic interpretations of *halakhah* (Jewish Law), dating to the sixteenth century, are distinct from those of the Ashkenazic. The major difference relates to the holiday of Passover that celebrates the Israelites' liberation from Egyptian slavery. During the eight days of Passover, no Jew is supposed to consume *hametz* (leavened) grain products, defined as corn, wheat, oats, barley, rye, millet, and spelt that have come into contact with moisture for more than eighteen minutes or that have been made with yeast. A number of the more orthodox Ashkenazi Jews also place beans, rice, lentils, peas, peanuts, garlic, and mustard, along with edible seeds, on the proscribed list.

While also abstaining from leavened breads, Sephardim do not include rice-based cakes, fritters, or other baked goods in the category of proscribed *hametz* because the main component cannot rise even with the addition of yeast. It is possible that this diet developed because the lands in which they initially lived could not support potato or root crops, and were best suited to rice cultivation. Sephardic rules also permit the consumption of legumes during this holiday. As a case in point, delicacies, such as *Frittada de Pressa* (fried leek pancakes) and nutty-flavored *Sodra/Sorda* (fava bean soup), are consumed with gusto at Sephardic ritual Passover meals.

Another difference between Sephardic and Ashkenazic cuisines can be found in the ingredients and preparation of *haroset/charoset* (a Passover dish symbolizing the mortar with which the Jews bonded bricks during their Egyptian captivity). The basic Sephardic version is often cooked down to almost a jamlike consistency. Whether cooked or not, Sephardic *haroset* is a combination of chopped dried fruits like dates or figs, nuts, and quince, mixed together with liquids other than, but also including, kosher grape or raisin wine. Like most holiday dishes, the Sephardic version varies from community to community in small details, such as the types of fruits, nuts, and spices used. In contrast, the Eastern European *haroset* is normally made from crisp diced apples, crunchy walnuts, and freshly ground cinnamon, mixed with sweet kosher wine. Then, too, a typical Sephardic *Sabato* (Sabbath) dinner might be built around salads, stuffed grape leaves, and couscous (a pellet-size product made from semolina flour), with fresh fruit for dessert, while that of the Ashkenazi might include pot roast or chicken, along with some kind of potato accompaniment.

Overall, Sephardic foods can be characterized as spicy and lively, citrusy yet honey-sweet, diverse, and sophisticated. Gail Rosenblum of the Minneapolis-St. Paul, Minnesota *Star Tribune* characterizes them as "edible poetry."[3] The dishes, because the Sephardim often lived "cheek-to-jowl" with their non-Jewish neighbors, actually reflect the foodways of the far-flung countries in which the Sephardim settled after being ousted from Spain and Portugal. The twist that makes them "Jewish" seems to be the High Holy Days and holidays' "tag" on some of the dishes. In fact, many of the most flavorful dishes are prepared for just those occasions. Among the cornucopia of recipes that Sephardim brought with them to the Americas are ones for dandelion wine and soup, roasted eggplant, poached figs, chopped date meringues, as well as foods given more exotic names, like toasted chickpea *Bilibis*, savory *Mina/Miginas* (beef, onion, and herb pie), *Mustachudos* (wine-soaked Passover cookies), *Risi Gialli di Sabato* (saffron rice pilaf for the Sabbath), *Fijones/Fajones* (bean stew), stuffed *Borekas/Booreketas* (sweet or savory turnovers), and *Pan d'Espanya* (orange sponge cake, a Passover delicacy eaten with *haroset*).

A few Sephardi found their way to Indianapolis from Monastir (now Bitola, Macedonia) between 1906 and 1913. Most were directed to this Midwestern city by the Industrial Removal Office (IRO), an arm of the Jewish Agricultural and Industrial Aid Society. Once a few Monasterlis had settled in, more followed in what has been termed "a chain migration." The men, "poor of purse," came first, boarding with others who shared their religion, language, and customs. When they had saved enough money, they brought their families to *artzot habrit* (the United States). By 1919, Indianapolis's Sephardim numbered more than two hundred.[4] At that point, they formed the Etz Chaim Sephardic Congregation. It was a tightly knit *kahal* (community).

According to Congregation records, "they were a singing and dancing people" whose numbers grew. More Sephardim came from Turkey, Syria, and Salonika, but never in amounts to equal those of the Ashkenazi. Some went into the wholesale produce business; some worked at the Kahn Tailoring Company; still others peddled linens door to door, then opened up retail shops; at least one made Greek-style *feta* cheese. The women, who typically married around the age of twenty, did not work outside the house. They cared for their families. They baked; they cooked—and, in America, they shopped.

In the Old Country, wherever that land might be, but particularly in the Middle East, women may not have gone to the markets often, if at all. However, in the United States, it was otherwise. Food shopping became a central and daily activity. It did not take the Sephardic women long to discover that Indiana's stores were always well stocked with products and produce. This bounty afforded them marvelous economical opportunities to make traditional dishes, as well as chances to innovate. Tomatoes, peppers, cucumbers, onions, quince, garlic, and early spring rhubarb formed colorful produce displays in green grocers' shops, as well as at local farm stands. Honey for locally grown and baked *kalavasa* (squash) that graced the table during the *Rosh Hashana* (New Year) celebration, came from local bee-keepers. After all, as Emily Frankenstein, writing on August 20, 1911, declared, Indiana had "the finest honey I have ever eaten."[5]

Until recently, the Etz Chaim newsletter had a cooking column authored by either Dolores Schankerman or her daughter, Stephanie Caraway. Every issue contained instructions for making a variety of Sephardic fare from countries the world-over, along with ones contributed by Congregation members. The published recipes run the gamut from Jerusalem *Pishkado Con Tomat* (Baked Fish in Tomato Sauce), to Moroccan Roasted Pepper *Bassous* (Tomato and Pepper Salad), from Dorothy Abraham's Apple Cake, to Florence Leshnover's Spinach Lasagna. They reflect the rich, varied, and creative Sephardic food culture well.

In the May/June 2008 issue, Caraway recalled, "My mother used to tell me about my Nona (Sophie Levy) making her own cheese at home. Mom said she would come home from school and find ripening cheese hanging in bags made from panty hose legs all over in the bathroom. Everywhere she looked were dripping bags of cheese curd. Mom never made her own cheese, but after hearing her description of Nona's cheesemaking, I felt as if I were there."[6]

In addition to her cheese-making skills, Mrs. Levy was obviously an accomplished cook, one who used her experience, and a drinking glass, to measure. Caraway recounted, in the same newsletter, "My mother chased her [Nona] around the kitchen with a measuring cup one day when she was making [Booreketas, as she called them]" to get the exact volumetric measurements for a recipe.

Michigan also had a small Sephardic presence. The first known Sephardic Jew to settle in Detroit was Joseph Papo. In 1911, he immigrated from Sarajevo, then part of the Austrian-Hungarian Empire. Following him, Turkish, Greek, and Syrian Jews arrived, so that by 1917, there were enough Sephardim to hold High Holy Day services. Many of the men found work in the automobile industry. Others set up retail stores to serve what was then called "the Spanish community." Through the years, the community has welcomed Israeli, Iranian, Egyptian, and South American Sephardim. All have blended their country-of-origin customs, traditions, and foodways into the larger "Sephardic Community of Greater Detroit."

Annabel Cohen, Michigan caterer and lecturer on Sephardic foods, shared a bit of her family history in an article for *Michigan Jewish History*, titled "Sephardic Treats." She wrote, "Even though my parents were born and raised in Brazil, many of the foods my mother prepared for my family were not South American at all, but Sephardic. Olives, olive oil, eggplant and spices were frequently ingredients for appetizers and main courses. Honey, nuts and lemon juice accented dishes. . . . My mother . . . has handed the tradition [of making *Borekas*] down to her three daughters."[7]

The bulk of Chicago's Sephardi came between the 1890s and the First World War. Some Syrians, who came for the 1933–1934 Century of Progress Fair, stayed. The early ones, however, were primarily from "Persia and Turkey," but never comprised more than 4 percent of Chicago's Jewish population.[8] Similar to their counterparts in Indiana, many went to work as peddlers, as lingerie merchants, and then into the garment import business.[9] By 1910, enough of them had arrived in the city so that they formed the Fraternidad Israelita Portuguesa (the Portuguese Israelite Fraternity).

In 1894, the *Chicago Daily Tribune*, somewhat inaccurately, reported that some "little Assyrian Jews" were participating in a neighborhood kindergarten program (run by the Women's Christian Temperance Union!) where "Mr. Khoisaat furnishe[d] once a week a comfortable luncheon for these children whose ordinary diet is uncooked vegetables."[10] However, efforts to involve Sephardi in the Maxwell Street Settlement, established in 1893 by Jacob Abt and Jesse Lowenhaupt, met with failure.[11] Apparently, the Sephardi were not terribly interested in what a settlement run by Ashkenazi had to offer in terms of social clubs, savings services, night school, cooking, sewing, or cultural activities.

Chicago, during those years, had no difficulty supplying the Sephardi with the necessities to prepare their traditional dishes. Close to where they settled in the Maxwell Street District, around Halsted Street and Roosevelt Road, they found produce overflowing store shelves. The women had their pick of fruits, beans, and vegetables transported by train, wagon, or truck, from as near as suburban farms, or as far away as South America and Asia. Chicago was the Heartland's market town. Meats and poultry were as close as any of the many kosher butcher shops. At that time, Chicago was the nation's meat-packing center, where the larger meat processors employed *shochets* to serve the Jewish community.

Famed home economist and food writer Jane Eddington gave recipes and preparation methods for spring table delicacies of artichokes, asparagus, and tender greens in her (Chicago) *Tribune* Cook Book column of March 31, 1929. Extolling the virtues of dandelions as a rich food source, she exclaimed, "And what a privilege to live in the country in dandelion time!"[12] In Chicago, however, Sephardic women needed to venture no farther than the local park or, perhaps even their own backyards, to dig the tender dandelions, which covered both lawns and fields in brilliant gold and were free for the picking, to use in traditional soups, salads, and wine.

It was also easy to gather the ingredients needed to make their wondrously paper-thin, Middle Eastern rice-flour bread with sweet milk. Milk, direct from bottling plants or kosher-run dairies, could be delivered to their doors daily, or even picked up from Pure Milk stations that dotted the Near West Side, while rice flour from the southern United States was inexpensive at the stores. The only thing missing in Chicago was a sunken Persian baking oven. The women adapted.

According to *The Journal of Home Economics* (1921), "in the Jewish sections of our large cities, there are storekeepers whose only goods are pickles. They have cabbages pickled whole, shredded, or chopped and rolled in leaves, peppers pickled, also string beans, cucumbers—sour, half sour, and salted—beets and many kinds of meat and fish."[13] But those prepared foods cost a great deal more than homemade. So, the Sephardic women undoubtedly canned and pickled their own fruits and vegetables to preserve summer's bounty. A toothsome mix of backyard green tomatoes, a few cucumbers, sweet peppers, and crunchy carrots, Michigan celery, Midwest turnips, and Chicago cabbage grown in fields right west of the Stock Yards, preserved in vinegar and pickling spices made up the healthy Middle Eastern medley called *Turshi*.

Uma damla (a little of this; a little of that)—spices from a Jewish peddler, sweet clover honey from the countryside, a fat, young chicken from the kosher butcher, some good olive oil, perhaps from nearby Italian shops, homegrown tomatoes and onions—plus a little chopping, a bit of sautéing, some gentle simmering, and they would have *Fricasada* (chicken braised in honey and tomato) for noontime dinner or supper. With a pinch of salt, another of pepper, one nice, firm New Jersey eggplant, a few yellow onions, some light oil, maybe four large tomatoes, and a pound or so of Texas (kosher) lamb, they would have the makings of *Berenjenas Ahobadas* (Eggplant Stew) for a filling meal or two. No one measured; they just knew.

Joseph Israel, originally from Cairo, Egypt, informed us that the Twin Cities (Minnesota) Sephardic community is "a small group, mostly transplants from other cities in the east, like New York, Boston, and countries such as Egypt, South Africa and Israel," who came to the Upper Midwest for better economic opportunities or because their (immigration) sponsors were there. Enough Sephardim now reside in the St. Paul and Minneapolis area to form a *minyan*.

Speaking about traditional foods, he told us that "Sephardi recipes have [always] been adapted with local ingredients." To illustrate, he passed along his wife's "great black-eyed peas cold salad," called *Lubia* in Arabic.[14] Israel claims, "No one at our table stopped at one helping. If there's leftovers—not likely—it tastes even more delicious the second day." This dish is typically served during *Shavuot*, the late spring Festival of Weeks celebrating the giving of the Torah to Moses. However, it can be eaten anytime, served with pita bread or alone. Composed of one cup of black-eyed peas boiled "al dente," two hard-boiled eggs, a generous bunch of parsley, a few green onions, freshly ground black pepper, with an optional dash of salt, the whole drizzled over with olive oil and lemon juice, this salad is "healthy, nutritious and very affordable, and *parve* [neutral] foods that can be eaten with either milk or meat) to boot," according to Israel. His wife, Matilde Cohen Israel, born in Colombia, South America, but raised in Brazil, "learned the basic recipe from her mom [Miriam Cohen], who told her that she learned it from her grandmother, Victoria, in Alexandria, Egypt, and it was traditional to serve the salad with pita, green salad with tomato

and cucumber seasoned with lemon and some olive oil, cheeses, yogurt, etc."
Matilde sometimes adds a "sprinkling of hot sauce, a bit of chopped [locally
grown] mint for aroma and taste (not too much, mint can be overwhelming).
It is a dish you can experiment with."[15]

In a recent news article for *American Jewish World News*, Israel summed up
how he views the Sephardi: "Being Sephardic is a state of mind in the broader
sense. We come from so many different countries with so many different influences, but there is a commonality among the way we do things, the food we
eat, our histories."[16]

At the same time that *Beteavon* (Good eating) wishes rang out in Chicago's
Sephardi homes when food was placed upon the table, many Germans and
German-speaking Jews across the United States, with *Gemütlichkeit* (homelike geniality), were exhorting their families and guests to *Essen Sie gut!* (Eat
well!). Irma Rosenthal Frankenstein, a Chicago-born woman of German-Jewish
descent, whose parents, Betty and Abraham Rosenthal, came from Frankfurt-
am-Main, often wrote in her diaries and journals about mealtimes overflowing
with such sentiments. For example, during the 1950s, she reminisced about
her family's open-heartedness at mealtimes: "On Sundays our parents kept the
roast goose or duck they were to have had for dinner at noon, for noon was
the accustomed time for dinner, hoping that our father's friends, our mother's
two unmarried brothers might drop in for a glass of beer or something good to
eat. . . . anybody who wanted could stay for Sunday night supper."[17] Like most
Germans, she learned early on that "the important things at a dinner party, I
am convinced are the food and the guests."[18]

Demonstrating that Irma's family was not unique, Michigan-born author
Edna Ferber recalled that her maternal grandmother's hospitality also extended
to friends along with relatives during the Jewish holidays and at other times.
In her autobiography, Ferber rhapsodized about the foods presented to those
guests: "The soup was almost always chicken soup with noodles (hand-rolled,
homemade, hair-fine) or beef soup with marrow balls, a clear strong golden
brew. . . . The eyes feasted on it first and immediately sent their message to the
stomach. 'Get ready, boys!' they telegraphed to the gastric juices. . . . Look at
this roast stuffed chicken, brown and crisp. I can see the slices melting away
from the glistening carving knife."[19]

That the German-Jews and German-Christians shared not only a language
and a mind-set, but also social customs, should not come as a surprise. By the
mid-nineteenth century, the German-Jews had assimilated the cultural values
and cuisine of their home country. After all, they had lived within Germany's

shifting borders for a millennium. So, if asked their nationality, they would undoubtedly have answered "German," or if they replied in Hebrew, they would have said, "Ashkenaz," which, simply translated, means "German."

The German-Jews also fit in well with other ethnic groups who had immigrated to the United States. Hermann Eliassof explained why: "The Jew possesses the capability of assimilation in a higher degree than many other people. His appreciation of liberty is keener and deeper, for his love of freedom was born in the flames of the auto-da-fe; his thirst for right and his hunger for justice took firm roots in the depths of his soul, in the darkness of dungeons, during centuries of cruel persecutions. Indeed, the Jew fitted well in the new conditions of the new world, and he quickly fell in line with the builders of the free American institutions, American civilization and commercial and industrial power."[20]

Following failed revolution(s) in 1848, German-Jews immigrated to the States in large numbers, primarily from South, West, and Central Germany— Bavaria, Bohemia, Austria, Hungary, Frankfurt. Writing about these immigrants, Ehrlich claimed, "Escapees from abortive political upheavals in central Europe flocked to the democratic environs of America, as did many apolitical refugees who fled from crop failures and devastating famines."[21] Unlike earlier German-Jewish immigrants, they were better educated. A large number were specialist craftspeople, retail and wholesale tradesmen, even lawyers and doctors. They oftentimes joined families and friends already in America, many in Midwest cities.

In September 1849, a reporter for a Jewish paper mentioned these facts. For his news item titled "Bohemian Israelites in Wisconsin," he wrote, "We learn from a reliable source that a number of highly respectable families have just arrived in New York from Bohemia, to form a colony in Wisconsin. There have been for several years past many families from the same country in the neighbourhood of Milwaukee; but the present party, we hear, mean to establish a congregation at once; and they came provided, as it is said, with teachers and other necessary officers to carry their intentions into effect. We hope to receive in a few months some more particulars of this enterprise, when we will communicate it to our readers. In the mean time, we wish the colonists all possible success."[22]

Most of the German-Jews who arrived after 1848 were solidly middle class, urban, and urbane. In this, they were quite like their Gentile-German neighbors. Part of the reason for the similarity was because many times these German-Jews, as Walter Ehrlich has noted, "felt impelled to throw off 'old fashioned' and 'European' ways. To many it was important to blend in. Not all Jews came to the US as observant Jews. . . . But as cannot be overly stated, in their overpowering determination to acculturate into American society, German Jews placed more emphasis on it than on maintaining age-old religious customs and practices. . . . To most Reform Jews, strict observance of *halachic* [Talmudic interpretations] dietary laws epitomized how archaic and obsolescent orthodoxy had become in the modern world."[23]

By the 1880s, more than 90 percent of the Jews in the United States belonged to Reform congregations. Reform Jews could make personal decisions about whether to keep kosher (*kashrut*); many chose not to observe the older, traditional dietary laws. Consequently, even food choices, culinary preparation, and meal presentations did not necessarily distinguish the German-Jews from the non-Jewish German majority, except perhaps, around the Jewish holidays.

Like others from the Old World, many German-Jewish women brought their treasured recipes with them to America. Imagine, for a moment, a warm summer day around the turn of the last century in the German enclave of any Midwestern city—Cleveland, Cincinnati, Milwaukee, Iowa City, St. Paul, St. Louis, Indianapolis, or Chicago. The streets overflow with the sounds of urban life. You hear peddlers crying their wares. "Peeeeaches! Riiiiipe peaches!" The tinkling bell of the ice cream man's push-cart . . . Newsboys shouting on the corners, "Extra! Extra! Getcher paper! Two cents for der paper." A policeman's high-pitched whistle . . . The staccato clacks of horses' hooves along worn red-brick paving stones promise deliveries of milk, fish, meats, and staples from local dairies, fishmongers, butchers, and grocers.

Almost every house has a clean, scrubbed porch claimed by the older generation for its own. The men sit and rock, chatting in German, commenting

Figure 1. *Bretzel* (pretzel) Seller, 1905

on this and that, reminiscing. Friendly greetings for their neighbors ring out. *Guten tag! Wie geht es dir?* (Good day! How goes it?). Exuberant annual nasturtiums (good for summer salads), bright pansies, and red geraniums spill out of forest-green oblong flower boxes affixed to the front window sills or porch railings. The double-hung windows have been opened wide to allow cooling breezes inside. If the women are lucky, a bit of fresh air will reach all the way back into their busy kitchens. There you will find mothers, in gingham house dresses and everyday aprons, impatiently wiping perspiration from their brows or smoothing a stray hair with the back of their hands, all the while kneading, chopping, dicing, mixing, or whisking. Their hot, hot ovens are baking—good, solid, German thick-crust grain breads; rich *brod torte* chock-full of freshly ground cinnamon, plump raisins, and sweet chocolate; egg-filled rice puddings studded with real vanilla bits; or *küchen* lavished with nuts and local in-season fruits. Enticing smells of *sauerbraten* (pot roast marinated in vinegar) or Frankfurt ring sausages with mashed potatoes and sauerkraut waft through the open windows, promising a hearty mid-day meal for the children who run home from play and the men who briefly return from work. *Komm schon!* (Hurry up!).

We took the following recipes from Ruth Dunie's cookbook as representative examples of such old-time German fare. Only one of these was specifically attributed to a woman we assume to have been in her social circle, but all may well have come from some of her German friends. Why a Lithuanian woman would mention that sauerkraut and potatoes would make a "good German dinner" makes no sense unless the recipe was handed along to Ruth with that specific comment.

Sour Kraut

Get one can *hot*—add ½ cup brn. sug. + white vinegar enough to make it tart. Cook for 10 min. Ring sausage put in the above to cook for ½ hr. gives good flavor. Put lid over pot during the cooking. Creamed I[rish] potatoes makes a good German dinner.

Rice Pudding

Take ½ cup rice + put 1½ cup water + let soak until grains swell on stove then pour off water + add 1 pt. milk + let cook to a jelly. Beat 2 yolks of eggs with 5 tablesps. sug. Stir into rice with 1 cup raisins, salt, vanilla. Bake + when done beat the whites of the egg with 2 tablesps. of sug. Put on top + put in stove again to brown.

Apple Kuchen (Josie M's)

2 eggs—well beatened.
1 cup sug.
½ " milk
2 " flour. 2 Tspoons B. P.
1 Tablespoon melted butter

Bake in long pan—Put cut apples, raisins, nuts, sug., cinnamon + butter on top.

Sherbert

20 cups sug.
2 whites egg
(Above) beaten stiff

Make lemonade, stir in the above + freeze. When half frozen stir in the beaten whites + 2 tablesps. cream.

Sometimes, too, German-Jews cooked foods specific to the Jewish holidays, such as Passover, when cakes made from unleavened *matzo* meal or potato flour, or *matzo* balls in soup, would typically be included in the celebratory *seder* meal. A mixture of traditional *matzo*-based dishes accompanied by New World foods, such as stuffed turkey, sweet potatoes, and tart cranberry jelly, would make enjoyable, and "international" eating. In 1941, probably on or about the 12th of April when Passover began that year, Irma Frankenstein jotted down just such a "hybrid" menu: "*Sedar party* . . . Even too busy to know if it was a nice party. Other people said it was. Served matzos glace, soup, turkey, green beans, cranberries, candied sweet pot., parsley pot., matzos cake, wine sauce."[24] Irma never recorded her recipe for *matzos glace*, or defined what the term meant, but we found no fewer than three similarly titled recipes for making *matzo*-based dumplings, in Ruth Dunie's manuscript booklet. The last two appear to be essentially the same, but the instructions are more complete in the third recipe. Perhaps Ruth asked for clarification of the method after she had initially written down the ingredients, looked them over, and found them somewhat sparse. It may also be, based on our interpretation of the last recipe and others labeled "glace" in Ruth's notebook, that to qualify as "glace" meant covering or glazing the dumplings with melted butter, goose fat, or chicken fat following their steaming.

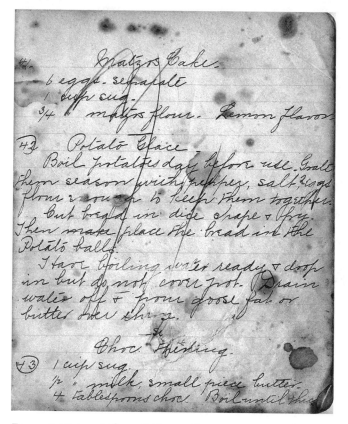

Figure 2. Matzos Cake and Potato Glace recipes in Ruth Dunie's cookbook, circa 1913

Matzos glace for soup

For 8 cups flour use 15 eggs—scald flour then add salt, pepper, ginger + goose fat. Make into balls.

Matzos Glace

2 eggs well beatened—pepper, salt
ginger to taste

To: 1 cupful matzo meal pour hot soup stock over it to steam and let stand one hour. After it is cold add parsley + nuts.

Matzo Glace

2 eggs well beaten, add salt + pepper + ginger to taste.

To 1 cup matzo meal pour ½ cup boiling soup stock over it to steam 1 hr. (Cover the bowl with lid to steam). After it is cold add parsley + chop nuts. 2 table-sps chicken fat last. Make into balls.

Certain German-Jewish recipes could be prepared for Passover and/or *Hanukkah* (the Festival of Lights), when oily foods are typically eaten. During those times, Germans might whip up *Pfannküchen* (pancakes) using *matzo*, as did one of Ruth's friends who shared the recipe with her.

Matzo Phon cake

Soak 1½ matzos. Squeeze dry—
Add pepper, salt to taste. 1 egg.

1 tsp. B. P., 2 Tablesps. sweet milk + enough meal (matzo) to hold together—Fry as batter cake in skillet with *hot* butter.

Other kinds of recipes German-Jews cooked were learned in the United States, either from cookbooks, newspaper columns, or women's magazines, or from friends or relatives. Henriette Davidis's book, *Praktisches Kochbuch für die Deutschen in Amerika* (*Practical Cookbook for Germans in America*), first published in the United States in 1879, was a favorite among German-speakers. Numerous American editions put out by various publishers attest to its enduring worth for German-American cooks. The publishers' initial nod to these women was to list measurements by volume instead of weight. Then, each succeeding edition incorporated larger numbers of ingredients specifically chosen "for the American kitchen." All of these changes and additions reflected the increasing acculturation of the cookbook's readers.[25]

While they may have cooked traditional dishes using traditional foodstuffs, Midwestern German-Jewish cooks also took advantage of the many fresh fruits and vegetables grown in, and transported to, the Heartland. A second-generation American-born woman of German-Jewish descent, Ruth F. Brin, of St. Paul, Minnesota, enumerated some of these:

Mother and the maid would have huge kettles boiling on the stove, filling the [kitchen] with steam while the temperature outside might be in the 80s or 90s. The smells were good because they were "putting up" canned peaches, pears, and applesauce. Sometimes when I walked through, I could see a cheesecloth jelly bag hanging on a broomstick with red juice from currants or other berries slowly dripping into a bowl. That juice would eventually become jelly. Mother canned tomatoes, and, from the apples on our trees, she made apple butter and sliced apples for pies. We had a plum tree that yielded jam and jelly. Mother also made dill pickles and bread-and-butter pickles. In those days, some canned goods were available, but there was no frozen food and almost no prepared foods. We bought bread at the bakery, but the pies, cakes and cookies were all baked from scratch, usually on Friday, baking day. Food was much more seasonal than it is today. We had apples, oranges and bananas during the winter, but no other fruit. Homegrown vegetables like carrots, rutabagas, turnips, cabbage and potatoes were most common in winter. Strawberries and asparagus appeared in the spring, but briefly.[26]

M. F. K. Fisher, noted food-writer, in her 1949 article titled "An Alphabet for Gourmets" had written: "Fish is a favorite of the Jews, because of the many prohibitions about preparing and eating meats. . . . Fish is convenient, too, because there is no prohibition against cooking a cold-blooded animal with cream or cheese or any other milk products, as is the case with red meats."[27] Although not Jewish, Fisher seems to have explored various ethnic cuisines rather thoroughly, so we felt her assertions warranted examination and testing. Consequently, we looked through our manuscript collection for fish recipes, to see whether they were, indeed, more numerous. They were. Then we decided to compare same-named dishes to test whether there were differences in terms of ingredients and spices. Indeed, various published cookbooks and recipe collections we examined showed that kind of variability. Could these be attributed to regional food preferences, to local traditions, and/or to affordability and accessibility?

In the Etz Chaim newsletter of May/June 2007, Dorothy Schankerman shared a recipe for Sephardic Jerusalem *Pishkado Con Tomat* (Baked Fish in Tomato Sauce). One from Rhodes for a dish of the same name, only spelled differently, was located on an Internet site devoted to Sephardic recipes.

Pishkado Con Tomat

  2 large pieces salmon fillet (2 lbs.)
  1 bunch cilantro
  Juice of 2 lemons
  2 cans tomato sauce (15 ounce cans)
  5 cloves crushed fresh garlic

dash pepper

2 tbs. Pareve (neutral, neither milk nor meat) chicken soup powder

Wash fish and place in oven-proof serving dish. Put garlic, cilantro, seasoning and tomato sauce on top. Cover with aluminum foil. Put into oven on 350 degrees for 40 minutes at least. Make sure it is cooked but do not overcook (it will become tough if over-cooked). Refrigerate a few hours and serve well chilled.[28]

Peskado con Salsa de Tomat (Rhodes)

1 3 lb. sea bass or other firm white fish, filleted

1 cup canned tomatoes, chopped and drained

2 medium onions, chopped

¼ cup chopped fresh parsley

1 large garlic clove, minced

½ cup dry white wine

½ cup tomato juice

¼ cup lemon juice

2 tbs. olive oil

Preheat oven to 350 degrees. Grease a 9 x 13 baking dish. Place the fish in the baking dish. Sprinkle the onion, parsley, garlic, salt and pepper over the fish. Cover with the tomatoes. Sprinkle over the top of the fish the wine, tomato juice, lemon juice and olive oil. Bake for 30 minutes, or until the fish flakes easily when tested with a fork. Serve immediately. Serves 6.[29]

Sea bass versus salmon is the immediately noticeable difference between the two recipes. The Greek Aegean island of Rhodes is a rich fishing area, so it makes sense that a recipe with origins there would call for a locally harvested fish. Sea bass is non-oily, with firm flesh and a mild flavor. Baking in white wine, with a touch of local olive oil, would ensure the fillets' succulence. The fish's white color, when fully cooked, would present a nice contrast to the recipe's green parsley and red tomatoes—a visual, and gustatory, treat.

Dorothy Schankerman's recipe uses salmon. Because she lives in Indiana, she might buy the Lake Michigan Coho or Chinook variety. Between December and the end of March, when those were out of season, she could always purchase wild or farmed salmon fillets. Salmon has a stronger flavor than sea bass or other non-oily fish, such as red snapper. Cilantro, too, has a sharper taste than curly parsley. Garlic would also add a pungency not found in the recipe from Rhodes. In the final analysis, this Jerusalem Baked Fish, like many other Israeli-Sephardic recipes we have read, makes a robustly flavored main course.

We then compared the recipe for "Fish in Tomato Sauce" from Ruth Dunie's circa 1914 cookbook to those above. This recipe, reproduced as written, with Ruth's assessment of "fine," reads:

Tomato Sauce Fish. fine

Take flour onion + butter to brn. then stir a little water to smooth. add box tomatoes to fish Red snapper—season sauce with pepper, ginger, parsley + put whole fish in long pan + bake in oven. Keep basting fish.

A pretty-colored fish, the red snapper has firm white flesh and a slightly nutty flavor. It is naturally found deep among the reefs of the Gulf of Mexico. Living in St. Louis, Ruth could easily have purchased fresh snapper at a (kosher) fish store because it would have come up from New Orleans by boat or refrigerated railcar. Her version, again most likely garnered from a German friend, gets its "kick" from the addition of ginger. Bohemian dishes often employed ginger, a tangy medicinal and culinary spice, so Ruth may have secured this recipe from a friend who initially hailed from that area. If fresh ginger were not available in St. Louis, as it most likely was not during the 1910s, Ruth could easily have substituted the powdered or pickled kind. In a pinch, she might have crushed a few commercially made ginger snap cookies. Unlike the Greek-Sephardic and Israeli versions, Ruth's recipe calls for a flour-based sauce, apparently cooked with the fish itself.

Irma's recipe for *Suz-und-Sauer Fische* (Sweet and Sour Fish) came from her mother, Betty. It, too, differs from one Ruth Dunie recorded. Ruth's was probably given to her by someone in her social circle that included South German Jews. The ingredients include aromatic cloves, a spice rarely found in Central or Northern German cuisine. This recipe also calls for flour-based gravy, whereas a light lemon sauce, more in keeping with other famous Frankfurt sauces, enhances Betty's fish.

Sour fish (Betty Rosenthal)

ginger snaps
1 large onion
water, let boil
raisins
½ lemon, little vinegar and sugar

let all boil
fish must be salted, then salt washed off. Let fish boil in the sauce at first quick, then slowly. Let boil about ¾ of an hour.

Sös (Betty Rosenthal's Sauce)

Juice of one lemon
3 yolks of egg
little parsley
teaspoon mustard
teaspoon corn starch stirred in little water
½ teaspoon sugar

mix with cold sauce of fish strained
then put mixture on to boil stirring constantly till it boils up—then let the whole thing grow cold & pour over the fish.

Sweet + Sour Fish (Ruth Dunie cookbook)

Cut fish [,] lay in salt. Take pot + brown onion with sug. Then add little water—to this add vinegar., sug., raisins, lemon + pinch of cloves. Then put in fish to cook until done. Remove *fish* + thicken gravy with flour.

The ingredients for these dishes would not have been difficult to obtain in any Midwestern city after the 1870s. Suitable fresh fish, such as buffalo, whitefish, or government-introduced carp, in particular, was readily available in both Chicago and St. Louis, directly from the lakes and rivers, transported up the Mississippi from New Orleans, or imported via refrigerated cars from elsewhere in the United States. Lemons arrived from California or Florida by rail; they were inexpensive compared to what they had cost in the Old World, where import taxes in Germany, England, and France had run high since at least the first half of the nineteenth century.[30] Spices, imported from around the world, could be purchased at markets, at pharmacies, or from peddlers.

Continuing our exploration of differences, we next turned our attention to recipes written by women of German-descent and German-Jewish immigrants all living in the Midwest. We compared Betty Rosenthal's recipe for *Brod Tort*, apparently one of her Frankfurt specialties, copied by her daughter, Irma Rosenthal Frankenstein, in 1898, to one appearing in Ruth Dunie's notebook. Both call for decadent amounts of chocolate and delicate, crunchy almonds, but Ruth's adds fragrant citron, along with tart grated lemon peel. Besides the obvious difference between brandy and wine sauces, the spices, too, are quite dissimilar. We suspect that Ruth borrowed this recipe from a woman who originally hailed from Bohemia. This region was a stop along the overland European spice trade route, and would have provided easy access to allspice, ginger, cinnamon, citron, and cloves. Too, a Bohemian, or at very least, a South German origin for this recipe's author, seems logical since, according to Ehrlich, most German-Jews in St. Louis, from pre–Civil War times on, came from the "western and southern German and Austrian states."[31] However, as different as they are, both recipes would have fit the "thrifty cook" model because they could use day-old bread.

Brod tort (Betty Rosenthal's recipe)

9 eggs
1½ cups sugar
3 bars chocolate
1 cup bread
little ginger
1 teaspoon cinnamon
almonds

bake in slow oven
Pour little wine over when cold

Brod Tart (Ruth Dunie's cookbook)

10 eggs.
1 cup grated choc. (sweet),
½ " " almonds.
2 " sug.
½ doz. slices citron cut *fine*.
1 lemon peel grated.

1 wine glass brandy.

4 Tspoons cinnamon.

2   "   cloves.

1   "   allspice.

Beat eggs + sug. Together until stiff, then stir in spices, choc. Lastly add 1 cup grated rye bread crumbs. Bake in Spring form.

A recipe for *Lepküchen* (spice cookies) recorded in Ruth Dunie's notebook as coming from "Minnie E." also bespeaks a South German origin with the allspice and cloves so often found in those baked goods. Because it employs European weight measurements, the recipe suggests it was one transported to the United States. Rich in molasses-based brown sugar, unnamed fruits, and a variety of spices, it stands in sharp contrast to the chocolatey "Brown Cookies" recipe, actually a different type of *Lepküchen/Lebküchen*, which Mrs. Friedman of German Frankfurt passed along to Irma Frankenstein.

Lep Kuchen (Minnie E.)

1 lb. brn sug

4 eggs.

1 qt. flour

1 Tspoon soda

1   "   cinnamon

1   "   allspice + cloves

fruits-

Brown cookies (Friedman's)

If desired leave out one white of egg for frosting

5 eggs

2 cups brown sugar

stir up well

melted bitter chocolate about 2 in. x 2 in. square

1 teaspoonful ground cinnamon

almonds & citron

2 cups flour

2½ teaspoonful and a half baking powder

oven not too hot

When flour in pan is yellow cookies are done

The common thread running through the recipes we have listed above is that they demonstrate the myriad artful and imaginative ways in which the Jewish cook might celebrate his or her identity. When certain ingredients were not available, substitutions were made; recipes were borrowed, tried out, assessed, perhaps "tweaked" a bit, then passed along. And in the passing, some of these hybrids became traditions. It appears then, as Joseph Israel advised, "food and culture are almost the same thing."[32]

3

Eastern European Jews
in the Cities

We buy cookbooks to read. We confess—our collection numbers in the hundreds. They range from reprints of American classics to original nineteenth-century editions. We also haunt flea markets, used bookstores, and the Internet for handwritten recipes and for books where recipes have been scribbled in the back or tucked between pages. Like the unnamed author of a 1909 *Chicago Tribune* column, we feel that "Much more intimate and personal is the cookbook which another woman, who is also a notable housekeeper, has compiled. There, written in her own hand are the recipes which she has tried and proved, perhaps altered in one or two instances to make them just right. Whenever she lunched or dined with her friends, and some particular recipe struck her fancy, she has asked for it, tried it, and entered it in her book."[1]

Now and then, we will compare the handwritten recipes to each other, and then to same-titled recipes in commercial cookbooks, just to see what differences time and geography make. Most often, the authors of the manuscript recipes have not identified themselves. These were, after all, their personal books. In some instances, the women have inscribed their names as if very proud of the contents and eager to let others know. On rare occasions, we might be intrigued enough with the contents of a particular manuscript to see if we can figure out the author's name, where she lived, or, at the very least, the dates during which she had compiled the book.

Often the recipes' use of brand-name products, such as "Crisco," or their titles, like "Jubilee Cake" or "Jenny Lind Pudding," give us an idea about the time period during which the author lived. We look, too, for regionalisms, such as the use of "lima beans" instead of the more southern designation, "butter beans," for locale-specific specialties, like "New Orleans Tea Cakes," or at cornbread recipes, which most often stipulate sugar in the North, but typically not in the South, that hint at where the writer lived. Occasionally—not always successfully, either—we try to cook a dish or two, just to experience those by-gone tastes.

Recently, we won an eBay auction for a handwritten cookbook. It was a standard composition notebook filled with more than one hundred recipes, sprinkled with a few comments, along with some mathematical figures scribbled in open spots. To entice on-line bidders, the notebook seller had scanned a page containing a recipe for "matzos balls."

The seller told us she had purchased the booklet we had just won at an estate sale in Tampa, Florida. She described some of the items she had seen in the house, such as correspondence between Edward Hiner of Peoria, Illinois, and Miss May Cooley, dated 1911, along with this notebook, then commented that the sale had been held at the home of a woman named Virginia Pickrell. She related that she thought that, at one time, Ms. Pickrell may have been married to the Atlanta antique dealer, E. J. Covington, owner of Covington Antiques and Repair, because she had seen personal letters from Mr. Covington to her, along with one of his financial ledgers. She added that she believed this estate sale had been "mixed," that is, it contained unsold items from a number of past sales in addition to Ms. Pickrell's personal possessions, so there was no way to tell whether the cookbook we had purchased had belonged to Ms. Pickrell or not, or to track how it came to be included in the Tampa sale.

When our booklet arrived, we saw that the faded, indistinct label on the front cover was incomplete because the last letters of the surname had been torn off. We believed we were certain of "Mrs. L. F. D—," but what had followed the "D"? The second line, however, unambiguously declared the contents to be "Recipes."

In leafing through the fragile pages of this mysterious book, we noticed that, although no recipes were mentioned as "holiday specific," they were the kinds of recipes that someone who ran a kosher household might have compiled. Not one mixed meat with milk; dishes were listed that could be cooked for the Sabbath and the major Jewish holidays. In other words, it had probably belonged to a *frum* (religious) woman.

A number of the recipes mentioned trademarked products, like Philips brand soup, Snowdrift and Crisco shortenings, Knox Gelatin, and Sun Maid raisins, all of which had been invented and marketed a bit before 1915. Then, too, a recipe for "War cakes" suggested that the time period during which this cookbook had been composed might have been when the United States was involved in the First World War.

Some of the recipes appeared to be German, and South German or Bohemian at that, based on the spices used and their descriptive names. However, they were written in phonetic German, for example, "scharff" for *sharfe* (sharp) and "melt" for *Mehl* (flour), as if the booklet's author had heard the word, then recorded it as it sounded to her. It took us almost no time to reach the conclusion that "Straben" should have been *Sträuben*, and described that famous Austrian fritter. But we had trouble figuring out "Phon," until we said it aloud. At that point, we recognized it as the German *Pfann*, and were able to identify the recipe for "Matzo Phon cake" as a distinctly Jewish adaptation of *Pfannküchen*, a sweet pastry served with powdered sugar, jam, wine sauce, or fruit compote. Sometimes, too, when the author wrote the word *küchen* (sweet pastry), she used an umlaut, while at other times she did not. We assumed that German was probably not her first language, or if she could speak it, she could not write it. As it turned out, we were both right and wrong.

Because the cookbook's author had written "Mrs." so prominently on the front of her cookbook, we surmised she was probably a newlywed, proud of her status in the community, thrilled to be married to a man she loved. We just did not know if her given name started with "L," if her maiden name was something beginning with "F," if her married name began with "D," or if "L. F. D." might have been her husband's initials.

We also assumed our author had solicited recipes from friends and relatives, since many were attributed to different people, including "Mama," "Sister," and "Aunt," perhaps at different times, maybe even over a period of years. It seemed to us that, at some point, she had organized those recipes into categories, although they were not labeled thusly, numbered them, then copied them into the booklet we now owned. Every recipe in the book we purchased had been crossed out, suggesting that the author was transferring them into yet another book, and did not want to skip or repeat any recipe. Scattered among the pages were notations and figures related to measurements and hem lengths in centimeters that led us to suspect she might also have been working as a seamstress or doing home sewing at a time when women's dresses were long, and that she was not a native-born American.

We decided to tackle the names attached to some of the recipes to see if they would lead us to a locale for our author. Running each one through the census lists for the entire United States, we were finally able to determine that the women for whom we had complete names appeared only in the St. Louis, Missouri records of 1910. And, with that, we finally had somewhere to start.

We were looking for a Jewish woman with the initials "L. F. D." who had lived in St. Louis sometime around that time.

Alerted to our quest, Diane Everman of the St. Louis Jewish Archives provided us with a set of the Lithuanian Orthodox B'nai Amoona congregation wedding records for the years 1911–1930.[2] Almost immediately, we found our elusive author! She *had been* living in St. Louis. Her name was Ruth Ginsburg. On September 21, 1913, she had married Isadore F. Dunie who, at the time, had been residing in the rich mining town of Leadwood, Missouri. We had misread the old-script "I" as an "L," consoling ourselves that this was, after all, easy to do.

Additional research into census, birth, death, cemetery records, and the Missouri History Museum stacks, along with a side trip to Hillsboro, Illinois, produced both concrete and tangential information about "our Ruth." Born around 1893, she emigrated from Lithuania in 1903 with her mother, Jennie, and six siblings, at the time when Eastern European Jewish migration was at its height. The entire family claimed Yiddish as a primary language, but were, according to immigration records, also able to speak English. Immigration records, which misspelled the family name as "Ginsberg," list their birthplace as "Kovno" (Lithuania), with an embarkation point of Southampton, England. When the Ginsburgs arrived at Ellis Island, they were met by the family patriarch. Mendel had come to the United States some three years before, and settled in Marietta, Ohio, where he ran his own grocery store in the Jewish section of that oil and gas boom-town. Like so many immigrants, he had worked and saved until he could send for his family. Around 1911, Ruth, along with her two oldest sisters, Rena and Ruby, by then out of school, moved to St. Louis, Missouri. They rented an apartment in the heart of the downtown Jewish neighborhood. Ruth and Ruby worked as retail clerks, while Rena was employed as a stenographer and bookkeeper. Then, in 1913, as we discovered, Ruth married.

After the birth of two children, Annette and Bernice, in Missouri, the Dunie family moved to Hillsboro, Illinois. They must have relocated to the Montgomery county seat sometime before 1920 because they were listed as living on Main Street, with a servant, in the federal census of that year. Ruth's occupation was listed as "none," but Isadore was shown as an employee in a retail dry goods store. The girls were five and almost three years old.

We pulled up in front of the Dunies' old address on Hillsboro's Main Street only to find it occupied by the town's newspaper. The publisher mentioned there used to be an apartment or sleeping rooms upstairs, but had no personal knowledge of the Dunies or of a Jewish community in the town at any time. He checked his paper's morgue to no avail.

None of the microfilm records for the *Hillsboro Journal* from 1919 through 1921, which we scanned at the local library, mentioned a "Dunie," gave any clue as to who might have been Isadore's employer, or identified any Jews who might have been living in that community. We read local news stories along with numerous advertisements for Swingle's Drug Store; Arnold's Grocery; George Shaffer, "the Reliable Meat Man"; Yoffie's Ladies Ware Shop; and Harold Weingand's Candy Store, but found nothing to explain why the Dunies had moved to this Illinois town, or even to suggest how they managed to secure kosher meat and poultry so far from a major city.

The sole newspaper clipping in Ruth's cookbook mentioned a "fireless cooker." Wording implied that the reader knew what the contraption was and how it would work. We did not, so we pored through newspaper archives. We located Mrs. Fridler's instructions for building a fireless cooker in her May 18, 1907 Letter to the Editor of the "In the Kitchen" column on page 7 of the *Chicago Tribune*. It is obvious from her directions that she had built her own cooker at some point. She wrote:

> To make at home a fireless cooker that will save time, fuel, cooking utensils, and also cook the food better, take a wooden box, any size desired, nail cleats one and one-half inch thick to all the outside edges, then fill in space between the cleats with old newspapers, fastened with tacks, until the surface will be even with cleats. Now tack heavy building paper to the cleats, completely covering the box and making a smooth surface. Make a cover to fit the top snugly, finish it with cleats, newspapers, and building paper like the outside of a box, and attach the top with hinges. This cover must fit so as to retain all heat. Have kettles of enamel ware if possible, with lids that fit in like on a pail.

However, Mrs. Fridler did not tell us how the cooker worked; she, too, must have assumed that everybody knew. Poking around more in newspaper and magazine archives, we discovered that this cooker was apparently a successor to the famous Aladdin oven, invented by Edward Atkinson and touted by him in a series of widely publicized articles during 1890.[3] A sawdust-lined box with water-filled copper coils, the Aladdin cooker was heated by a kerosene lamp, which raised the interior temperature to the point where it was possible to bake breads and cakes, and to "slow cook" one-pot dishes. Hyped as being a benefit to all women, it was supposed to emancipate them from the kind of constant stove supervision that contemporary cooking often required. This oven never really caught on, not because it did not work or because the foods baked or cooked in it did not taste good, but because it cost $25.00 at a time when this amount was more than many people made in a week, or sometimes even in a month.

Figure 3. The Ginsburg family. Ruth (top row center) with her mother, Jennie (middle row), Marietta, Ohio, circa 1905

When we discovered that a different, less expensive, commercial version of a fireless cooker had been available since at least 1910, we immediately saw how Ruth might have managed to serve her family a hot meal on Saturday afternoons without breaking the Jewish law forbidding work on the Sabbath.

The Duplex Fireless Cooker, developed by the Durham Manufacturing Company of Muncie, Indiana, seemed perfect for an observant Jewish woman who did not have access to a community oven where she could have her *cholent* (slow-simmered stew) cooked for her as in Europe, or any easy way to keep her wood or gas oven on low heat from sundown Friday until Saturday noon. This contraption, which stewed, steamed, broiled, and roasted meats, cooked cereals, and baked breads and pies, used preheated stones fitted into a metal box on top of which pans containing the food to be cooked were set. Once these were placed inside, the food cooked itself using radiant heat. Cooking times could be regulated by how hot the stones were made before setting into the box.[4]

At some point, for some reason, the Dunies returned to the St. Louis area, where Isadore opened his own retail dry goods store in the then-suburb of

Maplewood on Manchester, a broad street running parallel with the railroad tracks leading to the downtown city. He died unexpectedly in 1928, and was interred in the Dunie family plot in St. Louis. We visited the address given on Isadore's death certificate, and spoke to the current tenant. Intrigued with our search, he showed us around the building, where it became obvious that a family might have lived behind a small shop occupying the front part of the edifice. He knew nothing about the Dunies.

From the 1930 census, we learned Ruth and her two girls had moved from Maplewood. They were still living in the greater St. Louis area, though, with Ruth's occupation listed as "saleslady" in a department store. We were able to track her as late as 1934, when her younger daughter, Bernice, graduated high school. After that, she disappeared. It was frustrating. Although we had figured out where Ruth had lived at various points in her life, and what she did when in the workforce, we knew almost nothing about her as a person. And we had no face to put to the name either. We kept searching.

On the off-chance we had located a living relative, we sent a letter to a woman we thought might be Ruth and Isadore's granddaughter. Carol Christian has graciously shared treasured family photographs along with the following biographical stories about her maternal grandmother, Ruth Dunie, with us:

Grandma was born in Lithuania in a town she always called "Kupichek" (spelling phonetic). Her family fled the Russian pogroms. A story I remember her telling was that once when their village was being attacked, her mother told her to "grab a chicken and run"! I honestly don't know how the family ended up in the Midwest. . . . Grandma met her husband in the U.S. . . . Sadly, he died when my mother [Annette] was 12 and although the extended family helped Grandma Dunie as much as they could, she had to go to work to support my mother and my mother's sister, Bernice. I believe she worked in the hosiery department of a large department store [Scruggs, Vandervort and Barney in an era when all women wore hose and gloves] in St. Louis until she retired, [and] suffered a lot from varicose veins, having to be on her feet all day (according to my mother).

Grandma Dunie was a very sweet, humble woman who lived simply, always lit the Shabbos candles, went to synagogue, etc. Her apartment was filled with the descendants of a pothos plant from which she rooted cuttings to make new plants—they streamed around the windows all over her apartment. My mother followed in that tradition, and so do I. It gives me deep pleasure to have the babies of the babies of the babies of that plant in my house!

All of us, including Grandma D., usually went to my paternal grandmother's house for the Jewish holidays because they had a real dining room, which she didn't, as well as the funds and the help to prepare all those lavish meals. When we went to Grandma Dunie's for dinner, it was always the same meal: baked chicken parts (with golden brown skins), mashed potatoes, and a vegetable. I don't think we ever sampled any of the recipes she copied down as a bride.

Something that made me sad even as a child, and doubly sad as I think about it now, is that Grandma D. always apologized to us for not being able to give us as much Chanukah gelt (small amounts of money given to children during the holiday) as our other grandmother, as if it was some kind of a shortcoming on her part that she had limited income. It didn't matter at all to me or affect my feelings toward her but clearly it made her feel "less than." It was always Grandma Dunie who hemmed my skirts and, as my mother never tired of pointing out, did so with such skill that one never saw the threads showing on the front of a garment. And of course there was her babka (yeast coffee cake with cinnamon and chocolate), and her blintzes (thin pancakes filled with cheese or jam), and her chopped chicken liver. . . . [My cousin] told me a story about how when he was at the University of Chicago, Grandma Dunie sent him monthly care packages of her cinnamon toast. I realized when I read that that cinnamon toast baked in the oven was one my mother's specialties. It never occurred to me that it was her mother's recipe. It really was yummy: I think she buttered the bread (heavily) and sprinkled it (thickly) with a mixture of sugar and cinnamon, then baked it in a slow oven. It came out both crunchy and gooey.[5]

Based on information Carol provided, we knew Ruth kept the Sabbath holy, so we looked over her notebook recipes for ones she might have prepared. Among those was one for homemade raisin wine. Perhaps it was intended for cooking or baking, but most likely it was also meant for family *Shabbos* dinners and High Holy Day celebrations.

Every Friday, starting almost at daybreak, Ruth would have begun her preparations for the Sabbath. She would have baked and cooked and straightened the house. In the morning, she would have braided her sweet *challah* (bread), then popped the loaves in the oven until they turned a golden brown, sending yeasty aromas throughout the house. Then, pans of *küchen* filled with cinnamon and raisins, or a rich, moist chocolate cake, whose secret ingredient was mashed potatoes, might take their place, but only if Ruth were not planning to serve meat dishes during dinner since these desserts contained butter and milk.

Before the close of day, Ruth would have made certain the girls had changed their dresses, washed their hands, and combed their hair. She would have spread a clean white cloth over the table, then set it with her best dishes. At one end, she would have centered the *challah*, covered, perhaps, with a beautiful, handmade doily. At sundown, Ruth, herself in fresh clothes, would have lit two candles to welcome in the Sabbath, then intoned the *Bentsh licht* (prayer said while lighting the candles). Isadore, as the head of the household, would have recited *kiddush* blessings over a cup of wine to remind his family of the day's sanctity. *Gut Shabbos* (May you have a good Sabbath).

The evening's meal might have begun with an appetizer of *gehakte leber* (chopped liver) or potato glace (fat-covered potato dumplings), followed by a tasty pot roast. Then again, the main dish might have been *Sharfe* Fish whose recipe Ruth had learned from St. Louis friends. *Est gesunterheit* (Eat in good health).

Here are some of the recipes, taken from her own cookbook, which Ruth might have used:

Raisin Wine

½ yeast cake.
2 boxes Sunmaid raisins.
2 qt. water. into other raisins
add 2 cups sug.

Liver Paste

Calf liver, cooked until blood is out then ground fine.
2 stalks celery
1 large onion
4 hard boiled eggs.
parsely, pepper, salt.
2 tablespoons goose fat.
3   "   worstershire sauce.

Potato Glace

Boil potatoes day before use. Grate them season with pepper, salt, 2 eggs flour enough to keep them together. Cut bread in dice shape + fry. Then place the bread in the Potato balls. Have boiling water ready + drop in but do not cover pot. Drain water off + pour goose fat or butter over them.

Pot Roast

(one tblsp vinegar added with cooking)

4 lb. rump roast or shoulder chop makes an excellent cut. In an iron pot or Dutch oven put 1 whole onion cut-clove of garlic—6 bay leaves—Season roast with salt, pepper, paprika + ginger—Put 3 big spoons Snowdrift then onions+ all the above to brown. Meat must brown on both sides. Have lid on tight. Then after it is well brown, cover with water. Cook. Add ½ cup tomato soup (Philips). When meat is done, thicken the gravy with flour. Meat can be seasoned night before cooking—Potatoes can be cooked in gravy.

Scharff Fish

Cut fish + boil with pepper, salt, onions, butter (iron spoon), ginger. Then when done remove fish + have flour + water well mixed + stir in gravy, when boiled thick take from stove +stream in yolks of 2 or 3 eggs with chopped parsley. Pour over fish which has been placed on platters.

Rhetta G's Kuchen

1 kitchen sp. of butter
1 cup sug.
(Above) cream
3 eggs
2½ cups flour—2 Tsp. B. P.
1   "   milk.
vanilla + lemon.

Ethel Meyer's Kuchen

1 Kitchensp. butter
1½ cups sug.
(Above) cream
2 eggs
1 cup milk*
3   "   flour [,] 2 Tsps. Y. P.
Makes 3 cakes. Put sug. cinna. nuts, raisins on top of each.

* "⅔ cup milk" added in pencil

Whole I. Potato Cake

2 cups sug.

½ " butter

(Above) creamed.

2 eggs (separate)

2 cups flour. 2 Tspoons. B. P.

1 " nuts

¾ " Bitter choc.

1 Tspoon nutmeg.

1   "   cinnamon

1   "   allspice.

1 cup I. potato creamed + added last.

Ruth Dunie's family's flight from religious persecution in Eastern Europe is a story similar to ones told by other mostly Orthodox Jews who escaped to America between 1890 and 1915. Times were hard. Prejudice was rampant. One sure way to survive was to emigrate, *if* one could get the money for passage *and* the permit to leave. America, *di goldene medine* (the Golden Land), promised, if not riches, then, at the very least, freedom from bloody pogroms and forced military conscription. No matter how hard it was to make a living in the United States, very few Eastern European Jews returned to the Old Country, or ever wanted to return.

Finding some background for Esther Schechter, the author of an unique recipe for Huckleberry Pie that we collected in the Upper Midwest Jewish Archives in Minneapolis, led us to contact her grandson, Herbert. He shared a bit of his grandmother's harrowing journey from Russia, to Romania, and, finally, to St. Paul, Minnesota, with us:

[Esther] arrived in Minnesota about 1921–22. Her husband, [Harry], came to St Paul nine years before. They were separated because of the first world war, the need to accumulate enough money to bring a wife and two children across the ocean, and then the difficulties in leaving Russia. Esther and her two children, Louis and Irving, stole through the woods and across the border in the middle of the night by hiring a guide and bribing a border guard. Today the "guides" taking people across the US-Mexican border are called coyotes. She lived in a rooming house in Romania with her two children for about 6 months before she could continue the journey to America.

Harry came to St. Paul because the only person he knew in America lived in St. Paul. He was a man from their village. The man rented Harry a room in his house and took him to the South St. Paul meat-packing plants to help him get a job. Harry arrived not being able to speak the language and took a job for 5 cents per hour. By the time his wife arrived, he owned a business and an apartment building. This transition is a mystery because there is no one left who knows how he accomplished this.[6]

Judy Dworkin, of Kaufman's Delicatessen and Bakery, in Skokie, Illinois, tells the tale of her family's exodus from Eastern Europe that is fundamentally similar to both Ruth's and Esther's—to survive, they had to leave. Moreover, Judy's story is also rich in Midwest-based reminiscences—of Chicago's Jewish community around Maxwell Street, of family, and of the traditional foods her grandmothers prepared. We learned about it all seated in the busy bakery, surrounded by redolent whiffs of cinnamon, chocolate, and warm, sweet jams, talking over the incessant buzz of the bread slicer, and sampling first, a bit of chopped liver, then Judy's signature toasted *schnecken* (pastry roll with honey, nuts, and sugar, sliced, then baked), next, a poppy seed "dunker," and finally, a slice of still-warm, dark, moist, dense, and chewy rye bread, which her daughter, Bette, calls "Bohemian-slash-Czech."[7]

One branch of Judy's family was originally from Romania; the other hailed from Poland. Her paternal grandfather came to Chicago in 1911, perhaps because he had relatives or friends already living in the city. His wife and children stayed behind in Vienna, waiting for a boat to bring them to America. They were caught there by the outbreak of the First World War, surviving the miserable years of that conflict only because one of the sons "sneaked food." After the war, the family was reunited, but because nine years had passed, the father did not recognize his children! They all settled into Chicago's West Side, near Maxwell Street, along with thousands of other Eastern European Jews. Judy recalls:

It was a vibrant, vibrant community. . . . It was a whole world. . . . My [paternal] Grandmother W., and my aunts, my uncles, and my father all lived in the same building, which they had purchased, lost during the Great Depression, then bought back. In the basement was a closet—a cupboard—[with] floor-to-ceiling double doors. You opened that, and the cupboard was stocked with all the canned goods, jellies, jams, pickles, wines, and huge empty oatmeal boxes for noodles. . . . My father also made wine—Blueberry wine—for his sons' *bar mitzvah* (Jewish coming-of-age ritual for thirteen-year-old boys).

Every week my Grandmother W. made the *challah*; every week she made the *schnecken*. And the argument among her sons was "there's not enough raisins in it"; "there's not enough nuts in it." But, they [the *schnecken* slices] were gone by Sunday night! She made beet *borscht* (beet soup), and, of course, *Mama-*

lige (a Romanian cornmeal porridge). There's no recipe to it [*Mamalige*]. She used to make great big batches of it at a time, like a cereal. Of course, she was feeding twenty-three people at one time. She used a wooden spoon to make it. She'd flatten it on a plate with a pat of butter on there, and a layer of sour cream, and cottage cheese. It was eaten with a dill pickle.

My Grandmother W. wouldn't allow anybody in her kitchen. She was the boss of her kitchen. My mother and my aunt would do the shopping. They shopped every day. My great-grandmother, Little Bubbe, made *fleddel* (a pastry)—essence of strong tea, a layer of nuts, cinnamon, apples, in layers of dough around four inches high.

I remember going with my grandmother to buy chickens on the West Side [of Chicago] which were alive. And we fought over the little eggs that she'd throw in the soup. I used to go to her house every Friday and walk down to where the chicken markets were.

Both of my grandmothers were fantastic cooks. [They] made substitutions, but everything was from scratch. My Grandmother W. used to make a jelly, a combination of pineapple, and I think, apricot. And nobody's ever been able to duplicate it. [She] did not have measurements. She knew by touch. She made potato *kugel* (baked pudding). She made a dough from potato starch that was washed out. Nobody knows how. Unfortunately, most of the recipes are like that. Nobody took them down and nobody watched.

And she made bread—a big, braided *challah* with the braid on top, a double braid. She had a knife and she'd go (making a downward stabbing motion) with that knife into a table to hold the dough down for braiding, and then she'd start braiding, and that knife would hold it! It was an old, old knife, but I can remember her dragging that knifepoint through the dough and her hands moving so fast! Her bread was unbelievable!

My mother used to make beef liver. All I remember is you take a pound of beef liver in a brown paper bag and put it in the oven, and I'm sure you drown it in chicken fat. No goose fat. Chicken fat. I think it's a local kind of thing. And my Grandmother W. always used to make *gribenes* (cracklings). My son calls it "Jewish popcorn."

For Passover, my [maternal] Grandmother P. always made stuffed veal breast, and I made it for years, but nobody makes it anymore, and nobody wants to eat it anymore, either. . . . And I also made a recipe for *matzo* pop-overs. First you soak the *matzos*, drain [them], add ten eggs, and let it sit for hours—a 400 degree oven. . . . They should be served hot. The problem was that you had to have a hot, hot 400 degree oven, and it took a while. You were taking up space from other things because they should be served hot.

When my Grandmother P. used to go to the kosher butcher shop, and she'd get a veal breast, the veal breasts were so long (holding her hands about one foot apart). My cousin always put potato stuffing in [the pocket], but I like *matzo* stuffing. The *matzo* stuffing had *matzo* and egg, onions, celery, chicken fat, and, you know, salt and pepper. And, then, when you sew up the pocket, you rub the top and smear the pocket with chicken fat again. And, my grandmother told me to use a little bit of chicken soup in the gravy.[8]

The early 1880s saw a large number of Eastern European Jews primarily from Russia and Romania arriving in the Midwest. Some came through Canada, others via the Great Lakes; still others poured through immigration portals at Ellis Island, Philadelphia, or, less frequently, by way of Galveston, Texas. On September 25, 1881, the *St. Louis Globe-Democrat* published an article enumerating the Russian emigrants to arrive that week: a brewer, a locksmith, a watchmaker, a book-binder, a joiner, a tinsmith, a gilder, a carriage-maker, a rope-maker, a roofer, a cooper, a mason, a tobacconist, two painters, seven tailors, and five farmers. These were the "forerunners of a large number of artisans coming to this country," and help was asked of the German-Jewish community to find them employment.[9] Two hundred other Eastern European Jews arrived in St. Paul, Minnesota, in 1882 without warning, with more following quickly.[10] That same year, Milwaukee found the three hundred "destitute Russian peasants" who had arrived there in a condition "so lamentable that it [could] scarcely be described. Such destitution, suffering, squalor, and emaciation from low diet have ever been witnessed, even in countries where famine prevails."[11] Lizzie Black Kander, founder of the Milwaukee Settlement, wrote about those migrations: "Terrible pogroms in Russia had driven thousands of families to our shores, several hundreds finding refuge in our midst. Business all over the country was at a standstill and many people were thrown out of employment. And here were these immigrants many of whom had been well-to-do merchants, manufacturers and artisans, amid strangers in a strange land, entirely out of place with conditions in this country and unable to understand or speak our language."[12] And still more kept coming. About 15,000 Russian Jews fled to the United States between 1871 and 1880, then 18,000 more between 1881 and the end of 1882![13]

In 1902, the *Chicago Daily Tribune* was reporting, as if it were still news, that "a large part of Roumanian Jews, principally women, girls, and young children, stopped at Vienna today on their way to the United States. A majority of the emigrants intend to join relatives in Philadelphia and Milwaukee. All are pinched with hunger and wretchedly poor. They are enthusiastically confident, however, that in the United States their condition will be bettered. This party is only the beginning of what promises to be an exodus of Roumanian Jews during the next three months, owing, it is said, to oppressive legislation."[14] One year later, the same paper declared, "The Jewish immigrants come to stay. This is shown by the larger percentage of women and children among them. The men do not come over . . . to make money and return home to spend it there. The whole family migrates."[15] The *shtetls* (market towns) of Eastern Europe were emptying, or being emptied, of Jews, while America's cities were filling up to the bursting-point.

One would have had a difficult time distinguishing between an Eastern European Jewish town or village and the communities these refugees established in Midwestern cities: the smell of garlic, the aromas of ripe apples and oranges, the squawks of chickens, colorful outdoor markets with stands, stores, pushcarts, kosher meat markets, *matzo* bakeries, dry goods stores, tailor shops, pawnshops, the *schvitz* (communal bath house), and the people—hundreds and thousands of men and women marketing, going about their businesses, dawn to dark (except on the Sabbath)—were so alike. Over the clamor in the streets, in their crowded apartments, mothers crooned lullabies to their babies, or sang the bitterly ironic Yiddish lament, *Bulbes* (Potatoes):

Zuntik - bulbes! Montik - bulbes!
Dinstik uhn mitvokh - bulbes!
Donershtik uhn fraytik - bulbes!
Ober shabbes nokhn tsholnt a bulbe kigele!
Uhn zuntik vayter, bulbes.

Sunday - potatoes! Monday - potatoes!
Tuesday and Wednesday - potatoes!
Thursday and Friday- potatoes!
But the treat on the Sabbath, a potato pudding!
And Sunday, once again potatoes.[16]

Then, they would whisper a promise to their children—things will be different; it will be better in *di goldene medine. Sha! Sha! Gay shluffen* (Hush! Hush! Go to sleep). "The nickel theaters are more profusely spread through the district. Women and children throng the sidewalks. The people are more homelike in their attitude toward each other. They live nearby and call each other by their first names. Almost every other door is a little cigaret store or soda water stand with a delicatessen store combined. Every one of these places is packed with people who talk excitedly. As you enter you perceive long rows of books on the wall. In combination with this store there is also a private library and for 25 cents a month one can take out as many books as one possibly can read."[17] Life was in full swing.

In St. Louis, toward the end of the hot, humid summer, Ruth, too, would have been busy. Her cookbook tells us she was planning to take full advantage of the market's burgeoning stocks of succulent Midwest fruits and crisp, fresh vegetables for the chili sauce, pickles, and spiced brandied peaches she would put up for the winter.[18] As her attributions attest, she collected recipes from family and friends. The only "odd" one was the cucumber pickle recipe, which called for grape leaves and fennel. Those were ingredients Ashkenazi rarely, if ever, used. Perhaps a Greek or Italian friend gave it to her, or maybe it came from a Sephardic woman she knew. In any case, the grape leaves would have inhibited the enzymes that make pickles go soft.

In preparation for busy weeks of preserving and canning, Ruth might have purchased fruit jars locally manufactured by the Schram Glass Company in Hillsboro, Illinois. She would have at the ready a special pot for melting the paraffin needed to seal the containers, snug-fitting lids, along with little pre-cut cloth circles, pinked out of leftover scraps of gay, flowered cotton (from Isadore's store?) to cover the wax.

Chili Sauce (Mama's)

    24 l[arge] ripe tomatoes
    6 green peppers
    8 l[arge] onions
    8 Teasps vinegar
    8 Tablesps sug
    4   "   salt
    4 teasp. cloves
    4   "   cinnamon—red pepper-

Chop peppers + onions fine + slice
+ peel tomatos. Boil 2 or 3 hrs

Chili Sauce (Stella)

    1 pk. tomatoes—½ pk. onions (w.) ½ doz. bell peppers—1 teasp.
cloves gr. allspice, 2 red peppers—2 cups brn. sug. 1 qt. vinegar—¼
cup salt. Scald tomatoes. grind tomatoes, onions + peppers. Boil from
1½ to 3 hrs. stirring frequently.

Sweet + Sour beans (Mama's)

Cut beans lengthwise- ½ an onion Put in pot with 1 Tablesp. butter + let simmer- Then add water to cover—Cook 1 hr. and add salt to taste. 3 or 4 slices lemon-2 tablsp. sug 1 " vinegar pinch of cloves

Tomato Relish (Aunt Bea)

12 l[arge] ripe tomatoes, cut in small pieces.
4 l[arge] onions
7 grn. peppers
1 qt. celery
(last 3 above) cut or grind fine
1 teasp. cinnamon
1   "   cloves—
red pepper to taste
½ cup sug.
1 pt. vinegar

Mix all together let simmer 2 hrs. If quantity does not draw enough juice add a little water. Put in air tight bottles or jars.

Green Tomatoes

4 qts. green tomatoes
6 large onions
6   "   peppers—
½ cabbage
2 cup celery
2   "   sugar
1 tablespoon mustard
1   "   blk. pepper
1   "   salt
2 teasp. allspice, cloves (each)
1 qt. apple vinegar.

Heat slowly—simmer ¾ hr. after contents comes to a boil.

Tomato Preserve

Firm tomatoes. Scald them + remove skin. Put them in a colander so that the water drips from them. Then weigh them and to 3 lbs. of tomatoes take a 2 ¼ lb. of sug. Dice lemon thin it + put in a cloves+ allspice. You must be your own judge as to taste. Cook down close.

Pepper Hash

1 head cabbage chopped fine, 1½ tablesp. celery seed—3 tablesp. mustard seeds. 2 red peppers + 8 grn. peppers, 1 stalk celery chopped fine—3 onions

After cabbage is chopped, salt well so you can squeeze all the juice out of it. Then add other ingredients + cover all with ½ gal. vinegar that has been boiled—enough vinegar to cover it well. When cold, it is ready for use.

Chow-Chow

½ bu. grn. tomatoes
6 large onions
6 grn. peppers
1 red pepper
4 oz. mustard seed
2 tablesp celery

Grind or chop fine. Add ½ cup salt + let stand over night. Then boil this with 2 qts. vinegar till tender—when nearly done add 1 lb. sug. Put in jars.

Chow-Chow

1 doz. grn. peppers
2 qt. beans
1 cabbage
1 doz grn tomatoes
½ " onions
10 ¢ mustard ½ tablesp red pepper
10 ¢ vinegar- 1 " sug.

Cucumbers sliced

Slice + peel cucumbers + lay in salt over night also onions.
1 tablesp mustard seeds
whole spices
3 tabsp. gr. mustard
1 tea sp tumeric
1 cup sug
3 tabsp. flour
1 qt. vinegar + boil
together
1½ doz. cucum
" onions.

Cook 25 min.

Salt Water Pickles for winter

1 lb. salt
1 qt. vinegar—6 qts water. boil + pour over pickles at once

Salt Water Pickles

Grape leaves—fennel placed in jar. Stick cucumbers + put in jar.
Make strong brine of salt + pour over + add 2 Tspoons red pepper-½
cup vinegar. Put grape leaves + fennel on top Let stand for 4 or 5 days
+ try.

Vinegar Peaches

4 lbs. fruit. 1 pt. Apples.
1 " sug.
Use whole cloves.

Stir until you can stick straw.

Brandy Peaches

1 qt. alcohol.
9 lbs. sug, to ½ bu. peaches

Cook sug. to a thin (?)
cover sug. with water
bring to a boil

In St. Louis, at the time Ruth was compiling her cookbook, the Raskas Dairy Company had been in business a quarter of a century. Isaac Raskas, from Lithuania, had started the company in a "semi-rural area on the western fringe of St. Louis." Isaac began by selling milk door to door in a horse-drawn wagon. He, and his sons, Julius and Louis, became very successful, especially after they developed a special line of sour cream and soft cheese products. He took great pains to guarantee that all phases of the milk production met strict standards of *kashrut*.[19] Ruth may have ordered her dairy products from the Raskas family for any number of reasons. They were *landsman* from Lithuania; they spoke the same language; their products were kosher; and, best yet, milk, cream, and cheese were delivered to her door—certainly a time-saver for a busy woman with two children, who probably also helped out in her husband's store!

We found an interesting recipe for "Cheese Pie" with a sweet cookie crust in Ruth's collection. It would have been suitable for *Shavuot*, the holiday commemorating Moses' receiving the Torah, when dairy products are typically eaten, or, actually, almost anytime, especially since Ruth labeled it "ex[tra] fine." She had solicited the recipe from a friend or relative named "Hennie D." It did not specify any particular kind of cheese. Was it cheddar? Cream cheese? Farmer's cheese? Or just regular cottage cheese? Leafing through our old cookbooks was little help. There were recipes for pies made from all sorts of cheeses. However, during the research, we did learn that dairy products play an important role in traditional Lithuanian-Jewish cuisine. Then we discovered a pamphlet and a news column that we believe solved the puzzle.

We had already determined that Ruth's book had been written in St. Louis sometime around 1913 or 1914, perhaps even as late as 1918, but probably before she moved to Hillsboro, where she was living in 1920. For at least a portion of that time, America was involved in a world war. Everywhere you looked, the government was exhorting people to do their part for the war effort—in newspaper editorials and advertisements, on colorful posters hung at Ellis Island in 1917, printed in different languages, including Yiddish, that admonished immigrants to work for the war effort by being economical. The wording on all the signs was the same. The translation read, "You came here seeking freedom, now you must help to preserve it. Wheat is needed for the Allies. Waste nothing."[20] At this same time, the U.S. Department of Agriculture issued pamphlets titled "Make a Little Meat Go A Long Way," "Save Sugar: Use Other Sweets," "Use More Fish," and "Cottage Cheese Dishes: Economical, Wholesome, Delicious."[21]

It was this last circular, published in 1918, coupled with Jane Eddington's *Tribune* column, "Patriotic Cottage Cheese," mentioning how representatives of the U.S. Food Administration were going from state to state promoting the use of cottage cheese as a meat substitute, which strongly suggested that Hennie's pie called for that kind of cheese. Eddington also wrote that before the war her readers may have saved recipes for cottage cheese, but never used them because "there are cooking teachers who consider a cottage cheese pie unattractive and unpalatable." She continued, "The opinion is prevalent that we shall be able to eat more cottage cheese if it is cooked. New recipes are on the way from Washington for the cooking, so look out for their distribution and get your copy."[22] So, when we made Hennie's pie recipe, we used cottage cheese, thinking all the while how patriotic Ruth must have felt as she prepared it, doing what she could for the war effort in her adopted country.

Cheese Pie (Hennie D's) ex. fine

> 1 lb. cheese.
> 1 cup sug.
> ½ " cream
> 4 yolks added to cheese
> 2 Tablesp. flour - lemon + vanilla
> Whites of 4 eggs beaten stiff
> with pinch of salt—add
> 2 tablesps. sug. and fold in
> ½ tsp. of cream of tartar.

After this is well beatened stir into the cheese which must be ready. Have a *cookie* crust ready partly cooked before baking all together.

Ruth Ginsburg Dunie died January 6, 1969. She is buried in the same cemetery as her beloved husband, but in a different section. A kind woman, a simple woman, a religious woman, and a good cook, she left her family with warm, wonderful memories. She also left behind an extraordinary manuscript filled with legacy recipes. "May her memory be a blessing to those who treasure it."

4

Jews in Small Towns, on the Farms, and In-Between

As we leafed through one of our antique manuscript cookbooks, a faded magazine reproduction of a Victorian-era print fluttered out. The soft-focus picture shows a peasant family from somewhere, trudging through deep snow, heading somewhere else. In the background we note a small cottage. No smoke curls from its chimney. It has been abandoned. The father, who already looks weary, somewhat incongruously carries a rake over his shoulder. One son, undoubtedly the elder, lugs a basket of firewood. Perhaps they plan to camp along the road. Far behind, we see the mother, burdened by a huge basket strapped to her back. It probably holds everything of value that they possess. A small child, most likely a daughter, keeps close to her mother's skirts, as little children often do; another son, bent from the weight of his bundle, brings up the rear of this ragged parade. It is a sad picture of a very bleak time. And we could not help but wonder if our cookbook's author had saved this illustration because it reminded her of her own family's exodus from the Old Country.

Eastern European Jews left their homes, crossing vast expanses of terrain in all kinds of weather—some by rail; some hidden in the backs of wagons; some on foot—mile after mile, day after day, heading for a harbor where they could board a ship to take them to America. Most traveled light: the *Shabbos* candlesticks and tablecloth, perhaps; a few clothes, certainly; a package or two of home-cooked foods, absolutely. Who could trust what was served on the boat, even if they said it was "kosher"? When these Jews arrived at any of the New World's port cities, where did they go?

The majority headed straight for urban centers, where they ended up packed "like raisins."[1] Rabbi A. R. Levy of Chicago, writing for the *Reform Advocate*, articulated the widely held belief that "[f]rom the Russian pale of settlement to the crowded ghettos of America does not spell out liberty and freedom."[2]

A smaller number of Jewish immigrants, though, headed toward America's less congested towns and cities. Louis Witkin, originally from the Ukraine, but living in Superior, Wisconsin, explained why Jews clustered closely even there: "You didn't have to live in a Jewish area, but as a rule, you come to a strange town, you go among the Jewish to live—'cause you don't know anybody else, you know, and you're more satisfied to live among the Jewish."[3] Some opened shops; some practiced their Old World crafts if there were a demand; others peddled for a while to build up capital and/or to send for their relatives in the Old World. Lee Shai Weissbach notes, "Many . . . started out as peddlers. They settled for the same reasons the Germans did. . . . While the mass migration that began in 1881 affected the makeup of America's major Jewish centers almost immediately, it took perhaps a decade, and sometimes longer, for East Europeans to begin arriving in smaller cities and towns in significant numbers, especially away from the eastern seaboard."[4]

The German-Jews, although somewhat ambivalent toward these newcomers, rallied to provide whatever support they could—money, food, clothing, English lessons, citizenship and cooking classes. "These refugees from Russia are our brethren. . . . We are responsible for them to God, to our adopted country and to humanity."[5] That sentiment led to the development of philanthropic and social programs designed to help the Eastern European Jews settle in and become American.

The Baron Maurice de Hirsch Fund, established in 1891 in America, provided a variety of different kinds of aid to those newly arrived Jews: manual arts training classes, cooking classes, farming lessons, and loans. Eventually, different Jewish philanthropic agencies banded together, forming the Industrial Removal Office (IRO) in 1900 to assist them in moving out of Eastern cities. Those involved in these "de-congestion" efforts concentrated on Jewish men "who want[ed] to remove their families from that influence which threatens them with moral and physical deprivation and degredation."[6]

We suspect that it was through the work of the Baron de Hirsch Fund or the IRO that settlers such as Etheldoris Stein Grais's family found themselves in Minnesota. Etheldoris, who grew up in Hibbing, in the Masabi Iron Range of Minnesota, told us:

> I really have no idea how we got here [to Minnesota]. My [mother's] family came from Vilna [Lithuania] to New York, but my grandmother who was living in Vilna [with them] was from Russia. Once they got here [to America], then they were sent to Chicago. Why, I don't know. Then, somebody got word about Minnesota. My family went to Duluth. There was a large Jewish community there. Uncle Charlie heard about logging up north of Virginia [Minnesota],

so he went up there to explore. Then he got word about iron ore, and so they all left to mine. Soon a rabbi and a *shochet* came. They had a synagogue there. There were 156 [Jewish] families.

My father was studying pharmacy at the University of Minnesota when the [1918] flu came. He was ready to graduate, but the dean asked him to go up to Hibbing and help out—tell them what they could do, what medicines to use. . . . So he went, and he liked it there. He married my mother, and they moved to Hibbing where I was born.[7]

For the majority of the Eastern European Jews who applied to the IRO for help and then discovered they were to be relocated to communities "out West," their major question was how would they make a living? Why, "farming, of course" was frequently the answer. After all, the Bible documented that Jews had been farmers, herders, and warriors before they were forced from their original homeland. Wealthy banker Jacob H. Schiff informed the 1911 Convention of Jewish Farmers of America, "The Jew is by choice a tiller of the soil, and when the Jew was driven from his natural home, his first thought turned to this country and the soil. It is an honor to work and to help build up the country."[8] So, in the effort to relocate Jews, not only was biblical history invoked, but patriotism as well.

At that time, the Midwest had acre upon acre of rich, open, available, inexpensive farmland. The Jewish Agricultural Society, funded by Baron de Hirsch monies, provided loans and advice. "The selection of the kind of work to be done—truck, dairy, fruit or general farming—is left to individual choice. . . . The settlement of more than four or five families in any neighborhood is discouraged, unless it be where the older settlers have already inured themselves to the life and work of the agriculturalists."[9]

And so they went, if not exactly eager to try their hands at tilling the soil, then at least happy to get out of the squalor of their East Coast urban neighborhoods. The IRO efforts relocated any number of Jews to Midwestern states, such as Iowa, where by 1916, the Jewish population had risen to 9,000 from the 1,000 counted in 1878. As many as 500 to 1,000 Eastern European Jews were settled on Iowa farms alone between 1905 and 1920. Sixteen families were moved to land near Bad Axe, Michigan, which they called "Palestine," in 1891. Eighteen Russian and Romanian families were moved to Arpin, Wisconsin, in 1904 to establish a farming community; sadly, this venture was unsuccessful. Later, the IRO attempted to redirect 3,700 Jews to 74 towns and cities across the state; most, however, settled in Milwaukee. In Illinois, the Russian Colonization Society was established in 1891 to aid in the resettlement of immigrants from that area of the world, both Jewish and Christian. Rabbi Rubenstein, one of the members, stated, "We don't want them herded up in the great cities, but we want to scatter them throughout the country, so that they will become amalgamated with the people and lose their identity as Russians. We want to Americanize them and make them self-supporting." Toward that end, "Each head of a family will be provided with forty acres of good land and the necessary farming implements, horses, etc." on credit.[10]

Some Jews, though, did not need encouragement to move to the countryside. They simply wanted to farm. Brenda Weisberg Meckler's family left Russia for Boston, then moved to Cincinnati, and from there to an Ohio potato farm. This last relocation, involving her immediate family, along with her Uncle Mike, was because this uncle had conceived the rather romantic notion that "[a] Jew belongs on the land. It is honorable; it is healthy; you're your own master; nobody has you in his pocket."[11]

One of the handwritten cookbooks we own was written by an anonymous Midwestern Jewish farm woman. We cannot tell whether she was of German or Eastern European extraction, but from various hints she left scattered throughout her booklet, we suspect she lived in either Ohio or Indiana. Perhaps she reached the Midwest through the largesse of the Baron de Hirsch Fund, or joined family or friends already living in the area, or maybe she was the descendent or wife of a former peddler who had decided to settle down.

The cookbook itself seems to have been fashioned from a much larger ledger, probably by cutting it into horizontal thirds. This very fact speaks volumes about how thrifty our author was, and how difficult it may have been to secure a "real" notebook in which to jot the instructions for the dishes she wanted to prepare. "Cash money" for outright purchases was always scarce on a farm; farmers had to wait until they had sold their crops. In addition, our author started writing her booklet in 1892, the year the financial panic leading to the Depression of 1893 began. Her last entry came in 1898, the same year that the worst depression since the Revolutionary War officially ended. During this period, we somehow doubt that buying a book solely to record recipes would have been a high-priority item for this woman. We noticed, too, that her recipes did not call for any brand name or processed food products as Ruth Dunie's had done. We surmised that this was because they were too expensive, or unavailable. The recipe calling for "New Orleans Molasses" was simply to indicate molasses shipped through that port. This kind was considered the best.

One of our favorite recipes was recorded March 2, 1898. It is titled "Aunt Annetta's Recipe" and is for homemade yeast to be used in baking. Although commercially prepared yeast would have been available had our author lived in a city, on the farm she most likely had to make her own.

> Take 3 teacupsfulls of potatoes and a good handful of hops put in a bag and put in a gallon of water, boil. When boiled put in the liquor—
> ½ teacupfull salt
> ½ teacup full sugar
> 1 teaspoonful good ginger
> Set in a warm place to ferment

We imagine that, like many rural women, our author grew vegetables in a small plot near her house, and scoured the countryside for wild berries and fruits smelling of sunshine and summer. As warm days drew to a close, she, like Ruth Dunie, would have spent weeks canning and pickling fruits and vegetables. Her pantry shelves, and her root cellar, would then have provided the wherewithal to add variation to family dinners throughout the long, cold, Midwest winters, and acted as a safeguard in case the next year's harvests were poor.

Her recipe for "Chow-Chow," pickled vegetables commercially available since at least 1861 in Chicago and elsewhere, tells us what items she grew in her kitchen garden and on the farm, much like recipes of the same name often found in old Amish cookbooks.[12] Right before the weather turned cool, and night frosts threatened, our farm woman would have picked all the tomatoes, ripe or not. Because the growing season is so short in the Midwest, she would have had to start her lima bean seeds indoors if she expected to harvest them before autumn. They need three to four months to mature. She probably would have chosen the "bush" variety that suits Midwestern soils so well. She would have pulled her fat onions from the soil, then collected all the green peppers, little cucumbers, and string beans that remained on their vines, too. Her husband must have harvested a good crop of sweet corn the year she wrote out her recipe; her instructions called for a dozen ears. And then the spices—she may have ordered her pickling spices from the Sears, Roebuck catalogue if she could afford it, or purchased them from the grocer during an infrequent visit to town if she had the money or the credit, or obtained from an itinerant peddler, receiving them in trade.

Chow Chow

1 qt. green tomatoes chopped
1 doz onions
1 qt lima beans
1 doz. corn
1 qt. string beans. boil all separately
1 oz. white mustard seed
1 oz. celery seed
1 small pickles ½ lb of sugar
½ doz. peppers
bit tumeric powder
½ gal vinegar
1 box of mustard

Boil vinegar mix the ground mustard + tumeric together and stir in while the vinegar is boiling. Add other ingredients to and boil.

Catsups were not only used as condiments, but were often added to soups, gravies, and other sauces to season them. Olives in the recipe below add unusual and interesting visual- and taste-notes to this "Cooked Catsup" recipe. Grape catsup, as strange as it might sound today, was quite popular in the late 1890s. It was frequently served with meat or fowl, or added to baked beans or hash. Wild grapes, free for the picking, grew throughout the Midwest. The thick-skinned, dark purple, or deep red fruits called for in her recipe are sour if harvested before the onset of cooler weather. Our author would have picked them during the "dog days" of summer.

Cooked Catsup

1 Gal. ripe Tomatoes
4 Tablespoonsful salt
3   "   Black Pepper
3   "   Ground Mustard
1 Teaspoon Allspice
1   "   Olives
2   "   Red Pepper
1 Pint Vinegar

Cook 4 hours

Grape catsup

Wild sour grapes best to five pounds grapes
2½ gran. sugar
1 pt. Vinegar [,] 1 Tablespoon ground cloves, cinnamon, allspice, pepper and ½ Teaspoonful salt. Boil grapes in enough water so they won't stick. strain through colander add spice, boil until thick.

A woman's chili sauce was a matter of pride. Its flavor covered a multitude of sins, such as overcooking and dried-out leftovers; plus, it added zest to dinner foods. Interestingly, our author's recipe for this condiment did not contain any hot chilis, as might be expected from its name, only green peppers. Most likely, she would have used this relish as an accompaniment to chicken or fish.

Chilli Sauce

1 peck tomatoes
6 green peppers
6 onions
2 Teaspoonsful allspice
Cloves + cinnamon
2 Cups brown sugar
5 Cups vinegar
Salt to taste

Chop all fine Boil all together 3 or 4 hours.

The recipe that our author recorded for "Grape Tomato and Peach Butter" is actually two recipes: one for Grape Tomato Butter; the other for Peach Butter. Butters from tomatoes and peaches require less sugar than jams and are a perfect way to use up bumper crops of those fruits, especially when sugar is scarce or expensive. We suspect that "grape tomato" is a descriptive term for the fruit's size and shape, because what is now called a "grape tomato" is a hybrid developed during the 1990s. Sugar would have cut the acidic taste in the tomato butter, while the addition of a bit of vinegar might have served to prevent the growth of mold after the butters were canned.

Grape Tomatoe + Peach Butter

13 lbs Fruit to 8 lbs. of sugar for tomatoes use 8½ lbs sugar and some vinegar.

Besides handwritten recipes, our anonymous author pasted newspaper columns written by syndicated columnist Marion Harland and other domestic scientists throughout her book. Undoubtedly, reading these newspapers was how she learned about the most recent scientific cooking ideas, along with new ways to prepare foods, and, also kept up with the world's happenings. Although we found the recipes she recorded, such as for Roll Sponge Cake and Cherry Custard, along with the ones she clipped, engaging, primarily because they suggested what ingredients and foodstuffs she had "at the ready," what really fascinated us, because they told quite a bit about her life on the farm, were her handwritten medical concoctions.

Probably miles from a pharmacy or a doctor, when non-life-threatening illness struck, she would have been the one to whom her family turned for a cure. We can tell a lot about the types of ailments that worried or afflicted her and her family from the remedies she recorded. During the nineteenth century, there seemed to have been an epidemic of "dyspepsia" in America. This generic term described everything from indigestion, to stomach ulcers, to cancer. Oftentimes this malady was ascribed to devouring too rich foods, to eating tainted foods, and/or to eating too many spices or condiments. Cures were touted in newspapers across the land.

Dyspepsia! Dyspepsia! Dyspepsia!
WHAT IS IT? HOW IS IT CURED?
Dyspepsia is our National Disease—weak stomach, trouble[d] digestion, distress after eating, coative habit, bilious condition. How many suffer with it and its attendant symptoms of low spirits, bad taste, coated tongue, obstupified head, and attacks of headache? Yet, how few know how to cure it! Generally, because the bowels are constipated, resort is had to cathartics or laxatives. But such a condition was never cured by cathartics, whose only office is to weaken the digestion and impair the integrity of the entire assimilative system.

But HUMPHREYS' HOMEOPATHIC DYSPEPSIA PILLS—a simple medicated sugar pill—have cured hundreds of the worst and most obstinate cases. This is done simply by improving the tone and restoring the integrity of the digestive organs, from which result good appetite, regular habits, a clear head and buoyant spirit. Such a medicine is a gem, and only requires to be known to be appreciated.[13]

Apparently, on February 2, 1897, our author, not having a supply of Humphreys' pills, or any other patent medicine for dyspepsia at hand, became concerned enough about this condition to jot down a home remedy.

FOR DYSPEPSIA

Pour one quart of cold water in two tablespoonsfull of unslaked lime let it stand few minutes bottle and cool. When clear it is ready for use. Put three tablespoonsful in a cup of milk drink slowly before meals. Vary according to age.

If cattarh, coughs, or breathing problems afflicted anyone in the house, our author was prepared. Two of her recipes, which might have been used as expectorants or to allay asthmatic symptoms, called for locally available edible botanicals. Perhaps the dust, from planting and harvesting, or kicked up from walking on straw in the barn, caused someone in her family to develop breathing problems.

Recipe #1

½ oz Powdered flag root
½ oz Goldenrod flowers
½ oz Horehound
—

Dry rod in sun, Honey mixed with the above until a thick mass eat lump large as marble 4 times a day morning + last at night

Recipe #2

Oil Sweet Almonds
Syrup Violets
   "   Squills
in weight
Shake well take in mouth
15 drops Equal parts—

Our author may also have suffered from "tired blood," another common complaint during the nineteenth century. Is it any wonder women were exhausted? Typical farm and household chores included performing "stoop labor" like planting, watering, tending, and harvesting the garden, collecting eggs, milking the cows, skimming the milk, churning butter, making cheese, stoking wood fires, preparing three meals every day for her family and farm hands, doing dishes, washing, drying and ironing clothes, sewing, mending, watching children, putting up fruits and vegetables for the winter, and who knows how many more tasks.

Mention of the time and energy involved in growing, selling, canning, and preserving produce can be found in any number of Jewish memoirs. For example, Ben Rosenberg, a farmer in Benton Harbor, Michigan, recalled that in addition to her numerous other household-related chores, his mother, Gitche, also sorted and packed the strawberries his father, Samuel, grew and then sold at the Fruit Market on Benton Harbor's city wharf.[14] When crops were plentiful, this project would have taken days—time undoubtedly stolen from other necessary chores, with Gitche working until "bone-tired." Then, too, Brenda Weisberg Meckler recalls some of her family's effort in "putting up" fruits for the winter:

> We picked the last of the apples and the sour red cherries that were in the orchard across the road from our barnyard. Our house and yard were soon redolent of the spicy fragrance of apple butter and cinnamon, cooking to a rich, glossy thickness. The cherries became preserves, hoarded for serving with tea on special occasions. The gooseberries were turned into a tart sauce, stored against the day when we might have meat with which to enjoy it. And the currants were transformed into tiny rubies trapped in a sweet sea the color of molten gold. The grapes, too, became jelly, purple as the robes of kings. But the greatest magic of all was the jelly made from the peelings of the apples that had been turned into apple butter. . . . The cellar shelves were soon adorned with mason jars and jelly glasses sealed with lids of wax.[15]

During the nineteenth century, rejuvenation for the weary and work-worn often came from swallowing "spring tonics" and "blood purifiers." Had our cookbook author lived in an urban area, she might have purchased Paine's Celery Compound, which "wipes out unhealthy humors from the blood, opens up the skin and makes it due its full share in purifying the blood," from an apothecary shop.[16]

Instead, our farm woman needed to mix her own tonics. She wrote down two "blood purifier" recipes designed to increase energy. One of these specified ingredients grown in the Midwest that we might not consider edible, palatable, or even safe today, but which were commonly employed during times when medicines were often compounds made from herbs, spices, and other plants. The other, simpler one, called only for black alder. This tree was common throughout Eastern Europe, particularly in Poland, and so the recipe calling for this ingredient may have been one our cookbook author brought with her to America. Perhaps she intended to experiment to see which one worked better.

Blood Purifier

Yellow Dock
Sassafras bark
equal parts
steeped in water
—

Blood Purifier

Black Alder
steeped in water

Then again, if our author did indeed suffer from "tired blood," we suspect we understand why she recorded so many different recipes for candy in her book. While she may only have had a sweet-tooth, or was preparing for the day when granulated sugar prices dropped to the point where she could afford to make these sweets or anticipating the time when she would have a spare moment to make such frivolous comestibles, she may have been making and eating these candies for a temporary "energy-boost."

Candy

1 cup Molasses
½ Cup Sugar
½ Teaspoonful Baking Powder
2   "   Vinegar
Piece of butter large as walnut

Molasses Candy

1 Cup Molasses
1   "   Sugar
2 Tablespoonsful melted butter
1   "   Vinegar

Boil without stirring until it hardens in cold water. Then stir in teaspoonful soda. Never stir when cooling. Use New Orleans Molasses.

Caramels (excellent)

½ lb Brown Sugar
¼ lb Butter
¾ Cup grated chocolate
½ Cup sweet cream
½ Cup molasses

Mix all together. Boil until it hardens in water

We include another of her home remedies, solely for its historical interest, even though it is not really "food-related." This recipe was given no title in our farm woman's booklet. We had a great deal of difficulty figuring out its application. Was it a plaster for pleurisy? For pneumonia? Or something else?

5 cts Gum Camphor
½ oz Cod Liver Oil
1 oz Headlight Oil
¼ pt Wood Alcohol
Rub with above+ put white flannel on Ointment

The listed ingredients are potent and potentially lethal if ingested. Wood alcohol, poisonous if swallowed, was frequently used in varnishes and shellacs during the nineteenth century. It was also considered a skin "irritant" that could produce blisters. Pungently aromatic gum camphor had long been considered efficacious in stimulating circulation when applied topically. Cod liver oil, even today, is often considered "good for whatever ails you." This tonic was highly recommended for building resistance to diseases, but its use here in an ointment seems unusual, unless it enabled the other ingredients to be spread on the affected area(s) more easily. Headlight oil, a petroleum product distilled from cannel coal, was used in locomotive, signal, and miners lamps where bright, clear light was needed!

This particular ointment component truly was a real puzzlement. Then we found an 1869 article in the *British Medical Journal* that cleared up our confusion. Dr. John Mulvany had applied coal-oil to patients suffering from abscesses, inflammations, sprains, itches, and rheumatism. He wrote, "Petroleum enjoys an extensive and well-deserved reputation as an external application in rheumatism. . . . As a topical application to inflamed parts, it is, judging from my limited experience, unsurpassed by any other known remedy. It possesses also two other advantages which materially enhance its value as a remedial agent. First, it is always at hand; and, secondly, it is extremely cheap. Its mode

of action is simple, combining as it does, stimulant and astringent with ano-
dyne properties. . . . When rubbed on the skin . . . it produces a sensation of
numbness and of partial insensibility. . . . It does, however, unquestionably
relieve pain."[17]

We could almost hear our farm woman's thoughts, "If regular coal-oil is good
for rheumatism, then Headlight Oil must be better because it's more power-
ful!" So, she may have mixed up this ointment in hopes that it would give her
the temporary relief she needed to go about her tasks. In any case, once the
patient had been smeared, or had daubed herself, with this concoction, the
treatment site would have been wrapped with absorbent white flannel. White
was the color of choice because it was believed to retain heat better than col-
ored flannels.

A different group of recipes, purchased in a used bookstore, had been written into a notebook whose elaborately decorated front cover was edged with
curlicues and factory-printed with the following question: "Indications of Future Greatness?" Like the cut-down ledger cookbook, this one, too, seems to
have been composed during depression times. The author, whose name was
really "Hannah," but who was known as "Anna" to her family and friends, lived
somewhere outside Gary, Indiana, during the 1930s, and perhaps earlier.[18] We
know this because she had tucked a letter from a friend or relative into the
pages of her recipe book.

> Gary Ind
> Sept. 1931
> Dear Anna, Am sending you a Chili Sauce recipe.
>   1 pk ripe tomatoes
>   4 large onions
>   2 red peppers sweet
>   ¾ lbs sugar
>   1 pt vinegar
>   ⅛ tsp clove ¼ tsp cinnamon ¼ tsp alspice
>   ¼ tsp nutmeg 3 tsp salt sprinkl of red pepper   Boil 3 hrs
> Bertha stopped here to-night she says to ask you to save her a few
> tomatoe seeds.
>   Love to all from all.
> Emilie
>   Am going to Gary today to get some of the cement for the chimney so some
> day if Emil ain't busy try and come and fix it.

Whether Anna was Russian, German, or Hungarian, as many of the Jews in
Lake County, Indiana, around Gary were, we cannot tell, although we suspect

she might have been German, based on the recipes she recorded and their spices. We do know, however, that English was not her first language because in the back of the book she wrote what appears to be a grammar exercise:

GRAMMER

The dog guarded the young lambs "guarded" is a regular transitive verb active voice, indicative mode, past tense, singular number, 3rd person. The sun shall have risen "shall have risen" is an irregular intransitive verb, active voice, indicative mode, future perfect, singular number, 3rd person.

Anna apparently learned her lessons well because no recipes in her book were in any language other than English. This strongly suggests that whenever and however she had arrived in the Midwest, she had determined to become "American."

Besides the expected recipes for Jewish holiday dishes, and sweets, such as "Ginger Bread," Anna recorded directions for preserving meat.

Preserving meat

1 qt salt
2 tablespoon brown sugar
1   "   red pepper
1   "   black pepper
~~1 cup white sugar~~

Her recipe underscores the problems rural folk had in keeping meat for any period of time before the advent of kitchen ice-boxes and refrigerators. Attempting to understand some of the effort involved, we spoke with a friend who grew up in the same small town where she still lives about some of the meat preservation techniques that she remembers from "way back when." In a follow-up note, she emphasized, "It was a challenge to keep meat for more than a day or two. Fresh meat had to be placed in stoneware jars and covered with skim milk, and weighted with a stone to keep the meat under the milk. Or you had to preserve it by soaking it for 3 to 5 minutes in a solution of one tablespoon borax to a gallon of water, or rub it with powdered borax dry. If you potted meat, you'd cover it with a layer of paraffin to keep out the air. . . . It's a wonder more people didn't drop dead—well, maybe they DID!!—from various tainted foodstuffs."[19]

Even if a rural woman owned an ice-box or had improvised one from a covered shelf tacked to an outside window ledge, she might still have problems.[20] A covered shelf worked only in cooler weather; ice-boxes needed large blocks of ice to keep their contents cold. If farms were too far out in the country for the ice-man's delivery, some lucky women could go to their own cold spring houses or cellars for ice harvested from frozen lakes or rivers, then kept between layers of straw. Others were simply out of luck. As late as the 1930s, electric refrigerators were not yet standard kitchen appliances, even in cities. We learn this from Irma Frankenstein's diaries in which she recounted the purchase of her first electric refrigerator during the depths of the Great Depression in 1937.

> Met Victor [husband] at Gas Co. after 3. We looked at Electrolux Refrigera-
> tors—then over to Commonwealth Ed., looked at several refrigerators & then
> bot a Frigidaire—7 cu. Ft—cost 241.00 including 7.04 sales, payable monthly.
> . . . Right after lunch the Frigidaire came. Victor C. was much delighted with it,
> as I am. Showed me how to make it work & took possession of it like a grand
> new toy. It is a beauty and has many conveniences—automatic defrosting &
> temperature control, contrivance for loosening containers for ice-cubes, lever
> for loosening ice-cubes, Electric light inside the box. It will be a pleasure to
> use it & it is a pleasure to look at it. Does not take up very much room in the
> kitchen . . . The Frigidaire cost somewhere around $236.00 but we have 3 years
> in which to pay it. Of course, in 3 years we would have needed ice in the old
> refrigerator. There is a possibility that my frequent winter colds have been due
> in part to the difference in temperature between the warm kitchen & the cold
> place where the old ice-box stands.[21]

On April 8, 1932, Dr. A. W. Bitting related the following to a news reporter: "It's almost unbelievable what such an invention as that of the refrigerator [rail] car may do in changing the food habits of a whole nation. Prior to its development in 1869, by a Chicagoan, the major meat packing operations were conducted only during the cool months. Fresh meat could be cured only during the cold weather and nearly all meat for outside markets was pickled or cured. . . . Fresh meat was available in those days only in local markets as it was slaughtered. But the refrigerator car changed all that. . . . Meat was soon made available at all times and of better quality." He added that the same principle of refrigeration was just beginning to be applied to the transportation of poultry, eggs, and fresh fruits.[22]

Still, one of the major difficulties in rural areas around the Midwest remained how to secure fresh meat. If kosher meat were required, the problem was often compounded. Refrigerated cars frequently only carried deliveries to larger cities. Smaller towns and cities, even if on rail lines, might be out of luck. Orders had to be large enough to warrant the use of a refrigerated car.

Small-town and rural Jews living in the Middle West got around these obstacles. They would pack up their families, shut their businesses, and travel to larger towns and cities to be with relatives and friends during the High Holy Days and important Jewish holidays, because they might not have a synagogue or rabbi to perform religious ceremonies where they lived.[23] They would take these opportunities to buy kosher meat and poultry to carry back with them when they left after the holidays. Some observant Jews traveled to the large Midwest slaughterhouses that had kosher-processing divisions, or to kosher butcher shops in larger cities to pick up their own meat or poultry, then raced back home, hoping to arrive before their purchases spoiled. Others ordered their meats and chickens from slaughterhouses or kosher butchers, then had them delivered by U.S. mail or train. Still others waited until a *shochet* arrived at their farmsteads to slaughter livestock.

Molly Weisberg, Brenda's mother, sometimes rode the commuter train to Cincinnati to pick up kosher meat and poultry. Otherwise, the family did without. A typical meatless dinner was "cold *schav* (a soup of sorrel and sour cream), blintzes made up the day before, now fried to a golden crispness and topped with sour cream, canned tomatoes brought from the cellar, and late apples . . . baked in the afternoon."[24]

Abe Ruderman reminisced about his life as an onion farmer in Benton Harbor, Michigan, and what happened one time when he ordered chicken from the kosher butcher shop in Fort Wayne, Indiana. "One week before Christmas an order was placed for a freshly slaughtered chicken. Usually a package postmarked in the early forenoon would arrive in the evening mail. I forgot about the Christmas mail rush, and my package was delayed two days in arriving! The postmaster called me to tell me he had put my parcel in the back room—mailbag and all—as the stench was so terrible. I had to take the entire package home, clean out the mailbag, and bury the contents—and, of course, do without this delicacy!"[25]

In 1976, Blanche Halpern Goldberg, who grew up in Hebron, North Dakota, recalled similar problems with the delivery of kosher meat: "We imported the kosher meat from Minneapolis, but when it came out by train, and our store was across the street from the station, the stationmaster said, 'Jake, your package came.' [My father] said, 'I know, Pete. Dump it. It smells way over here already.' No refrigeration. How my mother managed to feed all those kids with very little meat, I still don't know."[26]

Joseph Ornstein, from the Polish Ukraine, was "an 'incurable farmer,'" so when he immigrated to the United States, he headed for the fields of Ohio.[27] He bought a derelict farm to which he brought his bride. They worked to make it productive. One year, crops failed; in another, crops were so bountiful all over the area that the market was flooded, and his produce brought next to nothing. Money was tight. Loans from the American Jewish Agricultural Society saved the various farmsteads they sequentially owned from near-bankruptcy several times. Eventually, the Ornsteins settled in Geneva, Ohio, where they were able to make a "go" of farming. At one point they, and other Jewish farmers in Geneva, produced "more than 60 percent of the area's grapes, and a large share of the peaches and other fruits."[28] The community was never large enough to employ a rabbi, a Hebrew teacher, a cantor, or a *shochet*. Joseph's son, Jacob Ornstein-Galicia, remembers, "A *schoichet* [alternative spelling] would sometimes come from Cleveland to butcher cattle and poultry. . . . [On the High Holidays,] it is pleasant to recall [the] bountiful meals—virtual feasts— served on those occasions. Farm wives vied with one another in producing traditional delicacies—stuffed cabbage; *hezel*, or stuffed derma; chopped liver; boiled chicken; beef *flanken* (a cut of meat from the short ribs); all polished off with an array of *tsimmis*, or compote, strudel, all rich in eggs and sugar; *Kichalech*, or cookies."[29]

Notions and potions, spices and extracts, and a thousand other things—who knew what wonders, what treasures, what necessaries, would be pulled from the peddler's pack or from the hidden recesses of his wagon when he knocked on your door? He brought the world. Lee Shai Weissbach states that "there was a great need for peddlers among the scattered farmsteads and villages of the American countryside, for until the early twentieth century much of the population lacked ready access to major commercial centers, where peddlers themselves obtained their wares, or even to country stores, where the peddlers sometimes kept their stock."[30] Myrtice Crews recalled the peddler "did business almost exclusively with women, and whatever they needed they could always find in the Jew's wagon. If they didn't have the money to pay for that they needed, he would trade for eggs or chickens or cured meat or canned vegetables and berries."[31]

Jewish peddlers, Sephardic, German, and Eastern European, like their Christian counterparts, roamed the American countryside, carrying news and goods from the cities to small towns and the countryside, and in the reverse. They were slaves to no time clocks. With luck, they could save enough to open a retail store, or bring their families over from Europe or Russia. Rabbi Isaac Meyer Wise recounted, "One afternoon I met on the street a man with a large, old straw hat drawn far over his face. He was clad in a perspired linen coat, and carried two large tin boxes on his shoulders . . . and dragged himself along with painful effort. I looked at him closely, and recognized my friend Stein. . . . 'Our people in this country, said he, may be divided into the following classes: (1) The basket peddler . . . (2) the trunk-carrier (3) the pack-carrier.'"[32]

Bernard Baum, who later owned shops in Kentucky and Indiana, recalls his first day peddling stockings to Kentucky farm women: "The first day I went towards the Bardstown Road, applied to many houses trying to sell some of my load, but were shown the door, and in some houses were introduced to a big dog. So I tramped till I were out of the city and succeeded to sell a pair of hose for 30 cents."[33] An unnamed Jewish man living in Chicago was interviewed during the Great Depression for the Federal Writers' Project. His story is titled "Pack on my back." He recounted how he came to the United States from Russia around 1870 at the age of eighteen with no skills. "The easiest thing to do was to peddle. . . . A great many men became country peddlers. There were thousands of men walking from farm to farm with heavy packs on their backs. . . . It was not an easy life. But we made pretty good money. We were all trying to save enough money to bring relatives to America."[34] And, with more luck, successful peddlers could also save enough to open wholesale businesses where other itinerants and retailers could buy supplies. As a case in point, "In Oshkosh, Wisconsin, the Segal family operated a wholesale distributorship that carried an eclectic mix of food products and related items, including 'canned goods, nuts, paper, produce, cheese, oleomargarine, dried fruits, salt fish, shortening, confectionery [and] oysters.'"[35]

In one of the antique diaries we own, a woman who recorded her name as "L. A. Rogers," and her location as "Whitemore Hill," which we believe was somewhere in upstate New York, noted: "Jan. 4, 1900. There was an extract pedlar staid here last night, he gave Bertha 3 bottles of extract." On October 29, of the same year, she recorded, "I went to Union and got my teeth. . . . The little pedlar is staying here tonight."

Peddlers often swapped some of their goods for a spot to sleep overnight, a few farm-fresh eggs, or even feed for their mules. Observant Jewish peddlers would look for places they might stay over the Sabbath, where they could fix and eat their *tseydo ladorekh* (food brought along for the road), for somewhere they could rest their weary feet and pray. As the same unnamed Jewish peddler recounted for the Federal Writers' Project:

The living expenses of the peddlers were very little. The farmers' wives always gave us plenty of food. I did not eat anything that was not kosher. But I could eat eggs and there were plenty of them. There was fresh milk and bread and butter. The farmers always gave us a place to sleep. In the summer we slept in the hay-loft. In the winter, if there was no spare bed, we would sleep on the floor. . . . The farmers were very lonely during the long winters, and they were glad to have anybody come to their homes. . . . There was no rural mail delivery in those days. The farmers very seldom saw a newspaper. They were hungry for news. They were very glad to see a peddler from any large city. . . . You see, I was a newspaper and a department store. . . . Yes, the peddlers with their packs did their share to make life more comfortable for the farmers, while they were ploughing the ground and raising food for America.[36]

We suspect that Ruth Dunie, while living in Hillsboro, Illinois, purchased the bottle of pistachio extract that her special cake required from a peddler. Extract of pistachio is not something readily available in general grocery stores, even today. In fact, when we searched newspaper advertisements, between 1910 and 1930, we found only lemon, vanilla, cinnamon, nutmeg, almond, anise, and rose extracts listed for sale. So, where else would she have obtained this essential ingredient except from an extract peddler?

Pistache Cake

> Bake. Hot water cake in layers.
> Leave the bottom whole but remove the centers of 2 upper layers.
> Beat cream until stiff, sweeten + mix in some pounded almonds.
> Put this in hollow cake.
> Ice entire cake with icing flavored with Pistache (1 drop.)

Itinerants worked out of and in Midwest cities, too. In fact, a reporter for the *Chicago Tribune* claimed, in March 1901, "The peddlers are to be found in every State and every large city in the country. . . . The men belonging to that class are almost without exception Jews of orthodox faith."[37] In a 1977 oral interview, Louis Witkin recalled that even during the 1920s, "Most of the Jewish people that came from the old country, they were peddlers. Most of them, they peddle junk; they [also] peddle fruit, and then, they had a couple of junk shops. You know, the Jewish people had the junk shops, and the peddlers come, and they pick up stuff, and they sell it, see?"[38]

The goods that peddlers sold in the cities might well have been things they had bought or for which they had traded out in the country: succulent strawberries, sweet cherries and Concord grapes, fresh onions, cloves of garlic, snap beans, or crisp apples. Then, too, some street hawkers sold items they had purchased in the city: Idaho potatoes, ripe bananas, oranges, golden pineapples, roasted peanuts, ginger candy, and fat Bohemian pretzels, or those they made on-demand, such as Iowa popcorn, hot dogs, and fizzy drinks.

Cities offered great opportunities for these mobile merchants. Alan Kraut says that "newly arrived immigrants preferred to make purchases from local merchants because they were unfamiliar with other parts of the city."[39] We would add that newly arrived immigrants and other city dwellers often preferred to make purchases of small items from door-to-door salesmen, rather than from local merchants. Prices were often cheaper, and you could always haggle. The *Chicago Daily Tribune* published an article titled "How a Jew Can Find a Jew," in which the unnamed author wrote, "A certain class of Jewish peddlers desire to deal only with people of their own race. They visit the houses of the poorer quarters of the city . . . yet, they never knock at the door of a room where other than a Jew resides. . . . On the doorframe at the entrance to every Jewish house there is nailed a little tin box—generally three or four inches long and one-half or a whole inch wide. . . . And it is by looking behind the street door that the Jewish peddler can tell whether or not one of his co-religionists dwells within the house."[40] They were savvy businessmen.

In Chicago, around 1900, the Maxwell Street District, in the Seventh Ward, was known as "the Hebrew quarter" or, less charitably, as "the Ghetto," in the press and in general conversation. More than 15,000 Russian Jews lived within that area "bounded by Sixteenth street on the south and Polk street on the north and the Chicago River and Halsted street on the east and west."[41] It boasted a "kosher fish market, the largest fish market in Chicago," newspapers, a theater, six synagogues, a kosher market, a "Horse market, where . . . peddlers of every sort who have need of horses patronize . . . [and] a Potato market [where] the potato peddlers buy their stock."[42] In her memoirs of growing up on Chicago's West Side, Marjorie Warville Bear wrote, "Not all peddlers had horse-drawn conveyances; some had pushcarts. One which pleased the children was the popcorn and peanut man who appeared at dusk when he would find more patrons sitting on the front porches. His sputtering oil flame and insistent whistle was the signal for trailing children. . . . [W]e were allowed only the hot roasted peanuts packed in green and red striped bags with two twisted ear-locked ends; the cost was five cents."[43]

The people of Chicago had been fond of popcorn going back at least to 1883, when a peddler, attired in a cap adorned with a broad brass sign reading "Popcorn," carrying a trumpet and two enormous bags filled with popcorn over his shoulder, told a reporter for the *Chicago Daily Tribune* that he sold out his supply of quart bags within a few hours. Its continued popularity is documented in a 1910 *Tribune* news column about a Jewish popcorn peddler who attempted to sell his wares at an outdoor church service.[44] Peanut peddlers, too, had a long history in Chicago. Back in 1869, that same paper had reported that German (Jewish?) peddlers were hawking both peanuts and oranges, and that the city received "a portion of its income from these itinerants" in the form of vendors' license fees.[45]

Chicagoans, and other Midwesterners, were also fond of pretzels, but only the big fat, handmade, soft ones, the kind the Germans ate when they drank their beer. Apparently Germans in other cities were just as fussy. A baker quoted in the *Atchison* (Kansas) *Daily Champion* stated, "The Germans won't buy any [pretzels] but the hand made, which, for some reason nobody has ever been able to make out, are sweeter and of a better flavor, even when the dough used is precisely the same [as in the machine made ones]."[46] So, the *bretzel* peddlers took to the streets with long sticks on which they had threaded handmade wares.

Itinerants with overloaded push-carts or lugging bulging sacks and hawkers touting their wares from behind makeshift stalls could frequently be found along Midwestern city streets during good weather. "A trip through some of the congested districts in Chicago on any summer day, and especially on a summer evening [would find that] the numerous stands . . . which sell soda water 'with one or all kinds of flavors' at 1 cent a glass are constantly besieged by children. The children of the poor apparently spend relatively more money on ice cream, soda water, cherries, pineapple, and numerous other kinds of fruits than do the children of the well-to-do."[47] But how could anyone resist buying "effervescent joy" from the seltzer water man's push-cart or a fizzy drink flavored with fresh-squeezed lemons or oranges from a temporary street stall thrown together from scrap wood that would be broken down at the end of the day? Who could pass up a shaved ice and sweet syrup "snowball," or a paper cone of rich ice cream from the "hokey-pokey" man? After all, these only cost one penny each. Through the summertime heat that threatened to melt even *Ingberlach* (crystallized ginger candy), the peddlers cried their wares. Tantalizing smells of sausages and onions sizzling on open charcoal grills permeated the muggy air—aromas that attacked your senses and remained with you for life.[48] Over the clamor and the din, you could hear, "Hot dogs! Red hots! Getcher red hot dogs!"[49] The tastes were ever so much better for being eaten out of doors.

And, so, day after day, year after year, until they got tired or settled down, these mobile merchants moved through their neighborhoods and beyond, meeting the desires and needs of their customers, linking countryside to city, and in the doing, helped shape Midwestern Jewish-American life and foodways.[50]

5

How to Cook . . .

When thousands upon thousands of impoverished Eastern European Jews descended on Chicago, Rabbis Emil G. Hirsh and Liebman Adler of the two largest Reform synagogues in the city urged their congregants, mostly of German extraction, "to engage in a large scale philanthropic effort to find employment, to raise the living standards, and to 'Americanize' [your] less fortunate Jewish brethren."[1] Their listeners rose to the challenge. They started the Maxwell Street Settlement House. They instituted social clubs, savings clubs, drama clubs, and book clubs. They opened day nurseries and kindergartens. They established the Jewish Training School that taught German "for the express purpose of influencing its pupils to disdain and abandon the use of Yiddish, a so-called German 'jargon.'"[2] They ran soup kitchens.[3] They conducted cooking classes. German-Jews and those of German-descent founded similar institutions in every large city where Eastern European Jews lived, the Nathan Morris House in Indianapolis and the Milwaukee Settlement House being two. The Young Men's Hebrew Association of Cincinnati undertook "a practical work for the improvement of Jewish immigrants. It will establish night classes for adults. . . . The children are not included in the plan, but their parents will be encouraged to send them to the public schools."[4] However well-meaning these efforts, they were frequently met with resistance and contempt from the very people they were intended to help. If Eastern European Jews were to be assimilated, it was to be on their own terms.

Walter Ehrlich pointed out, "Eastern European Jews also sought to become good Americans [like every other immigrant group]. At the same time, though, they were determined to maintain the customs and traditions of their Judaism—which meant *Orthodox* Judaism. But with it was a way of life and a culture—which some refer to as 'Jewishness'—that had set them apart from others for centuries."[5] Those desires oftentimes ran in direct opposition to public school curricula, to the aims of Progressive-era reformers, and, sometimes even, to American ideals as they were then formulated. The Jews had fled from upheavals in Eastern Europe but landed in the midst of a social and cultural revolution in America!

The Progressive era, roughly 1880–1920, saw sweeping social reforms in the areas of temperance, education, and domestic science, all ostensibly for the "good of the nation" and for "the health of the nation." City streets teemed with the ragged—beggars, orphans, prostitutes, drunkards, and the garden-variety poor. They also abounded with social workers and settlement houses. Visits from social workers and social work students were so frequent throughout the area surrounding Chicago's Hull-House that Jane Addams declared they had "become obnoxious."[6] In 1910, the *Chicago Tribune* reported:

> The social settlements are a feature of Chicago life. They are neighborhood centers established for the purpose of improving the condition of the surrounding community in manner of living, in morals, in social condition, as well as in other ways. . . . There are twenty-three of these institutions in the city, the two oldest being Hull house and Gads Hill Center, both of which were established in 1880. . . . These institutions seek to maintain religious, educational and philanthropic enterprises and improve the conditions in industrial centers. Gymnasiums, clubs, classes, coffee houses, workingmen's clubs, theaters, industrial museums, with shops for various handicrafts, women's clubs, cooking, sewing, and household instruction, penny savings banks, and other things of like nature are included in the list of their activities.[7]

Nine years later, after even more immigrants had landed in the city, that same paper reported the "social settlement workers and the child welfare associations [did] not find their task of educating the appetites of the foreign-born lately come among us an easy task. . . . Food is one reason why the foreign-born like to live in colonies when they settle in Chicago. Then they all can be near to the baker, the butcher, and the grocer of their own race, and the colony being closely packed, these purveyors find it worth while to cater to the tastes of their compatriots. . . . There is a kind of tribe element in the economies of the food problem."[8] Early on, efforts to improve the diets of the urban poor had extended to holding classes on nutrition, how to cook, and what to cook. Their foodways were subjected to scientific analyses in terms of cost and content. Not surprisingly, W. O. Atwater, special agent of the U.S. Department of Agriculture, found, "In the case of families of limited income the choice of foods was necessarily governed by their costs. . . . In many instances the houses were found to be untidy, and the food did not appear appetizing. The need of training in housekeeping and cooking was apparent. . . . The conditions of the families in the congested districts of Chicago and other cities can undoubtedly be improved by education. The housekeeper should be taught how to prepare and serve food. In this way the diet may be made more attractive and more wholesome."[9] In other words, Atwater was suggesting "Americanizing" the dietary habits of the immigrants. Chicago philanthropists and club women responded. It seems they agreed with the sentiment expressed by the writer of a 1909 *Chicago Tribune* column: "Pity the woman who does not know how to cook—she has missed half her birthright. Never to know the thrill of grati fied pride in one's own achievements when the batch of bread comes from the oven brown and light and deliciously odorous. Never to sit down at the table to a perfect meal that her own hands have prepared and her own brain has planned."[10] The Domestic Science Association conducted cooking classes for this purpose; Mrs. Levy Mayer taught Jewish girls how to keep house and prepare (American-style) meals, while Miss Isabel Bullard instructed Jewish women on how to make chafing-dish viands that included Pineapple Toast, "the poor man's dish" of Codfish à la Newberg, plain omelettes, and Eggs à la Newberg.[11]

Chicago public schools, and, indeed those across the nation and in Canada, incorporated domestic science classes into their regular curriculum. Lizzie Black Kander wrote that this was not without problems, however:

> The cooking school forms an important adjunct to the [Milwaukee] Settle-ment. It occupies two rooms and one serves as a model; and while we are only equipped for 12 pupils, many of their mothers as well as their older sisters and friends who come [from the] kitchen to the baths, visit the classes and linger around, interested, and eager spectators.
>
> The ages of our protégés range from 13 to 15 years. All of them attend the public schools, but do not attend the Public School Cooking schools mainly because they are not far enough advanced. Either they are not long in this country, or their attendance at school has been often interrupted, to enable them to help mother or to do the housework while mother goes out to help support the family, to tend to the babies, or if they have been more fortunate in the selection of their parents and can afford to attend school long enough to be eligible to the Public School Cooking School their strict adherence to the Mosaic ethical and dietary laws, would prevent them from attending.[12]

One effort to adapt curriculum to the needs of observant Jewish children in Chicago in 1904 included purchasing separate sets of crockery, one for *milchig* (milk) and one for *fleischig* (meat) dishes, as well as additional kitchen utensils, and procuring kosher meat for use in public school cooking classes. Dr. Dudley, a Chicago public schools trustee at that time, opposed these purchases, protesting, "It won't be long before the Mohammedans and Buddhists will come in here and want meat cooked in their particular way."[13]

A few years later, public school students produced cookbooks featuring ethnic dishes, including what was called "Jewish" food, under the direction of their home economics teachers. The rationale for these projects was to show students, and presumably their mothers through them, how their traditional, "foreign" foods could be adapted to American ideals using the best, most recent scientific methods and standards. This idea was borrowed from Anna Cooley's *Teaching Home Economics*, so, although it was not a Chicago-innovation, it was applied citywide.[14] One such classroom-authored cookbook was compiled in 1931 at the Orr school. It included "Kwogle (Potato Pudding), Jewish." The recipe was published in the *Chicago Tribune*:

4 large potatoes.
3 eggs.
1 small onion.
6 ounces fat.
2 tsp. flour.
1 tsp. baking powder.
Pepper
1tsp. salt.

Grate the potatoes and the onion. Press the water from the potatoes through a cloth. Melt the fat, add the rest of the ingredients, and mix well. Heat a pan with the fat. Put potatoes and other ingredients into a warm oven and bake. Service for eight.[15]

In 1897, the *Milwaukee Sentinel* wrote about Mrs. Simon Kander's efforts to teach the children of Russian Jewish immigrants how to sew and become "Americanized."[16] The scope of her efforts expanded, so that by 1899, Lizzie Black Kander and the Milwaukee Jewish Mission women were running the "only Kosher cooking school" in the West.[17] We read Kander's 1898 manuscript booklet in which she outlined the curriculum for her "Kosher Cooking School." She initially structured it for women or girls who would work in households that employed servants, but it also became useful for those who might one day supervise their own household help. The "Rules for Housekeepers" began with instructions for "Housekeeper #I: 'Get kindling & coal. Build the fire.'"[18]

The Jewish Mission that Kander ran was an outgrowth of a study circle formed under the auspices of the National Jewish Council of Women. The curriculum was again aimed at Eastern European Jews, who, according to the article were "as particular in their observance of the 'kosher' laws as high caste Brahmin." Emphasis was placed on cleanliness, refinement, and the preparation of food that would be palatable—all "the little touches that go to make up the difference between existing and living."[19] By 1900, their programs had reached the stage where "the women of the Mission united with the Sisterhood of Personal Service to form 'The Settlement' to better serve the underprivileged Jews of Milwaukee's Haymarket neighborhood."[20] Like organizations and sisterhoods have done since the time of the Civil War, the ladies sought to raise funds by writing and selling a cookbook. Myrtle Baer, later the editor of the famed *Settlement Cook Book,* mentioned, during a 1963 interview, "Mrs. Kander taught cooking as part of the Americanization course. She needed a text book of American recipes and cooking methods, and this resulted in the Settlement Cook Book. At first each girl was given a book. Then it developed and grew popular as other people wanted the book and were willing to buy it. The proceeds went to the Settlement."[21]

In addition, the ladies planned to use the book in their cooking classes. After being turned down by the settlement's (male) board of directors for the monies needed to print the book, they sold advertisements to finance its publication. The first edition of what came to be called *The Settlement Cook Book* contained twenty-four cooking lessons and five hundred heirloom (German) recipes, and came out in 1901.[22] This early twentieth-century book changed forever the way multiple generations of Jewish immigrants cooked by demonstrating how American ingredients could be incorporated into traditional Jewish dishes, and by showing how American ways of cooking could be applied to Old World foods to make them "more palatable" and healthier. For the Eastern European Jewish women, it became an introduction to American life and the American kitchen. For many Jews today, it is *the* Jewish cookbook. In fact, when we were soliciting heirloom recipes from women in Michigan and Wisconsin, they told us they still use *The Settlement Cook Book.*

We consulted our 1903 facsimile reprint copy of Kander and Schoenfeld's *The Settlement Cook Book* to see if any of the recipes appearing there were also in Ruth Dunie's booklet, under either the same or different names. Among

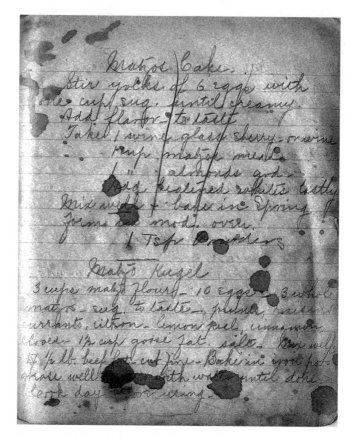

Figure 4. Matzos Cake and Matzo Kugel recipes in Ruth
Dunie's cookbook, circa 1913

others, we found one that Ruth recorded for an egg-rich, fruit-laden pudding
she called "*Matzos Charlotte*," as well as one for "*Matzo Kugel*." We compared
them to Kander and Schoenfeld's recipe for "*Matzos Pudding*." *Matzos*, in place
of lady fingers or sponge cake from regular flour, made this dessert suitable
for a Passover celebration.

Ruth's recipe for *Matzos Charlotte* called for both wine and wine sauce, so
she probably used her mother's recipes for those ingredients. Of those that
Ruth jotted down calling for wine and wine sauce, all suitable for Sabbath
meals, only one was credited to her mother, Jennie. We assume, however, that
the other non-attributed ones were also her mother's because they use many of
the same spices and fruits. During the nineteenth century, the Baltic countries
were known as grape-growing regions, so it makes perfect sense that people
living there would have developed recipes to use these sweet, nutritious fruits

that could be kept over the winter. It also makes sense that when Lithuanian Jews came to the United States, they would have brought that custom with them. Wine, after all, is and was an important part of Jewish holiday traditions.

For puddings

Wine Sauce (Mama's)
To every yolks of egg use 1 table spoon sug.
½ cup of water in eggs.
½ " of wine—cinnamon bark + currants

Beat whites to froth + stir in last.
Mix wine mixture + yolks of eggs together and allow to come to good boil—Let whites boil in water—when cool mix together.

Wine Sauce

Sug. enough to make wine sweet. 4 eggs.
Cinnamon bark
Wine. If too strong add a little water.

Matzos Charlotte

8 matzo soaked in wine + water
1 cup goose fat. Place a lining of matzo in pot to be covered with sug. cinnamon, almonds, raisins + currants apples—to form layers. Beat 6 eggs with 1 cup sug. + add ¾ cup meal—Cut through several times so that sponge will go between each layer.

Matzo Kugel

3 cups matzo flour—10 eggs—3 whole matzos—sug. to taste— prunes, raisins currants, citron—lemon peel, cinnamon, cloves—1½ cup goose fat. salt—Mix well.
½ lb. beef fat—cut fine—Bake in iron pot
Grease well + cover with water until done.
Cook day before serving.

Kander and Schoenfeld's recipe for "*Matzos Pudding*" reproduced below is similar to Ruth's in that it uses *matzos*, goose fat, apples, and wine. However, it calls for far fewer fruits and *matzos* than Ruth Dunie's, and avoids cinnamon altogether. Was their recipe specifically adapted for the less wealthy Jewish women who were attending settlement cooking classes? Or was something else at work?

Matzos Pudding

3 matzos (soaked, pressed and stirred until smooth).
½ cup white wine,
1 cup goose fat,
Grated rind of a lemon,
10 eggs beaten separately,
2 large apples (peeled and grated),
½ teaspoon salt
Sugar to sweeten

Stir one-half hour, and lastly fold in the beaten whites. Grease form well, bake in a moderate oven one-half hour and serve with wine sauce, six eggs, one cup weak wine, sugar to taste. Stir constantly until it thickens as it is apt to curdle.[23]

Could other recipes provide additional data about what was happening during this time period? We examined Irma Frankenstein's recipes from 1898, along with others from our manuscript cookbook collection dating between 1892 and the 1930s, then compared those to ones printed in newspapers, women's magazines, commercially printed cookbooks, and fundraising books during the same temporal frame. It seems that, overall, earlier recipes oftentimes had more spices.

We began our inquiry into possible reasons for this phenomenon by looking at recipes for pot roasts and stews because they are so fundamental to cooks' repertoires. Irma Frankenstein wrote down a recipe for this dish in 1898.

Eingedämpft Fleisch

Let fat get hot. Put in meat & let it grow brown on one side; then turn & let other side brown. Put in sliced onions, little celery, little carrots & let it boil. If meat cooks slowly no water is required. If it cooks fast one must add water. When tender thicken gravy with flour & water.[24]

At first, we thought perhaps Irma had simply neglected to note the required seasonings when she was recording the ingredients, but their omission was too consistent throughout her cookbook. Did traditional German and German-Jewish foods use seasonings beyond salt and pepper? Looking through vintage recipes, we were able to determine that German cuisine, while not terribly high in spice amounts, typically called for parsley, thyme, laurel, chives, caraway, cardamom, mustard, aniseed, cinnamon, pepper, and horseradish where appropriate. So, what happened to the seasonings in the recipes Irma recorded from her mother, newspapers, and women's magazines during 1898?

When we ran across a 1974 *New York Times* article by M. F. K. Fisher, we believed we had found a clue. Fisher stated: "Good Victorian ladies, following the lead of Queen Victoria, saw to it that their immigrant kitchen help skimped on salt as well as fat, served clean gravies instead of fancy Frenchified sauces, and simple steamed puddings instead of soufflés. A forthright style of cooking, based somewhat indirectly on revolt from the Old World extravagances and from the elaborate dicta of famous male chefs, emerged gradually in the American Middle West. It was ample, with no frills."[25] Perhaps this was the reason. Fisher, after all, was describing what she believed was happening in American society during the nineteenth century in the Midwest. We decided to test if her assumptions were correct, first in regard to recipes and cookbooks available in America, then to recipes and books in and from the Heartland, and finally to Jewish Midwest recipes. For that, we again turned to our collection.

The Jewish Manual, published in 1846 and attributed to Judith Cohen Montefiore, contains a recipe for stewed brisket that demonstrates that Jews did not typically eschew seasonings and added generous amounts of other ingredients, such as fruits, when they were available. The purported author of this book lived in England, but supposedly collected her recipes from all over Europe, wherever Jews resided. Onions, lemon, allspice, pepper, salt, nutmeg, and mushroom catsup added zest to the simple stewed steak and brisket recipes that were recorded.

Brisket Stewed With Onions and Raisins

Stew about five pounds of brisket of beef in sufficient water to cover, season with allspice, pepper, salt and nutmeg, and when nearly done, add four large onions cut in pieces and half a pound of raisins stoned, let them remain simmering until well done; and just before serving, stir in a tea-spoonful of brown sugar and a tablespoonful of flour.[26]

In 1871, Esther Levy published what has been identified as the first Jewish cookbook printed in America. Her recipe for "Beef A-La-Mode" called for claret wine, along with a number of different spices, while the one for beef stew included salt, pepper, ginger, mace, and mushroom catsup.

Beef A-La-Mode

Take a piece of nice fat beef. Cut up some smoked beef. Let each piece be near an inch thick, dip them in vinegar, and then into a seasoning, ready prepared, of salt, black pepper, all spice, and cloves, all in fine powder, with parsley, thyme, savory, and marjoram, shred as small as possible, and well mixed. With a sharp knife, make deep holes to insert pieces of fat, called larding, into it; then rub the beef over with the above seasoning, and bind it up tight with tape. Set it in a well-tinned pot, over the stove. Add three or four onions, fried brown, to the beef, with two or three carrots, one turnip, a head or two of celery, and a small quantity of water. Let it simmer gently ten or twelve hours, or until extremely tender. Put the gravy into a pan, remove the fat, and keep the beef covered; then put them together, and add a glass of port wine. Take off the tape, and serve with the vegetables; or you may strain them off, and send them up, cut into dice for garnish. A teacupful of vinegar should be stewed with the beef.

A Good Brown Stew of Beef

Take a piece of beef, about three pounds, and one pound of good veal. Cut it into small pieces, and fry with some onions, quite brown. Put all in a saucepan with a quart of water, and stew till tender; add some pepper, salt, ginger, mace, onions, and a spoonful of mushroom ketchup, thickened with a little brown flour. Some persons think it good with a tablespoon of vinegar. Serve up with forcemeat balls.[27]

Two recipes listed above call for "Mushroom Ketchup," but, rather surprisingly, we could not locate instructions for making that condiment in any of the above-mentioned cookbooks. Perhaps this was because it was easier and safer, given the poisonous nature of some mushrooms, to purchase it ready-made. Indeed, editor Sarah Josepha Hale, in *Godey's Magazine* of 1840, had advised her readers, "Mushroom is most esteemed; but the difficulty in our country of obtaining the right kind of plant, (some are poisonous,) renders a recipe of little consequence. It is better to buy this catsup at the shops."[28] We eventually found a recipe detailed in a *Chicago Daily Tribune* article of 1895. It was written before large-scale commercial mushroom production began in the United States, and so directs the homemaker to forage for these edible fungi.

Mushroom Catsup

Gather the mushrooms in dry weather, for if taken in wet weather or soon after rain the catsup will not keep. Choose large, ripe, and perfectly fresh ones, cut off the ends of the stalks, and throw away any that are worm-eaten. Break up the mushrooms into small pieces, put them into a pan—an earthenware one for preference—and mix them well with salt, allowing three-quarters of a pound of salt to one peck of mushrooms. Turn them over with a wooden spoon at intervals, leaving them to stand for three days. Drain off the juice at the end of that time, but do not press the mushrooms, and simmer it for half an hour in a very clean stew pan. Pour it out, and leave it till the next day, strain it again, and to every pint of liquor add one-quarter of a teaspoonful of mace, the same quantity of ground ginger, and a little cayenne. Let it simmer for another half hour, allow it to go quite cold, then carefully pour it off, taking care to leave all the sediment behind; put it into perfectly clean dry bottles, and add a dessertspoonful of brandy to each quart bottle. Have new and sound corks, and seal them over thoroughly to exclude air. It is best to fill the bottles quite full, and keep them lying on their sides.[29]

Although the methodology for preparing the catsup appears to be fairly standard, this particular recipe seems rather short on spices. Earlier ones we ultimately found for this sauce had called for more varied ingredients, such as nutmeg, allspice, cloves, garlic, peppercorns, onions or shallots, larger amounts of mace, and alcohol. In fact, beginning around 1880, we noted a real change in the amounts of seasonings used in most foodstuffs, at least in published recipes. In 1844, Henriette Davidis wrote a cookbook whose original title was *Praktisches Kochbuch* (*Practical Cookbook*). By 1879, her *Practical Cookbook* had been transported to America, reprinted fifty-three times, and retitled *Praktisches Kochbuch für die Deutschen in Amerika* (*Practical Cookbook for Germans in America*). Obviously, the reprint editions were geared for the American-based German-speaking market, which included non-kosher-keeping German-Jews. Later still, her book was translated into English, and recipes for the "American Kitchen" were added. These included ingredients available in the United States. Therefore, in later editions, recipes for and from other ethnic groups, such as the following one for "Irish" stew, made from meat remnants, calling only for onions, cloves, pepper, and salt—not a great deal of added spicing, but some.

Irish Stew made of Roast Meat Remnants

A rare piece is the best for this purpose and the sinews should be carefully removed from it; cut into small cubes and for each plateful of meat take 2 platefuls of sliced raw potatoes, ½ plateful of onions, pepper, salt, a little ground cloves, mix well together and cook in soup stock, shaking frequently until done. The kettle should be buttered and then make a broth from the bones of the roast with water and whatever gravy is left; cover the kettle tightly.[30]

Another recipe from Davidis's later edition book is for "*Beef a la mode*." The title implies a French origin for the dish. Strictly speaking, beef stewed in wine is *boeuf à la mode*, but by the nineteenth century, this distinction had broken down to the point where any stewed beef was tagged with "*à la mode*." It really was what we would call "pot roast." Note the use of wine—in this case, claret or white wine, along with salt, pepper, cloves, vinegar, bay leaves, and lemon. More spices are used here than in the "Irish Stew" she recorded. Could this be attributed to the recipes' different "ethnic" origins?

Beef a la mode

Take about 8–10 pounds of the round, pound it, rub with salt, pepper, and ground cloves; it can also be larded if wished. Put about 2½ ounces of kidney suet . . . into a kettle, heat it, put in the meat, dredge a tablespoon of flour over it, and roast until brown all over, turning from time to time. Then pour in from the side enough boiling water or better still half claret and half water to partly cover it, then put the lid tightly and cook slowly, turning it after the elapse of 1½ hours, adding a cupful of pickles cut into cubes, together with 1 spoonful of vinegar, 4 bay leaves or a few lemon slices, cover again and cook slowly until tender, which will usually take from 2–2½ hours. . . . In France this kind of a roast is served with a tomato sauce; in Bavaria, with a mushroom sauce, using for this purpose the broth from the roast.[31]

Fannie Farmer's classic work, the *Boston Cooking-School Cook Book* came out in 1896. Her recipe for "Beef Stew" calls for only salt, pepper, and vegetables.[32]

Also in 1896, *The Chicago Record Cookbook* published Mary Meeker's recipe for "Stewed Beefsteak" where only onions, salt, and pepper are listed.[33] The *Chicago Record* was a daily newspaper that published recipes sent in by readers. Every now and then, these were compiled into a cookbook, which sold for $1.00. Mary Meeker was one of the contributors to the published volume. That same year, *The 20th Century Cook Book,* by Montgomery (Alabama) Jewish authors Mrs. C. F. Moritz and Miss Adèle Kahn came out in a fifth edition. Seasonings in Moritz and Kahn's "Irish Stew" recipe have also been reduced to salt and pepper, along with whatever flavors the simmering meat and vegetables imparted.[34] And it was not just the so-called "Irish" stew recipes that employed few seasonings, either. The phenomenon seemed to be pervasive.

But why were spices suddenly eliminated from recipes and pantry shelves? Fisher's explanation that Americans were copying the British in their revolt against "Frenchified" foods at a time when American nationalism was running high did not seem totally adequate. We looked for other factors.

Perhaps seasonings had vanished because so many people in the nineteenth century suffered from gout, a painful condition they attributed to eating rich, highly flavored foods, and to alcohol consumption. Maybe they fell out of favor because so many people developed dyspepsia, that generic term for all sorts of stomach ills from indigestion to ulcers to cancer, which they also attributed to eating highly seasoned foodstuffs and overindulgence in alcohol and rich meals. Or could it have been that they were "poisonous"? After all, Charles de Saint-Évremond back in the seventeenth century had claimed they were, and there was nothing to prove things had changed during the past two hundred years.

PHILOSOPHY OF THE TABLE

Regard all cook's mixtures, such as ragouts and hors d'oeuvres, as a variety of poison. If you eat a little of them, they will do you only a little harm; if you eat much, the pepper, the vinegar, and the onions will surely spoil your taste, and in the end affect your health.[35]

Perhaps seasonings, spices, condiments, and extracts fell out of favor because they were frequently tainted with adulterants thought not only to cause stomach problems, but all sorts of ominous, unnamed blood diseases. A contemporary advertisement for Dr. Price's Flavoring Extracts claimed, "The poisonous flavoring extracts in the market are one of the wolves in sheep's clothing which ruin the stomach, causing dyspepsia and blood diseases before the consumers have discovered their true character."[36] Then again, perhaps herbs and spices and the condiments made from them disappeared because urban Americans no longer had easy, inexpensive access to them.

Indeed, a survey of newspaper columns in the *Chicago Inter-Ocean,* a paper that regularly detailed the produce, fruits, vegetables, meats, and sundries available at local markets, and a survey of ads in the *Chicago Daily Tribune* beginning in the 1870s, reveal very few listings for herbs, dried or fresh. Early advertisements appear to suggest that *cost* may well have been a contributing factor in their disappearance. In 1898, a single package (size not indicated) of sage, savory, thyme, or marjoram cost four cents. Nutmeg cost two and one-half cents per ounce, and a packet of bay leaves or ginger root sold for six cents—all at a time when the average working man's wage was fifteen cents per hour, with women's wages less. These high prices may well have been due to the McKinley and Wilson Tariff bills of 1890 and 1894, respectively, that had slapped steep taxes on imported goods, spices included. So, was it health, economics, access, changing tastes, or something else that caused seasonings to vanish from American kitchens and meals?

We will argue that, although all of the factors we have listed above impacted the use of spices and condiments, the major reason behind their disappearance was due to reform efforts spearheaded by nineteenth-century crusaders. Many of these reformers operated in the hard science/social science disciplines, the temperance, suffrage, settlement, and philanthropy movements, as well as the domestic science, and/or health care fields during the Progressive era.

The late 1800s saw a huge influx of immigrants to America. Immigrants often traveled light, as we have already noted. If the women brought recipes from their homelands, they were not necessarily in books, but in their heads. When possible, they adapted these remembered recipes using foodstuffs available in their new homeland. Not all immigrants came as family groups, though. Sometimes, they came alone. Cooking was typically a "woman's job," but many young women came to the United States before they had learned to cook, and may not have had their mothers around to consult. Early on, these women, if they could read, oftentimes looked to daily news columns, women's magazines, and cookbooks for recipes and instruction. For those who were not fluent in English, recipes could be found in any number of foreign-language papers published in the United States. These recipes, whether in English or another language, reflected the most up-to-date scientific ideas about cooking.

Also, as aforementioned, settlement houses and other philanthropic agencies tried to teach immigrant women the fundamentals of American-style cooking, shopping, and hygiene to help in their assimilation. Their efforts were concentrated on the poor, many of whom were illiterate and unskilled. The poorest heralded mostly from Italy, Ireland, and Eastern Europe. Once through the immigration process, many crowded into filthy urban slums. The poor had limited access to healthy, fresh foods, and so were often sickly.

They also suffered from dyspepsia. Their stomach complaints were sometimes blamed on the large amounts of spices and condiments that were required to mask the flavor of cheaper, tainted meats, poultry, and fish, or to the spices and condiments they used in cooking their traditional foods. Oddly, the stomach problems of the poor did not elicit sympathy like when members of the middle class had similar complaints. Instead, some sociologists connected poor people's digestive ills with criminal behavior! For example, a 1910 advertisement for "Shredded Wheat Dishes" reads:

DYSPEPSIA OUR NATIONAL DISEASE

Wherever men and women are allured by the fascinations of business life and social endeavor away from the simple and natural life it is not an exaggeration to say that nine out of ten of them are either sufferers from chronic indigestion of from occasional derangements of the stomach or bowels. Many sociologists declare, indeed, that most of our crimes may be traced to indigestion.[37]

There were three other common beliefs: (1) The kinds of foods the immigrants had eaten in the Old Country were not necessarily good foods according to the best modern scientific research and standards, as evidenced by Bertha Wood's book, *Foods of the Foreign Born in Relation to Health*, that analyzed immigrant diets and found them seriously wanting in many instances.[38] (2) Tuberculosis and other diseases were exacerbated by malnutrition; the poor were malnourished, contracted a variety of diseases, then spread them to others, costing the economy many dollars in health care, productivity, and lost wages. (3) The poor needed to be educated in how to become American. "Americanization" meant being taught what to eat, and how to cook, so the émigrés and their children would stay healthy enough to support themselves and contribute to the economy.

In the Midwest, settlements, like Hull-House, the Maxwell Street Settlement, Indianapolis's Nathan Morris House, and Milwaukee's Settlement, were established to help with reform efforts and the process of turning foreigners into Americans. Their attempts sometimes met with resistance from the immigrants themselves, especially in the area of food. Jane Addams, in a discussion about her early efforts to feed the poor at the Hull-House Kitchen, sounded surprised. She wrote, "We did not reckon, however, with a wide diversity in nationality and inherited tastes . . . perhaps the neighborhood estimate [around Maxwell Street] was best summed up by the woman who frankly confessed, that the food was certainly nutritious, but that she didn't like to eat what was nutritious, that she liked to eat 'what she'd ruther.'"[39]

Around this same time, scientists, like Louis Pasteur, discovered the link between bacteria, germs, and disease. They began to worry about the Three Fs: "flies, fingers, and food." They also worried about *Salmonella* and *E. coli* invading meats and poultry, causing widespread sicknesses or even death. The scientists' concerns were shared by physicians, nurses, and domestic scientists, alike.

Mary Lincoln, a noted domestic scientist, cautioned: "Care must be taken not to expose food to the action of bacteria, unpleasant odors, or contact with unclean substances. Scrupulous neatness in personal habits of those who prepare food, and cleanliness of all utensils used, and storage places, are no minor matters. The preservation of the body, the temple and instrument of the soul, can be secured only by observing the laws of hygiene in all our habits, especially in the choice, preparation, and eating of our food."[40] Then, another domestic scientist, Ellen H. Richards, reported that 75 percent of spices had been adulterated. She noted that sawdust was regularly added to mustard; dirt was added to pepper, and alum, copper sulphate, carbonate of lime, ground gypsum, kaolin, barley, rice flour, corn, oatmeal, and/or horse-feed was often mixed with flour.[41] Out and out fraud was also prevalent. For example, flour mixed with vinegar was frequently sold as German mustard. In truth, criticism of food products ran so high that some companies felt compelled to assure the public that their products were pure. The Knox Gelatin Company combined reassurance with education. Their 1895 ad reads: "You have no doubt noticed while pouring hot water on some gelatines, a sickening odor which will arise from it—this never will happen in pure gelatines—and shows that the stock is not pure—so is unfit for food."[42]

Not only commercial products were contaminated. Meats were often tainted, and/or processed under unsanitary conditions. Recall Upton Sinclair's 1906 blockbuster book *The Jungle*. Sinclair's book undeniably had a huge impact on public perceptions about the meat-packing industry and cleanliness. In fact, it laid the foundation for more than a few government regulations. Sinclair was somewhat taken aback, claiming, "I aimed at the public's heart, and, by accident, I hit it in the stomach."[43]

Adulteration and contamination were so pervasive, something had to be done. And here is where the reformers and crusaders made their inroads, and not just among the poor. According to Lorine Swainston Goodwin, in *The Pure*

Food, Drink, and Drug Crusaders, 1879–1914, the various reform movements began slowly around 1879.[44] They reached their zenith around 1920, when a flurry of regulatory laws was passed in response to their activism.

As we have mentioned before, during the Progressive era, "reform" was a buzz-word. Reform efforts touched upon almost every aspect of life: from religion to health, and from economics to cooking. One rallying cry was: Cleanliness is next to Godliness, and Cleanliness is "American." Others were: Sanitize your kitchen and sanitize your life! Improve your diet, and improve your health! Moderation is the key! Over the years, the crusaders' message spread—via newspapers and magazines and later across the air waves.

Taking to heart Jean Anthelme Brillat-Savarin's oft-repeated phrase, "Tell me what you eat, and I will tell you what you are," an idea Ludwig von Feuerbach famously paraphrased in a succinct verbal pun, *"Der Mensch ist was er isst"* (Man is what he eats), some domestic scientists, like Mary Lincoln and Fannie Farmer, established cooking schools to promote scientific cooking methodologies and hygiene. At their core, these were attempts to shape and change food habits, behaviors, and attitudes. Toward that end, more than a few domestic science authorities wrote cookbooks that were widely disseminated and widely read. Some, like Marion Harland, Sarah Tyson Rorer, and Maria Parloa, even penned columns for syndicated newspapers and women's magazines. Newspapers typically sold for a penny or two, while magazines cost a dime, so these advice and recipe columns were aimed at the literate, expanding middle class, and at the aspiring-middle-class woman.

Domestic scientists sometimes acted as public health watchdogs, too, as they did in 1899, when cautioning that 6,500,000 germs had been found in a gram of stale bread.[45] But a number of them advanced a somewhat more strident and radical message. An article published in *The Iowa Citizen* states in part: "There are a great many people who use neither salt, pepper nor any other condiment in their victuals, and the taste for un-seasoned food is growing. The desire for strong condiments is just as unnatural as the craving for tobacco or ardent spirits. Pepper, nutmeg and allspice all contain poisonous principles, and people would be much healthier without using the seasonings."[46]

Domestic scientists at that time promoted the idea that every woman could and should learn to cook, not only for themselves and their families, but especially if they were employed in someone else's kitchen. In truth, that was one of the underlying reasons *The Settlement Cook Book* was written. Wealthy and middle-class women also needed to know how to cook in order to supervise their household help. Hence, standardization was crucial. It was both a democratic model, as well as an efficient, factory-like approach to cooking. It also guaranteed the creation of dishes untainted by foreign influences. If people used good, healthful, carefully selected, plain American ingredients, and followed the printed instructions to the letter, then dishes would taste the same time after time, across the land, regardless of the cook's ethnic heritage or social class.

Other reforms, especially ones linking diet with intemperance, or connecting condiment use with illness, were also placed on the table. For example physicians, such as Dr. A. Wilberforce Williams, writing for the *Chicago Defender* newspaper, often discussed the link between the excessive use of condiments, spices, and seasonings, and various illnesses in his columns. Barbara Haber found that although Sylvester Graham, preacher and diet reformer, had died in 1851, his recommendations to avoid stimulants, including coffee and tea, along with condiments were still advocated by many people decades later, including Seventh Day Adventists and domestic scientists.[47]

However, the most vocal and successful of the food reformers and honorary member of the Women's Christian Temperance Union, the one preaching moderation in life habits most vociferously, bolstered by German-based scientific research, was Dr. John Harvey Kellogg. Kellogg was a Seventh Day Adventist and vegetarian who founded the Battle Creek Sanitarium and Health Spa in Michigan. He also developed a specialized food line that included peanut butter, meat substitutes, and, of course, cereals. Dr. Kellogg believed that seasoned foods had "deteriorating effects" and were "injurious" to the individual as well as to society. In fact, he once commented, "Many a mother is bringing her boy up to be a drunkard by giving him highly seasoned and badly selected foods. Mustard, ginger, and pepper are not fit to be taken into the stomach."[48]

In 1893, his wife, Ella Eaton Kellogg, a Seventh Day Adventist, nurse, vegetarian, leader in the Women's Christian Temperance Union, author, domestic scientist, and hugely influential woman, published an extremely popular cookbook called *Science in the Kitchen*. In it, she wrote, "True condiments such as pepper, pepper sauce, Worcestershire sauce, ginger, spice, mustard, cinnamon, cloves etc. are all strong irritants. The use of condiments is unquestionably a strong auxiliary to the formation of a habit of using intoxicating drinks. A more serious reason why high seasonings lead to intemperance, is in the perversion of the use of the sense of taste. An education which demands special enjoyment or pleasure through the sense of taste is wholly artificial. It is coming down to the animal plane, or below it."[49]

According to Josephine Hunt Raymond, in 1897, a cooking school related to the Battle Creek Sanitarium was operating on 47th Street in Chicago. She

Figure 5. Battle Creek Cooking School, Battle Creek, Michigan, circa 1898

added, "The teachers are graduates of the Battle Creek Sanitarium School of Cookery."[50] We assume this cooking school promoted Kellogg's philosophy and taught enrollees how to prepare vegetarian dishes. However, we could find no data at all about this school in local newspapers.

In May 1899, the Battle Creek Health Food Store opened in Chicago. It featured a line of food products developed by Dr. Kellogg. This store, with its attached kitchen *cum* restaurant, apparently shut after approximately one month.[51] It could have been that Chicago was not yet ready for this kind of reform Thereafter, Chicago grocers, like Selig-Cooper, simply stocked pre-packaged Battle Creek Sanitarium foodstuffs for those who wanted to buy them.

Despite the criticisms that "healthy" food bereft of spicing tasted about as appetizing as shredded tree bark, bland foods, promoted mostly by vegetarian reformers and temperance advocates, became the vogue among certain segments of the populace. As testament to the increasing popularity of the vegetarian philosophy, no fewer than eighty references to vegetarians and vegetarian products were found in a survey of *Chicago Daily Tribune* articles published between 1898 and 1899. Vegetarian cookbooks, also, enjoyed brisk sales, especially since vegetables, beans, and nuts provided inexpensive alternatives to costly meats and more-than-likely adulterated wheat flour.

Earlier, it had been discovered that 10 percent of all the spices, including cloves, cinnamon, allspice, or pimento, imported into the United States could be found on saloon counters—placed in bowls for drinkers to chew in order cover the smell of alcohol before heading home or back to work.[52] Social reformers declared that spices were obviously covering up wide-scale intemperance. We found an interesting essay or speech concerning this issue among Lizzie Black Kander's papers composed around 1918 by a Mrs. Branton titled "The Survival of the Best." In it she argued to her audience at the University of Wisconsin-Madison, "Formerly, we had a bread-diet, much dependence was placed on wheat; plain food was the rule. Such food requires a great deal of pepper, salt, vinegar, and other condiments; it is pleasant only when some liquor is used as a complement. It was thus essentially a liquor diet. Now, however we have a sugar diet. Food has been increased and cheapened enormously. The sweet dishes are essential parts of each meal; the other foods are arranged around these, just as formerly they were arranged [around] alcoholic beverages. A sugar diet is not so costly as a liquor diet; hence one who live[s] on it will have a great advantage in many lines of industry."[53]

Then, too, culinary reformers connected bad cookery and greasy foods with intemperance, along with the antisocial behaviors, such as sloth, wife-beating, and thievery, which obviously resulted from it. An article in the *Chicago Tribune* stated:

> It sounds absurd to say that there is a direct relation between bad cooking and vice, crime, divorce, disease, and insanity, but it is a solemn truth that such a relationship exists. Especially is evil cooking responsible in a considerable degree for the intemperance that abounds in the poorer sections in the city. The apostles of good cooking say the use of drinks in these less favored regions of the city comes largely because of the unsatisfied condition of the man's stomach. . . . After a dinner of a greasy joint, greasy potatoes, pie, and tea that has been stewed until it is puckery and bitter, he has a sense of heaviness and surfeit that again demands the relief of alcohol. . . . Dr. F.X. McNamara said: "Indigestion is the great curse of the American people. It is due to badly cooked food. Raise the standard of cooking, teach the youthful Housekeepers how to utilize food products with the least waste and how to make food not only wholesome but how to make it dainty and toothsome, and much domestic wretchedness and misery will go away and never come back."[54]

Temperance advocates, social reformers, health care professionals, domestic scientists, and vegetarians kept promoting their messages, and much of the public marched along in lockstep. Connections between the use of spices and alcohol consumption were kept in the forefront of society's consciousness through newspaper articles and magazines. For example, on August 20, 1877, the *New York Times* reported that George W. Bungay delivered an address at a meeting of the American Temperance Union. According to the reporter, Bungay asserted that "hard times and labor problems were directly attributable to the rum trade. He did not confine himself to a general condemnation of the liquor traffic, but hotly denounced the use of such familiar articles as pepper, salt, mustard, vinegar, cakes, candies and other confectionary as well, since, he believed they all bred intemperate habits in the young."[55] That the American people had been led to believe there were real connections between liquor use and adulterated food products is also shown in a letter to the editor of the *Chicago Tribune*, dated October 14, 1876, titled "Adulterated Spices." In it, the author, echoing the beliefs of who knows how many others, wrote that in order to mask the taste of adulterated sugar, flour, pepper, mustard, and cinnamon, housewives were reduced to using brandy, a practice that, the writer asserted, inevitably led to an appetite for stimulants of another nature.[56]

At this time, many educated people, especially those of the middle class, subscribed to a linear model of evolution that ranked societies hierarchically from Savagery through Barbarism to Civilization, with humankind far above the "brute" animals. And they also believed that civilized people exhibited moderation and control in all areas of their lives.

This model was underpinned by the old Lamarckian idea that certain traits, such as drunkenness, health, intelligence, and even poverty, were inherited. It was even thought that undesirable traits could be bred out of the human line through judicious mating practices. Eventually, this concern with heredity and cultural evolution shifted from improving society by rearing healthier children to creating fitter families, within fitter nations, that would be superior to others less fit, and, hence, lower on the evolutionary scale. Ultimately, these notions resulted in a more expansive type of eugenic reform that encompassed both heredity and environment, or nature via nurture.

So, these notions led to a push to do something to improve Americans and their lives, by eliminating bad cooking and foreign dishes. Spices and condiments had to go. If that were accomplished, it was believed that any number of domestic and social ills would disappear. Reforms would start with the women and children by teaching them how and what to cook. After all, Catharine Beecher, early domestic scientist and author of *The American Woman's Home; or Principles of Domestic Science,* had claimed women could reshape society through their work at home and in the kitchen. In fact, the Enterprise Manufacturing Company, picking up on this idea and taking it a step further, declared the kitchen to be the engine-room of the home—the place where energy, health, and happiness were manufactured.

In response to concerns about social, economic, and health issues related to food and its preparation, domestic science classes were added to the regular public school curriculum across the nation starting around the 1890s. These classes were designed to benefit American society by teaching the latest scientific methods of cooking, meal preparation, and hygiene. The recipes the students were taught, however, were often short on seasonings and condiments for all the reasons previously mentioned. Indeed, as Adelaide Hoodless wrote in her 1898 book, *Public School Domestic Science*, students were taught that "The use of such condiments as pepper, curry, pickles, vinegar and mustard is decidedly harmful. Salt is the only necessary condiment. The blending of flavors so as to make food more palatable without being injured is one of the fine arts in cookery."[57]

The reformers' effects on American cuisine and lifeways extended well beyond the nineteenth century. In 1906, the Pure Food and Drugs Act was passed in response to Sinclair's exposé of the meat-packing industry, to Ellen Richard's study of food adulterants, and to public pressure placed on legislators. By 1917, the temperance movement had gained enough of a foothold that it precipitated the passage of the Eighteenth Amendment. Starting in 1920, alcohol was legally available only by medical prescription. Prohibition lasted until 1933, when the Eighteenth Amendment was repealed. Yet, the repeal did not totally lift the *de facto* prohibition on seasonings and condiments, or suspicions about them.

Julia Child once wrote: "Cookbooks are the history of an epoch. They show how people prepared and ate the ingredients available to them. Cookbooks provide answers to social, political, and economic questions about the society for which they were written."[58]

And they are, indeed, all that and more.

In 1898, Irma Frankenstein compiled her cookbook, taking many of the recipes from newspapers and women's magazines that showcased "American" cuisine. Written by nineteenth-century domestic scientists, they exhibit the expected dearth of spices and condiments. A Reform Jew of German extraction, Irma, like others in her familial and social network, did not keep kosher, yet she always considered herself Jewish. Her generation looked to its elders for guidance, but was, nonetheless, willing and eager to move beyond the confines of home and neighborhood, beyond the strictures imposed by Old World beliefs and traditions. Irma was also an American, who embraced progress, who wanted to be up-to-date and modern. In other words, she belonged to that first native-born group eager to adopt the "new." And, during the late nineteenth century, the "new" affected almost every sphere of life, including foodways.

Ruth Dunie's recipes represent a slightly different phenomenon. Ruth was a Lithuanian immigrant who kept kosher. Her social network consisted of family and friends with whom she shared a language along with European-based cultural and religious customs. Her recipes were primarily for cooking

Jewish holiday and High Holy Day meals, even though they were not labeled as such. Although compiled during the early twentieth century, they included traditional European-Jewish recipes that seem to have been brought to the United States, then passed along essentially unchanged. Therefore, they called for more spices and condiments than were in vogue at the time she wrote her cookbook. It appears that Ruth adapted the recipes she collected only so far. The changes we noted involved the substitution of American measurements for European in most cases, along with the inclusion of a few brand-name products, commercially produced yeast, and baking powder. We also noticed she included some recipes for baked goods that, at first glance, appeared distinctly "American." Upon closer examination, we believe they are quite close to their European counterparts, and so, do not represent much, if any, adaptation to then-current American taste. For example, the recipe titled "Gold Cake" is almost indistinguishable from that of a dense, moist *gelb küchen* (pound cake), popular the world over; Ruth's "New Orleans Tea Cakes" are comparable to Eastern European *rugelach,* and her "Bird's Nest Pudding" recipe seems to be no more than an English name for an apple *kugel,* a dish that spread from Germany, to Poland, and from there to Lithuania. We suspect she chose to record these particular recipes because of their similarities to foods with which she was already familiar. Ruth's manuscript recipes, then, formed a link with her past, and demonstrated resistance to the kinds of sweeping change reformers were promoting, at least with respect to what she must have considered an essential part of her Jewish identity, that is, "traditional foods."

6

When to Cook . . .

The children remember. Although they were small, a trip to their Bubbe's house meant love and food—always. The two were inextricably connected. Hugs and kisses, quickly followed by hustling them to the table with, "*Ess, mein kinderlekh*" (Eat, my little children). Sunday breakfasts were an unchanging feast: lox, bagels, bialys, cream cheese, sliced tomatoes, smoked sablefish and chubs, fruit in season, freshly squeezed orange juice, and potato chips. Potato chips? After years of silently wondering, they asked. Bubbe answered with a story: "In the Old Country (and we only ever knew that "the Old Country" was six hours from Warsaw, but in which direction, and by what conveyance?), in the Old Country, we were poor, so poor we had to slice the potatoes very, very thin to fry. Then I came to America, and I found they had done it for me!" And that was why potato chips sat in a large bowl on the breakfast table surrounded by all the other store-bought delicacies—a reminder to be thankful for the bounty she had found in America.

Bubbe was a good cook—no, a great one—and she cooked for every major Jewish holiday, and for the minor ones, too. Her life seemed to revolve around that calendar—and her family. The Albany Park neighborhood in Chicago where she lived in a three-story courtyard building was predominantly Eastern European Jewish. The *shul* (synagogue) was a few easily walkable blocks away. Papa went daily once he had retired from working as a union tailor at the Hart, Schaffner & Marx Company. Their routines rarely changed.

Every week, Bubbe would stop at the bakery to pick up bread, doughnuts, cakes, or other sweets for Papa. She was not a baker. Next, she visited the *yatke* (butcher shop). Following a long, involved discussion of the merits of one chicken over another, of this piece of *flanken* over that one, she directed the butcher to make sure he marked each package with the name of its content, in Yiddish, of course. Then, she dragged all those white paper-wrapped packets home, in every kind of weather, in her collapsible, wheeled shopping cart, in triumph. She prided herself on having beaten that *gonif* (thief) at his own game; she had secured the best cuts of beef, the best chickens, the ones he kept hidden in the back where nobody could see, the ones that for some never-articulated reason she felt he did not want to sell to her or anybody else. She ran a kosher kitchen.

Bubbe's preparations for Passover, the most important holiday of the Jewish year—and so, of her year, too—began far in advance. They started with cabinet cleaning. She cleared the shelves of every loaf of bread, every cracker, every piece of cake, every crumb. Out it went. She directed Papa in packing up the everyday dishes, then supervised his *schlepping* (lugging) of the best dishes, only used for that holiday, from the basement storage space. By the time *erev Pesuch* (the eve of Passover) rolled around, and the family had announced themselves with "*Gut Yontif!*" (Happy Holiday!) at the door left open for Elijah, Bubbe had been cooking for days, but working for weeks. This dinner was her triumph!

Her table was set with a pure white linen cloth on which was centered the symbolic *Seder* plate. On it a hard-boiled egg in a burnt shell, some romaine lettuce, celery sticks sitting in salted water, a cooked chicken neck, freshly grated horseradish dyed with beet juice, and *haroset* of cinnamon-sprinkled apples, and walnuts, mixed with wine were arranged.[1] Off to the side sat a plateful of three *matzos*. When no one was looking, Papa sneaked the *afikoman*, the middle piece of *matzo* snapped in half, wrapped it in a napkin, then hid it, but not so well that one of the grandchildren could not find it and claim the dollar reward. A copy of the blue Maxwell House *Haggadah*, the Jewish religious text setting out the order of the Passover Seder and accompanying prayers, then free with a can of coffee, and saved from year to year, topped each special Passover dinner plate. No eating without praying. *Yarmulka* (traditional Jewish male head coverings) lay in a pile next to Papa's chair at the head of the table, in case someone had forgotten his. To Papa's right was an open bottle of impossibly sweet "Kosher for Passover" wine, which would eventually fill everyone's small cup four times.

As the sun set, Papa called the family to table. Course after course of wondrous food emerged from Bubbe's small kitchen. Her famous chicken soup always came first. She made it from scratch by boiling up a hen ("an old one"), with some carrots ("a few is all"), one sliced *tsibele* (onion), *a bisl* (a little) kosher salt, and *a bisl* celery ("not too much"), until the fat globules, as large as quarters, floated across the golden broth's entire surface. Her *matzo*-balls were dense and chewy "sinkers," puffed up to the size of baseballs. You almost needed a knife and fork to cut them.

At one time Bubbe chopped up her own *gefilte* fish from fresh Great Lakes whitefish purchased at a place we knew only as "the Fish Market" down on Devon Avenue in the heart of another Jewish neighborhood. *Nu*, where else? They had the best fish. In later years, she apologetically served "store-bought, from a jar." Each oval piece arrived at the table chilled in its own aspic, hand-decorated with a carrot slice and a sprig of curly parsley. Every time she served those fish balls, someone had to reassure her that although they were good, they were not anywhere as good as the ones she used to make. Like the dinner, this, too, was a ritual.

We had no idea what was involved in making this classic appetizer, except a lot of work, until our friend, Jane, sent us a video titled *Gefilte Fish*. The older woman in the film, a grandmother named Elizabeth Silverstein, related that she used to make *gefilte* fish because:

It's a healthy food, very nourishing, and it's very tasty. It's a traditional dish and typical "Jewish," and it seems like everybody likes it. Even a lot of the Gentiles like it, too. When I was a small child, we used to have *gefilte* fish on Friday nights, and I used to go with my mother to the fish market, and we always had to get a live fish to be sure it was fresh. Of course, we had to clean it. . . . First we'd get a big kettle, and we'd line it with sliced onions, and sliced carrots and [more] onions and parsley. The younger generations are making it, but they don't use the old-fashioned way; they use the new-fangled way with the Cuisinart, and with the part [attachment?] so that you don't have to chop. (Holding up a large, wooden bowl and a metal half-moon chopper) This is the chopping bowl I used, that I've had for the last 65 years, and it's still good, and this is the chopper. It belonged to my mother-in-law and she passed it on to me, and this is probably 100 years old because she brought it from the Old Country, and we would chop and chop and chop that fish. Chop; chop; chop. And we would chop until the fish stuck to the chopper, and sometimes we'd have to chop for over an hour, and this [chopper] I will probably pass it on to one of my granddaughters if she'll want to make *gefilte* fish. Well, later on in years, when I was married, and making the fish myself, I got a food chopper. It was one of those choppers you'd have to attach to a table or to a chair, and then we would grind the fish. (Holding up a chopping attachment and wooden pestle) This is the chopper—the electric chopper. It's an attachment to my can opener. . . .

I stopped making *gefilte* fish because my health does not permit it. That's why I stopped. I think it's better if you make them [*gefilte* fish balls] yourself. I think the homemade tastes better than the bought fish, but it's still very, very good.

Elizabeth's daughter-in-law, Marcee Silverstein, next demonstrated how *she* made *gefilte* fish. She started with "six pounds of whitefish, a little bit of trout, and buffalo belly" ordered the day before from the fish store. She cleaned them, made a stock of the heads and bones, ground the fillets two or three times in a food processor, formed them into balls, then boiled them in the stock for about one hour. She believes "It's the mixture of the buffalo, the whitefish, and the trout that gives the [*gefilte*] fish its consistency. I guess I could have made it easier on myself and bought the fish in a jar, and doctored it up a bit, like some people do, and it would have tasted as good—well, not quite as good, let's be honest—but I think making the fish yourself is a test of love, or—well, it just makes me feel good."[2]

A legendary cook, Etheldoris Grais offered us a recipe for "Gefilte Fish 'Minnesota Style.'" To qualify as such, it must be made solely from local whitefish and pike. She emphatically declared that *no one* in Minnesota uses buffalo fish; although it is pulled from the river in batches, it sits rotting on the shore. Because this recipe, along with the one following, calls for sugar, we place the origin of both somewhere in what is now southern Poland.

Gelfilte Fish

A poached Fish Ball—with a filler—
Served on Sabbath or for Holiday meals!
by Eastern European Jews
Traditionally made from white fish & pike!
from the "Minnesota Area"!

For Stock: Fish Trimmings— (Head, Tail, Fins & all bones)!

2 carrots—whole
2 stems Fresh Dill
2 onions—chopped
2 qts. water (or more to cover)

2 lemon slices
2 stems from Parsley S + P to taste
3 stalks celery—with leaves
1 tsp. sugar

Place in large wide pot! Bring to boil & skim. Cook covered for about 40 minutes. Taste for seasoning.

Etheldoris also provided us with an alternative recipe, one that could be made with whitefish, or a mixture of trout and pike. She pulled it from her large loose-leaf binder, simply labeled "For Fish" with a "side" of "Red Horseradish Sauce." She commented that, for Passover, she only uses *matzo* meal.

3# chopped fish (Fillets of whitefish or trout and Pike)
About 1 tsp. salt
⅛ to ¼ tsp. pepper
3 T. matzo meal (or breadcrumbs)
1 tsp. sugar
Optional: 1 carrot ground fine
1 onion
2 eggs slightly beaten
¼ cup water (or more) to make a light texture

A. Have your market grind fish—or use a meat grinder or processor—When using a processor be careful not to grind too fine— *You need texture!*

B. Process carrots (if using) + onions—Add seasonings + Matzo Meal! Add eggs one at a time—add water!

Wet hands—and shape into oval balls. If too loose add a little more matzo meal. If too sticky, add a little more water! Drop into simmering broth—add more water if needed to cover all fish balls!

Cover—simmer 1½ to 2 hours! Taste after 1 hour to correct seasonings- (add more salt, pepper and sugar to taste). Turn off heat; let cool.

While cooking, occasionally shake pot—so fish balls won't stick.

Yield: about 15 balls

To Serve: Line plate with greens; Top with fish balls. Garnish each ball with slice of carrot. Garnish tray with fresh dill and parsley! Serve with Red or White Horseradish—or Red Horseradish sauce.

Red Horseradish Sauce

¾ cup mayonnaise
2–4 T. prepared horseradish
⅓ cup Ketsup
few drops *fresh* lemon juice to taste
ground black pepper

Combine ingredients in bowl! Serve with Gefilte Fish Balls.

During the too-short afternoon we spent "talking food" with Etheldoris, she showed us how to scale a fish, advised how to make excellent *matzo*-balls, gave us some of her wonderful specialty recipes, informed us that really good cooks only used kosher salt, and confided that occasionally she would "make *gefilte* fish balls into patties, and fry them. You sauté them in a frying pan, or sauté onions over them, or a red sauce. You can put a tomato sauce over the top with lemon juice and bake it a little in the oven. I think that's an Iron Range thing."

She also shared the recipe for her version of a Sephardic Passover dish called "Persian *Charoset*," which she had developed for a cooking class. The sweetness of the wine and fruits is tempered by the spices, and somewhat off-set by the vinegar. The flavors play off one another.

¼ cup almonds
¼ cup pistachios
¼ cup walnuts
¼ cup pumpkin seeds
¼ cup hazelnuts
¼ cup pitted dates
¼ cup raisins
½ cup apricots
½ cup pitted prunes
½ cup dried cherries
½ cup sweet red wine (kosher for Passover)
2 teaspoons wine vinegar
1 pomegranate or 1 teaspoon pomegranate juice
¼ teaspoon rosewater
a pinch of *adviech* (a Persian spice mix that consists of 1 teaspoon ground cinnamon, ¼ teaspoon cardamom, ¼ teaspoon ground cloves, ¼ teaspoon ground ginger)

Chop all the fruits + nuts in food processor. Add liquid ingredients + spices + cover + chill. Serve at room temperature.[3]

On the trail for additional Passover recipes, we asked Judy Dworkin for the *matzo* pop-overs recipe, which she said she typically served with stuffed veal breast. These crispy culinary marvels are, indeed, puffy despite being made from unleavened flour. The "rise" comes from the large number of eggs in the recipe. Their hollow, soft, somewhat chewy interior is immanently suitable for spreading with sweet jam, or for sopping up meat juices.

Pop-over Recipe

1 box matzoh farfel [matzo broken into small pieces]
10 eggs
1½ Tablespoons of oil or chicken fat

Soak the farfel in hot water, drain, add eggs & oil/fat. Let sit for 1–2 hours until all the liquid is absorbed. Fill well-greased cupcake tins ¾ full. Bake for 1 hour at 450 degrees.[4]

We looked to Ruth Dunie's cookbook for others. There were so many! Her notebook included more than a few recipes for those quintessential Passover dumplings—*matzo*-balls. We found it interesting that these particular recipes called for chicken fat, instead of the goose fat that had appeared in some of Ruth's other recipes. Perhaps the ones specifying "goose fat" were temporally older, from an era when geese were more readily available. Raymond Sokolov mentions in *Fading Feast* (1998) that food customs originated on farms; then, as American farmlands were gobbled up by city expansion, and as farmers discovered it was more profitable to raise chickens, goose production declined.[5] Or perhaps these recipes came from one of Ruth's German friends, since Germans considered goose fat an excellent flavoring.[6]

Generally served with chicken soup, *matzo*-balls can be dense and chewy or light and fluffy, depending on any number of factors—the cook's preference for a certain consistency; whether the dough is well chilled before handling; whether the balls are dropped into boiling liquid, then covered, partially covered, or not covered at all; or whether they are partially cooked before being added to boiling chicken soup.

We whipped up Ruth's *matzo*-ball recipes. As directed, we dropped the dough-balls into boiling chicken soup stock. Because she did not stipulate how they were to be cooked, we left them covered, but with the pot lid cracked, for fifteen minutes. We found them good, with an interesting (unusual to us) taste produced by the addition of ginger and paprika, and a texture with which we were also unfamiliar because of the addition of almonds, but noted both recipes produced the heavier, chewy kind(s) of dumpling.

Matzo Meal Balls

5 eggs well beatened—
Take one [egg] shell + measure 5 times of water.
Salt, pepper, ginger, parsley
paprika to taste.
Almonds if desired.
5 Tablespoons chicken fat.

Enough meal to roll into balls for soup.
Stock must be boiling—Then drop in balls to boil *15 min.*

Matzos Balls

1 cup meal
1 tsp. salt, ginger, pepper + parsley
chicken fat ¼ cupful
1 cup boiling water
3 eggs

Make into balls.

Coming up with ideas for comestibles that meet Passover rules regarding *hametz* (leavened) foodstuffs is a challenge for any cook. For example, "What can you serve for breakfast or dessert?" But other factors figure in as well, such as "How do you make a cake rise without leavened flour?" Ruth collected recipes to solve all those problems.

For breakfast, she might have served her family fried batter-cakes, very similar to pancakes, but made with *matzo* meal. We decided to try this recipe. If one of us had to be the fry-cook, the other had to be the guinea-pig. After eating one plain, "the guinea-pig" decided the cakes needed "jazzing up." So, he smeared strawberry jam on one, ate another with honey, and tested still another by drowning it in maple syrup. He declared the plain *matzo* batter-cakes "immensely improved" by these additives.

Matzos Batter Cake. (Mrs. Summer D.'s)

To 1 pt. sweet milk use 3 eggs well beaten. Add a little salt, sug. and enough matzos meal to thicken for fry.

For dessert, Ruth had recorded two lemon-flavored cake recipes. Although the directions are spare, and we cannot reconstruct the method she used, the baking temperature, or time, we can, nonetheless, mentally taste its eggy richness, kissed with a hint of citrus. Perhaps the "lemon flavor" she used in the first recipe was also an extract she had purchased from a peddler.

Matzos Cake

6 eggs—separate
1 cup sug.
¾ " matzos flour. Lemon flavor.

Potato flour Sponge Cake (fine)

12 eggs (separate)
12 level spoonfuls sug. beaten with eggs (½ hr.)
10 tablespoons potato flour (level)
½ orange juice
½ lemon
½ " rind. Add whites last. Grease pan.

Like the children's Bubbe, Ruth seemed to organize her year around the Jewish holiday calendar. Among other recipes, she wrote down and borrowed ones that would be suitable for the early fall holiday of *Rosh Hashanah* (the Jewish New Year), when fruits were often the sweet notes at the end of a meal. These could do "double-duty" for *Tu B'Shevat*, the early spring festival that has been called the "New Year for Trees," when eating dried fruits is customary, or even for the fall *Sukkot* (Festival of "Booths"), when cucumbers, dates, and melons are generally eaten. The large number of different fruits and the amounts used bespoke Midwest bounty, not just in terms of local harvests, like figs and currants, but the ready availability of produce brought from California or Florida by rail. We checked the prices of fruits in local markets from between 1914 and 1918. It appears that prunes, dates, and raisins all cost around ten cents per pound. Without factoring in labor time, Ruth's recipes would not have been terribly expensive.

Fruit Cake

1   cup butter
1¼   "   sug.
1¼   "   molasses
4   "   flour
1   "   sour milk
4 eggs.
1 Tspoon soda.
1 Lb. seedless raisins,
2   "   currants,
1   "   figs,
1   "   prunes,
1   "   dates. ½   "   citron,
1 lemon grated,
1 tumbler jelly.
½ pint brandy,
2 tablespoons cloves,
2   "   cinnamon
2   "   mace.
1½ nutmeg.

Mix fruit + flour altogether.
Bake 3½ hrs. in slow oven.
Line pan with greased paper.

Prune Pie

Cook prunes well. Remove seeds.
add after well mashed raisins, citron;
almonds, cinnamon, sug. + 1 egg.

Date Kisses

(Mrs. Leibermuth)
1 lb. standard pulv. sug.
Whites of 5 eggs beaten to a *stiff* froth
Add sug. gradually + beat for ½ hr.
Juice of ½ lemon. vanilla.
1 package dates cut *fine*.
½ lb. almonds   "   "   + blanched.

Bake in gas stove moderate oven.
Grease pan *well*. Drop with Tspoon.

Date Kisses

(Aunt Ida's)
Whites of 4 eggs. beaten *well*, then
Add 2 cups sug. pulv. + beat 20 min.
2 cups nuts
1   "   dates cut fine.

Drop in greased pan.
Bake in slow oven.

Date Tart

Beat 2 cup sifted sug. With yolks of 12 eggs. beat ½ hr.
Then add 1 lb. dates cut *fine*,
1½ Tspoon allspice, cinnamon, 2 squares Bitter grated choc. Or
cocoa. 1 cup of matzos flour sifted *fine*, or cracker meal 1 teasp B.P.
grated peel 1 lemon, nuts if desired. Juice of 1 orange, + lastly the stiffly
beaten whites.

Bake slowly in Spring form.

Date Cake

(Sister's)
1 cup nuts—2 eggs.
1   "   sug.
1 tablesp. butter
(Above) cream

1 tsp. soda in

1 cup boiling water to be poured over

1 "   stored dates cut *fine*.

2 "   flour—

1 tsp. Y. P.

Bake in long pan + cut in sq.

Moderate oven.

Etheldoris shared her own recipe for "My Q cumber Soup," which is suitable for *Sukkot*. She told us, "I've been making this recipe for over thirty years!" Garlic and onions provide the tang. Decorating with darker green dill and parsley emphasizes the light green color of the soup. Visually, it is a marvelous interplay of summer shades and textures. It is also a time-saver, especially during frenetic holiday preparation periods, because it can be made a few days in advance.

My Q cumber Soup

Serves 10–15

Ingredients:

4 to 5 good size cucumbers

Peel 4 cukes—cut up into cubes

(Save 1 cucumber to be used in final blending)

1–2 cloves garlic crushed

1 large or 2 small onions diced

also add 3 green onions—white and green stems included. You can add chives if you have them in your garden.

1 large leek cut up. Long green stems cut off.

3 stalks celery—peeled and diced!

2 to 4 T. butter (or margarine). Butter gives a better flavor!

6 to 8 Cups of chicken stock or vegetarian chicken stock to completely cover vegetables.

2 stems of parsley—cut up.

1 piece of dill.

Method:

Sauté all veggies in melted butter—onions, celery, leeks, garlic, green onions, and chives until translucent or opaque.

Add 4–5 T. flour to vegetables and cook 3–4 minutes, stirring constantly until flour is cooked

Add diced cuke and add stock to completely cover vegetables.
Mix well and bring to a low boil. Cook until cukes are translucent.
Remove the stems that haven't dissolved.
Correct seasoning, mainly salt and pepper.
Take out 2 cups of vegetable and stock mixture and set aside.
Blend in blender on blend the rest of the ingredients.
At the end add the 2 cups you have put aside, peel last cuke, cut in
½ length-wise and spoon out seed. Cut in chunks.
And add remaining liquid and buzz on grate. This gives the soup
extra texture.
Refrigerate overnight. The next day, correct the seasoning to your
taste.
Add 1- 2 cans of carnation milk and stir well.
The Q Cumber Soup is now ready to serve. This soup can be kept in
the refrigerator for 3 to 4 days.

While we were up in Minnesota, we also took some time to go through the
Eloise and Elliot Kaplan Family Jewish History Center collections in Minneapolis. In a fundraising booklet, titled *Kosher Cooking*, authored by members
of the Women's League of B'nai Abraham Synagogue, we found Corrine Keslin's
recipe for "Pot Roast," proper for *Rosh Hashanah* or *Shabbat*, but not for an
Ashkenazic Passover meal because it contains legumes. We thought Keslin's
recipe unusual because it calls for pickling spices and lima beans, quite unlike
the spicing found in Rose Mass's more typical Jewish slow-cooked stew of lima
beans and meat called "*cholent*."

Cholent

(Rose Mass)
1 lb. dried lima beans
3 lbs. chuck, brisket, or short ribs
3 lbs. potatoes, or ¾ c. barley
3 onions, sautéed
1 carrot, shredded
3 T. olive oil or schmaltz
2 T. flour
2 t. sea salt, or kosher salt
Dash pepper

¼ t. ginger
1 bay leaf
1 clove garlic, minced
Paprika to taste
1 T. dried parsley

Lima beans must be soaked overnight and then drained. Cut meat into large pieces. Spread ⅔ of vegetables on bottom, then meat, and remainder of vegetables on top. Add oil or schmaltz. Seasonings are mixed into flour and sprinkled over the above. Add boiling water to almost cover all ingredients. Cover and place in 200 degree oven and it can cook slowly for about 24 hours. My alternative is 5 hours at 350° oven. Can be served on dinner plate or in bowls. Vegetables are on the bottom; put meat on top.[7]

We asked a waiter, who had earlier told us his parents were Minnesota farmers, about lima beans, and whether they were often pickled in local dishes. Since we were asking, we also inquired about spinach because we had seen a number of spinach-based dishes, including omelets, on restaurant menus and in local Jewish sisterhood cookbooks, such as the 1983 *Adath Caters to You— All You Can Eat* cookbook published as a fundraiser by the Adath Jeshurun Synagogue Sisterhood. Etheldoris Grais had co-chaired this venture, reminding those who purchased the book, "*Mitzvah shel s'udah*" (Make every meal a religious experience).

The waiter assured us that lima beans were a popular crop in the state, and that he did not find pickling them unusual. He said his mother grew lima beans "because my father likes them." Spinach, too, was claimed to be a favorite local vegetable, growing easily in Minnesota's alkaline soils. He stated that his mother grew spinach because she could plant it in the spring and then again in the early fall, thereby getting two harvests of that vegetable that takes around forty days to mature before the miserable cold of winter set in. So, we present the following recipes for "Pot Roast" and "Syrian Spinach Souffle," despite its title, as having distinctive "Minnesota flavors."

Pot Roast

(Corrine Keslin)
3 lbs. chuck roast
1 tsp. salt
⅛ tsp. pepper
1 tsp. pickling spices
1 lb. dried lima beans
5 carrots, cut into ½ inch slices
Salt and pepper

Brown meat well on all sides in hot shortening in large skillet or Dutch oven. Add onions, garlic, 1 cup water, catsup, salt, pepper and pickling spices tied in cloth bag. Simmer, uncovered for 30 minutes. Cover, simmer for 2½ hours. Add water as necessary during cooking to make 3 cups liquid. Remove meat, add lima beans. Place meat on top of beans. Cover and simmer until beans are tender, 2 to 2½ hours. Continue to add water during cooking to keep beans covered. Add carrots the last 30 minutes. Yield: 6 to 8 portions.[8]

Syrian Spinach Souffle

(Betty Husney)
2 cups spinach, fresh or frozen
3 eggs
1 lb. dry cottage cheese
1 onion chopped
3 tbsp melted butter

Saute chopped onions in butter. Add spinach and ¼ of cheese mixture. Place in a buttered 2-qt. casserole. To cottage cheese add 3 eggs and 3 tbsp butter and beat well. Place remaining cheese on top. Bake at 3500 about 45 minutes.[9]

Marilyn Feder also contributed a recipe for "Carrot Tzimmes" to B'nai Abraham's fundraising endeavor. The name "*tzimmes*," which means something akin to "mish-mosh" in Yiddish, accurately describes this baked casserole. *Tzimmes*, which sometimes contains only vegetables with dried fruit, can be baked or stewed. Unlike those, Feder's version is a mixture of vegetables, starch, and meat. Originally from Turkey and well-known throughout the world, carrots, both white and orange, grow easily in the Midwest, keep well, and are normally a fairly inexpensive vegetable to purchase in stores or farmers' markets. Sweet potatoes, a tender New World tuber, are commercially produced in the southern United States, where the weather is warm and frost-free during the growing season. Around the time of the Jewish New Year in September, they are plentiful, and cheap. Feder's carrot- and sweet potato-based beef dish is, therefore, thrifty, as well as being suitable for *Rosh Hashanah* dinner, when sweet foods symbolize hope for a sweet new year, for celebrating *Sukkot* and the Sabbath. Because it can be prepared beforehand, and is essentially a one-pot dish, it is a real time-saver.

Carrot Tzimmes

8 carrots 5 sweet potatoes 1 onion 1 lb. lean beef. Season to taste, cover with water and bake in covered [pot] at 350° oven until meat is tender. Pour ½ cup honey over top. Heat through. Thicken with 2 tsp. potato starch in 1 cup cold water. Pour in casserole and bake. Can be prepared ahead.[10]

We copied one last recipe found among the pages of that same synagogue book. It was a handwritten, anonymous one for "Mock Strudel," appropriate for a Sabbath dessert or for any Jewish holiday where fruit is traditionally served. We were unable to determine why it was called "mock." Was it because, unlike traditional German strudels, it uses no butter, so is *parve*, or because it calls for preserves and/or a poppy seed filling rather than for the more typical fresh fruit(s)?

Mock Strudel

1 cup sugar (bring to boil and cool)
½ cup milk
Add ½ cup oil. Add two eggs + beat well.
Sift 4½ to five cups flour with 2 tspn. bak. powder + one tspn. bak. soda—1 lemon, orange + vanilla flavor—grated rind of lemon + orange, roll out to rectangle, + spread with either strawberry or cherry preserves or poppy seed filling (plus tbsp. honey + yolk of egg). Roll up + bake in a 9 x 13 pan, 325° oven, about 45 min.—or until done fairly brown.[11]

Ruth Dunie listed a variety of dishes that could be prepared for *Hanukkah* (the Festival of Lights), the joyous eight-day winter celebration during which fried foods are typically eaten. Her "Dough-nuts" would have been sweet, with goodly portions of both sugar and nutmeg.

Dough-nuts

½ cup butter
1   "   brn. sug.
½ " luke-warm water
¼ Tspoon nutmeg
2   "   B.P.
Flour enough to roll out
2 eggs—salt.

Sträuben, or "Straben" as Ruth identified the recipe, sometimes called "Pennsylvania Dutch fried dough," is frequently served warm, dusted with confectioner's sugar, at county fairs, carnivals, and flea markets. Making certain the oil temperature is correct can be problematic. Too hot, and the oil "spits" when the dough is dropped in; not hot enough, and the dough absorbs the oil. Occasionally made one day ahead, *Sträuben* can be reheated in a toaster or toaster oven.

Miss Hoffheimer's Straben

1 pt. flour
1 tsp. salt
milk to batter
4 yolk added + stirred in separately
the 4 whites well beaten + added lastly.
2 tablesp. sug.
Cook in deep fat.

Apple Fritters are often topped with warm compote or applesauce. They work well for both breakfast and dessert. In 1910, syndicated columnist Jane Eddington gave recipes for Apple Fritters, *Apfel Kuchen*, and *Apfel Strudel*, and wrote that because apples were plentiful "no housekeeper need be at a loss during the coming months for economical desserts."[12] Then in 1914, that same home economist had further advised her readers to "acquire the foreign habit of calling fruit a dessert."[13]

Apple Fritters

Peel + cut apples.
Batter: 4 eggs, sug 1 cup well beaten.
grated peel of lemon.
separate whites + add before sifting in flour.
Enough flour to make stiff batter.

Ruth's recipe for "Candle Salad" would have made a novel dish for the *Hanukkah* table. At the time she recorded it, it probably was some American home economist's recent innovation with no connection to any holiday, either Christian or Jewish. The earliest newspaper reference we found to this salad was 1916, when it was mentioned in an Iowa newspaper as one of the dishes served at a society banquet.[14] The lack of explanation about this salad suggests it was familiar to the paper's readers, but special enough both to merit mention *and* to be served at a gala event. A few years later, food columnists touted it simply as a nice salad to accompany Christmas meals.[15] Articles from 1929 and 1933 refer to it as "well-known." Then, by the 1980s, it was prominently listed in a number of newspapers as a fun children's "food craft project" for *Hanukkah*. Variations through the years included substituting a doughnut for the pineapple ring, scattering cranberries around whatever base was used, and adding a demi-round slice of green pepper to represent the "candlestick finger-hold," or embedding the whole "candle" in gelatin.[16]

Candle-salad

Put salad leaves on plate, with a full slice of pineapple and in the middle of the pineapple put half of a banana, with the rounded end up. On the top put the mayonnaise. Then put a quarter of a crystalized cherry, which gives the appearance of a lighted candle.

Joseph and Matilde Israel passed along two recipes they serve "on *Rosh Hashanah*, for *Shabbat*, for company, or whenever." Although the recipes are heirloom ones, with possible origins in Egypt among the Sephardic Jews, they have been updated to incorporate items such as "angel-hair pasta," pine nuts, and basmati rice. Nonetheless, all the ingredients are readily available in Minnesota and throughout the Midwest. Joseph advised the "Rice with *Fideos* is [a] treat by itself or with vegetables, meatballs, stews, etc. Matilde serves this when we have company, during holidays, Shabbat, etc. I remember my mother making this rice, and also decorating it with roasted pine nuts or bits of walnuts, or roasted pistachios. Matilde does the same, and also decorates it with some finely chopped parsley. I also [remember] my mother-in-law cooking [it] the same. No one can remember the origins of this delicious recipe."

Rice with Fideos (Angel Hair Pasta for soup)

Ingredients:

1 cup of basmati white rice

2 nest-shaped angel hair pasta, (Can be found in Greek market. The regular angel hair pasta is too coarse.)

Cooking oil

Salt

Optional: Turmeric, Paprika

Preparation:

Sauté crumbled pasta in the pot intended for cooking rice with a little cooking oil, 1–1½ spoonfuls, for [a] few minutes. This pasta cooks very quickly.

Add 1 cup of rice in the same pot, add 2¼ cups of water, some salt. For some color you can add a pinch of turmeric or paprika; not too much. Stir once.

Bring to a boil, cover pot and let steam on a low flame until rice is done; no water and the rice is flaky.

let cool, or not.

Bon appétit

Joseph also told us the "Stuffed Artichoke Hearts" recipe is "[o]ne of our favorite[s]. Original recipe was from my mom, Mary, and adapted by Matilde. The original recipe calls for fresh artichoke, which required a lot of preparation to remove the leaves, and the choke from its heart, coat with lemon to [keep it] from turning blackish, etc. Now, Matilde uses frozen artichoke hearts, all ready for stuffing and cooking."

Stuffed Artichoke Hearts

Ingredients:

1 pack frozen artichoke hearts (buttons), can find at a Middle Eastern or Greek grocer.

½ pound ground lean beef

½ pound ground veal

1 egg
Large lemon or lemon juice
Tomato sauce, medium can
Chopped yellow onion
Breadcrumbs
Sea salt
Black pepper
Parsley
Ground cumin
Allspice
Olive oil
sugar

Preparation:

Remove frozen artichoke hearts from freezer and place in fridge overnight to defrost, do not defrost in microwave, as this causes the artichoke hearts to start cooking and they become soft and mushy.

Combine the chopped beef and veal (you can also substitute chopped turkey or chopped chicken for the beef) in a mixing bowl; add finely chopped onion, finely chopped parsley, egg, season to taste, add a pinch of allspice and ground cumin (not too much cumin as it will overwhelm the taste).

Knead the mixture well to pasty consistency, add breadcrumbs if necessary to hold together to make meat balls. Let sit for few minutes.

Spray PAM in a large frying pan, one with cover, place artichoke hearts, and arrange them cup side up.

Make meat balls to fit inside each artichoke heart, not too big to go over the edge, enough meat for it to sit inside the heart.

There's always ground meat paste left over; make tiny meat balls, the size of a large gum ball, and place in pan.

Add contents of small tomato sauce can to pan, kind of pouring the sauce over the stuffed artichokes; drizzle about 2 spoonfuls of olive oil over the contents; a pinch of sugar to balance acidity; lemon juice from ½ a large lemon.

Cover and simmer over a very low flame, until meat is well cooked, and artichokes are firm. Over-cooking makes the artichoke pasty and mushy, not very appetizing, a good bite to the artichoke is almost heavenly.

Serve with white basmati rice, our favorite, or by itself, a piece of pita is always needed to get the last of the sauce. Decorate with some chopped parsley for a good presentation, and *voilà. BETEAVON.*[17]

Annabel Cohen's "paternal grandmother, of Turkish descent, taught [her] mother whose family was from Poland, to make *Borekas* for her only son." In her article, "Sephardic Treats," Cohen presents two tempting recipes for this Sephardic *pastelle*: one with the more traditional cheese mixture, the other given "a Michigan twist by adding dried cherries to the filling." These tasty turnovers can be served with a dairy meal on *Shavuot*, on *Hanukkah*, or for breakfast.

Borekas

1 lb. flour
¾ cups peanut or vegetable oil
½ to ¾ cup hot water
Glaze (below)
Egg Yolks
Oil

In a medium bowl, place flour, oil and half the water. Use your hands or a wooden spoon to mix the dough. Add remaining water and mix until moist; the dough is ready when it pulls away from the sides of the bowl. (Dust your hands with flour to remove the sticky dough from them). Cover the dough with a towel and let it rest at room temperature for one half hour.

Dust your hands with flour. Pinch off a teaspoon of pastry and, with your fingers, flatten it into a round about 2 inches in diameter. Combine filling ingredients and mix well. Drizzle a little butter over filling. Place a teaspoon of filling into the center and fold pastry into a half moon. Seal the edges with a fork. Brush oil on a cookie sheet. Place the borekas on it (not touching). Brush egg yolks to glaze the tops of the borekas with filling. 1, Use apricot preserves glaze for filling 2, heating the preserves in the microwave for 1 minute. Bake at 400° until golden (about 25 minutes). Serve hot or at room temperature.

Filling 1:
8 ounces cottage cheese
4 ounces grated kaseri cheese
2 ounces crumbled Feta Cheese (preferably Bulgarian)
1 large baking potato—peeled, boiled and mashed well
3 eggs
a handful of chopped parsley
Salt and pepper to taste[18]

Filling 2:
3 ounces ground walnuts
2 tablespoons dried Michigan cherries
Grated zest of 1 small orange
½ tsp. cinnamon
¼ tsp. nutmeg
2 tbs. sugar
melted butter
2 cloves chopped garlic

Etheldoris told us her "Meat Blintz" recipe, suitable for a Sabbath dinner, "came out of Chicago," and that she had never seen another like it. The blintzes are similar to French crêpes, thin, light pancakes. The preparation is a multistep process, well worth the fuss.

Blintz Batter Recipe

3 eggs
1 teaspoon vegetable oil
dash of salt
1 cup water
1 cup all-purpose flour
½–1 teaspoon sugar
¼ teaspoon baking powder

Method:
Beat eggs, add liquid together. Use a blender. Add the flour, baking powder, sugar and salt. Don't overbeat. Refrigerate 30–60 minutes.
Heat 7 or 8 inch non-stick skillet with sloping sides.
Grease lightly with vegetable oil. Pour just enough batter (about 2½ Tablespoons) in skillet to cover bottom. Tip from side to side to spread

until the bottom of pan is completely covered. If there is too much batter, pour off the excess. Cook on one side only, until slightly brown and dry on top. Use a spatula to loosen edges. Drop onto a white tea towel, fried side up. When leaf is cooled, put on a square of wax paper and stack until ready to fill. Leaf should be thin.

Ingredients for Meat Filling:
Left over Roast Beef or 1 cup roasted beef, ground coarse
1 egg
½ cup diced medium onion—sautéed
5 Tablespoons fresh parsley, chopped

Method:
Mix all together. Add a few Tablespoons of chicken stock if necessary to moisten. Sauté, use non-dairy margarine or oil (no olive oil). For the perfect taste, use rendered chicken fat (called *schmaltz*).
Place 1 rounded tablespoon of filling on blintze wrapper.
If you prefer a larger blintze, use 2 Tablespoons of filling.

To Serve:
Serve as a main dish with chicken mushroom or beef mushroom gravy.

Etheldoris did not give us a recipe for mushroom gravy, but Ruth Dunie's book contained an unattributed one. The title, "Creole Sauce," hints at an international flavor achieved by simmering and blending exotic spices, but which are not found in the actual recipe. However, given the time frame during which it was recorded, making a sauce with catsup, Worcestershire sauce, and garlic had become fairly exotic and daring.

Creole Sauce

Brn. ½ cup flour then add water to thin.
1 Tablespoon butter
2   "   catsup.
1   "   worcestershire sauce,
salt, pepper to taste—little sliced
garlic if desired.
Use with veal. with mushrooms.

While we were in Minneapolis, we also looked into the University of Minnesota's Upper Midwest Jewish Archives' cookbook collection. We found a group of recipes archived under the name of Esther Schechter. Written in what we thought was Yiddish, they appear to have been compiled sometime during the 1960s, although they are undated. We selected the recipe for Huckleberry Pie for inclusion in this book because its English title had been noted on the page, and because huckleberries are a Midwestern fruit. To our surprise, when we had the recipe translated, the language was not Yiddish at all, but phonetically spelled English written with Yiddish characters! Interestingly, too, the translator noted that the recipe called for sugar and, then, a for a smaller measure of something written as "sweet10." Did she mean to specify Pillsbury's artificial sweetener of that name that became popular during the 1960s?

The archival cookbook collection of Esther's handwritten recipes contained no biographical information about her. So we asked her grandson, Herbert Schechter, first, if his grandmother had typically written in this fashion. He replied, "When I was in the military service, Esther wrote to me in her English with Yiddish characters. It was then that I realized her mispronunciation of words was not an accent but how she thought the words should be pronounced. Later in life, I taught her to write checks and write out the numerals in English. She had a list of numerals from one to one hundred (one, two, three, . . .), so she could spell them properly on the check."[19]

Then, we asked about Esther's cooking. He told us:

[Esther] was one of 12 children, and while growing up in her native Russia, helped her mother with the cooking for the family. . . . I have many recollections of her cooking in her kitchen, and, of course, eating many wonderful meals at her home. . . . Her daughter, my aunt, Doris Schechter Kirschner (of blessed memory), was a home economist. In later years, she attempted to create recipes from Esther's cooking. Esther cooked by touch, feel, and taste with no recipes. When she cooked, she did not measure. The batter had to have a certain consistency. She cooked by eye, taste, and feel. Doris watched her mother cook, and measured or weighed each ingredient to get an accurate listing of ingredients. It was her intent to develop a cook book.

Esther lived in a small home with a small kitchen. It is a wonder how she was able to cook so much with so little space. Her only working area was the kitchen table. The pots and pans were hung on nails pounded into the wall going down the basement stairs. She made her own noodles. I remember coming into the house and seeing white dish towels (made from flour sacks) spread over all the tables in the house with dough on them drying. In fact, everything was made from scratch.

On her back porch she had a 5 gallon can of cooking oil and a 30 pound drum of sour salts (citric acid). What anyone would do with 30 pounds was another mystery, but a good cook can not have too many or too much seasonings for a good borsht. Although I have eaten borsht prepared by many, none have succeeded in making a better borsht than Esther. . . . She did use all kinds of Minnesota vegetables in all kinds of dishes.

In addition to her cooking talents, she sewed. She made suits and coats from patterns she made from newspaper. She laid the newspaper on the floor and the person would lie down in it. She would then trace the outline to make the pattern. They apparently did not have pattern stores in Europe, or, [perhaps] as a product of the Great Depression, she would not buy anything she could make herself. Curtains and draperies were child's play for her.

I remember visiting one time when she was in her 70s and remarked that the living room looked different. She replied that she had just painted it (herself). In order to do this, she took the bus to the paint store, bought the materials, took the bus back, walked the two blocks from the bus line, got out the ladders and painted the room. Of course, you must remove the draperies, curtains and rods, clean and wash them, and then rehang. I get tired just thinking about all that. She was truly an amazing woman![20]

And so, we are left to wonder if the recipes archived under Esther's name were a collaborative effort, not unlike the one Stephanie Caraway recounted involving her mother and Nona detailed in chapter 2. Did Esther jot down the ingredients and methodology, and did Doris dictate the measurements once she had determined the correct amounts? One of Esther's other grandchildren seems to think that Doris, who was interested in alternative sweeteners, may have calculated the "sweet10" amount, which Esther then wrote down. In whatever fashion this recipe came into being, it represents the tradition of passing treasured recipes l'dor v'dor (from generation to generation) as expressions of Jewish identity, and the innovation that is so often found in Jewish cuisine.

Esther's recipe does, indeed, call for huckleberries, similar in taste to blueberries. Minnesota boasts both wild and cultivated varieties of this luscious fruit that turn deep blue and sweet toward the end of summer. It seems that, today, though, huckleberries, which have to be gathered and are slightly "seedy," have been mostly replaced by prepackaged blueberries in baking recipes; indeed, this recipe would work equally well with the substitution of that fruit. Although we have no idea what time of year Esther might have baked her huckleberry pie, it would have been quite suitable for an end of the summer Sabbath dessert, for *Rosh Hashanah* in September, or for *Tu B'Shevat*, if the berries had been frozen.[21]

Huckleberry Pie

(Esther Shekhter)[22]
2 cups berries
1½ cup[s] water

Cook for 30 minutes in a covered saucepan
Heap berries then burst: mash with a potato masher.
Then add 4 cups sugar or 4 teaspoons sweet10
[or Sweet-10?][23]
Then 4 Tablespoons lemon juice or to taste
¼ cup flour. Cook until thick. Pour into pie shell—one shell
without a top
Bake for 10 minutes at 450. Reduce the heat to 350. Bake another 30
minutes.

Sauce for Huckleberry [Pie]

2 pounds fruit
1 cup cold water. Cook for 45 minutes. Keep covered close.
Skin should burst.
1½ teaspoon sweet10 [or Sweet-10?] and cook another 15 minutes.

In the final analysis, then, we believe the recipes we have reproduced in this chapter represent the mosaic that is the Midwest Jewish community. They are distinctly and firmly grounded in cultural and religious traditions, both Ashkenazic and Sephardic, yet show a great deal of creativity and individuality. They also demonstrate how adaptable the cuisine really is to local conditions, available produce, and resources. Reading through them, we can visualize any Bubbe, Nona, or Großmutter, in her kitchen before any Jewish holiday, or on any day of the week (except, perhaps, Saturday), having looked at what was available in the store, market, or garden, substituting this for that, and tweaking "the balance of ingredients until she can announce both to herself and the child who is her kitchen apprentice: ' . . . Like this, it tastes right.'"[24]

7

. . . And When Not to Bother

Be it Ashkenazic *challah* or Sephardic *panderica* ("bread of the rich"), bread has always held a central place in Jewish life. Breads of every shape and variety are made and served for the Sabbath, holidays, and daily consumption: rye breads in Eastern Europe and Russia; rice-flour breads where some of the Sephardi lived; wheat breads elsewhere. For the poor, it truly was the staff of life. There is an old Jewish saying that a rich man is one who puts meat on the table once a week. The rest of the time, his family eats bread (or potatoes, depending).

In ages past, bread-making was an essential skill passed down from mother to daughter. It has been called both a science and an art. But who has the time to bake bread on a regular basis anymore? Too, even at the turn of the last century, it was often cheaper to purchase bread than to buy the ingredients—flour, yeast, sugar, eggs, salt, oil—and *then* spend five or more hours making a loaf.

In the Old Country, to save time and effort, you might buy your bread directly from a local woman who made it, money permitting. For example, Herbert Schechter recounted that, "as a young married woman, [Esther] baked bread that she sold in the neighboring village."[1] Then again, in larger towns or cities you could make your purchases from a commercial baker. Either way was certainly easier than making it yourself. The popularity of bakeries, today, may be due to a similar phenomenon, in addition to one other. "It's the convenience factor, *plus* people not knowing how to do it anymore," suggested Bette Dworkin, owner of Kaufman's Bakery and Delicatessen.[2]

But what about *matzo* bread? Of course, if you are Jewish, you must have *matzos* for Passover. Yet, does anyone make *matzo* bread at home for the holidays anymore? We could not locate any instructions for making this flatbread cracker in the recent cookbooks we consulted or in contemporary articles we

Figure 6. L-R: Judy Dworkin, Bette Dworkin, and Herb Fingerhut, Kaufman's Delicatessen and Bakery, Skokie, Illinois, 2009

reviewed. However, we did read that the Jewish Children's Museum in Brooklyn, New York, in conjunction with the Chabad-Lubavitch Tzivos Hashem children's organization, hosts a yearly *matzo*-baking workshop, which serves strictly as an educational exercise, since the *matzos* cannot be eaten on Passover.[3] So, we asked Joseph Israel whether, to the best of his knowledge, Sephardic women, known for their home-baking, made *matzos*. Apparently not, but he did inform us, "I remember in Egypt the matzah made in the kosher for Passover bakery (open only before Passover to supply the community) was very thin, round and delicious; it would remind us of the kind of unleavened bread eaten during the exodus; round and thin, and very crisp with a wholesome taste and texture."[4]

Because we wondered about the actual process of making this characteristically Jewish bread, and how it had changed over time, we checked newspaper archives. In 1884, the *Cleveland Herald* devoted a news column to those very questions.

In some of the European countries people are more careful and extremely particular about the flour when originally prepared. The head of the family purchases his own flour, takes it to the bakery, and superintends the manufacture of his own Matzos, which are prepared by hand without the use of any machinery, the dough being reduced to the desired thinness by means of rolling pins. In some parts of Europe . . . the preparation of the Matzo begins with the sowing of the seed for the flour. Daily visits are paid to the field, and after the grain is cut the utmost precaution is taken in thrashing in order to exclude all foreign substances. Then the head of the family takes his own grain to the mill and superintends the manufacture of his own flour.

The process of baking the unleavened bread [in the United States] is rather an interesting one. It begins with the preparation of the flour, which must be thoroughly sifted first in order to keep it pure and free from any foreign substance; then the dough is prepared by a simple mixture of the sifted flour and water, which is filtered. The dough is then placed in a breaker and pressed to the thickness of ordinary sole leather, it then goes through two successive rolling machines until it is rendered very thin, about twelve feet in length and one in width. A roller is then run across it which perforates the entire piece. A man then steps up with a heavy iron cutter, who immediately cuts the entire length of this dough into large circular pieces, which are instantly transferred to the adjoining room, where about fifty at a time go through the process of baking and are afterward packed away for future use. They are usually shipped out of the city in boxes specially prepared for them, but to Clevelanders they are delivered in large baskets.

The men who are employed about the bakery are not all of Jewish faith . . . but before entering upon their day's labor, they are obliged to clear their pockets of all articles of food or drink they may have about their person, for if anything in the way of ordinary food should come in contact either with the flour or the prepared Matzo, it would immediately be declared unfit for use.[5]

That same year, the *Milwaukee Sentinel* reported that there was a single bakery in the city making *matzos*. Owned by Julius Kohn, it operated out of a "two-story frame building. . . . The front part is occupied by a small, square salesroom. Then comes apparently a family room and kitchen, and in the rear of that is located the bakery, with its apparatus. For it must be remembered that nearly all the work is performed with machinery. . . . Up a short flight of stairs to a room above . . . a good-natured workman is piling up the freshly-baked bread. And what a sight! Piled high to the ceiling, the room is two-thirds full of un-leavened bread, and a workman is still further increasing the amount by basketful after basketful, just hot from the oven, which crackles sharply on being subjected to the cool atmosphere." Kohn told the reporter it took approximately two minutes to bake each "disk" of *matzo*, and that he would produce around 25,000 pounds that year, with each pound of 8 or 10 disks selling for 10 cents. It took him three months of almost daily baking to produce that amount. Only the perfect ones were sold for use during Passover and at *seders*; others would end up as flour "for cooking purposes." He always hired four teams of men and horses to deliver the matzos throughout the city.[6]

Four years later, Rabbi Dov Behr Manischewitz opened a small *matzo* bakery in Cincinnati, Ohio, to meet the holiday demands of its Jewish population. The operation grew quickly, eventually requiring the replacement of its coal-fired ovens with gas to better control baking temperatures and the addition of portable traveling-tunnel ovens to handle production. Manischewitz may also have introduced the now-familiar square *matzo* form since this could be machine-stamped more efficiently than a round or oval shape. It certainly wasted less dough. The company eventually branched out into making other kinds of crackers, kosher wine, and different kosher products, such as *gefilte* fish in a jar.[7]

In the *Gefilte Fish* video, Marcee's daughter, Jill Silverstein-Newman, discussed the merits of using premade fish versus making it from scratch. She mused:

> It smells like fish . . . but it doesn't even have the consistency of fish. It's not flakey; [it's] kinda all mashed together. It looks kind of like a *matzo*-ball that's all wet and mushy. . . . I don't make *gefilte* fish very often. As a matter of fact, I've never made it at all in my entire life. If I ever need any or I'm going to serve some with dinner or on a holiday, I usually take it from the refrigerator, from the jar (holding a jar of Manischewitz *gefilte* fish toward the camera).
>
> You know, there are a lot of reasons why I don't make it myself. It's mostly the time element involved, and, to be honest, I can't stand the smell of fish in the kitchen when you're making it. . . . One of the reasons I take my *gefilte* fish out of the jar is because my life style is so significantly different from my grandmother's, and also my mom's, that it's really a necessity. Eventually, I will be the one making it for my family. But it really would not surprise me even when it was my turn to start making it, I'd still use my Manischewitz *gefilte* fish because there's just a balancing of things, and you have to decide which is more important. I know that someday I'm going to learn how to make it from scratch and the reason why is "tradition." There's really no other reason why I can think of.[8]

So, it seems prepared foods and baked goods, like *matzos* and bakery breads, became popular because of lifestyle changes involving population and employment shifts from the countryside to cities, time constraints, and, to be quite honest, talent. Not everybody can cook or bake.

To serve just those people who could not, would not, or had no time to bake, Sarah and Max Pratzel opened a bakery almost a century ago in the north part of downtown St. Louis, Missouri, at the time when it was a predominantly Jewish area. Over the years, Pratzel's Bakery has become an "institution," as we heard more than once during our stay in the area. Ronnie Pratzel, grandson of the founders, started working in the bakery as a child, and he remembers, "Most of the business was [originally] in St. Louis, but [there was] some in East St. Louis [Illinois, which] was a Jewish community a long time ago."[9] The bakery has moved a number of times, always following its clientele. "The migration of the Jewish population in this city has been westward, westward, westward—anchored by Orthodox synagogues." However, the bakery's business now encompasses just about everybody who wants a top-notch product, be it elephant- or butterfly-shaped cookies, upside-down cupcakes, old-fashioned *apfel strudel*, or Jewish breads. Ronnie related, "We get calls all the time from Lincoln, Nebraska, from elsewhere—they want what we particularly do."

We sat in Ronnie and Elaine's small office/command center at the bakery on Industrial Drive talking about bagels, those rolls with the holes, which have made it into mainstream America's diet. A black-and-white framed portrait photo of Max Pratzel, who had come to St. Louis during the "big migration" in the early 1910s, oversaw the conversation. "My grandfather came from Russia, and my grandmother came from Poland. They had family here probably. This was, and is, a family business; Grandma stayed in the bakery. She was always there. We were the bakery that made pastries, not just bread." But, what bread! Hand-braided *challah*, those big, fat loaves essential for *Shabbos* dinner, with a translucent egg wash—Knot rolls, Kaiser rolls, Onion rolls, Hot Dog and Hamburger buns, you name it. Marble rye, Sour Dough, and *Tzizel* rye all made from a sour culture borrowed from another Jewish baker almost a century ago. This last is generously dusted with golden Midwest cornmeal, and was voted the best rye bread in St. Louis. Elaine interjected, "Ronnie's grandfather invented the *Tzizel* bread." Ronnie then related the story of that innovation. "*Tzizel* Rye Bread is one of our biggest sellers. The logo was an ear of corn on a field of red and orange. It said 'Corn *Tzizel*.' I don't think bakers in the Old Country made it that way. You know, at the end of the day, the bread you had left? He cut the end[s] off and he'd bring the bottoms home. The bottoms were covered in cornmeal. And he thought, 'I can do that with the whole loaf.'" And, too, they make *Tzizel* bagels—what bagels! Ronnie continued, "Bagels are the single largest unit we make. We boil our *Tzizel* bagels." When asked about the meaning of *Tzizel*, Ronnie replied, "Where does it come from? It does not mean 'round.' I guess [my grandfather] made it up." Ever curious, we consulted a Yiddish dictionary. Although there is a Yiddish word, *tzibel*, meaning onion, it makes no sense to apply it to cornmeal-covered breads that contain no onions. The closest we could come was *zissele*, actually a girl's nickname meaning "sweet." But was *tzizel* derived from that word or concept? In the final analysis, maybe Max really did make it up!

Ronnie next talked about the production end of his business. "We don't bake on the hearth with our bagels anymore, though. In the 1930s, '40s, we were a large production bakery. We used twenty-foot boards [and] double ovens. You couldn't buy a bagel machine in the '60s, you could only rent them, so my dad rented a bagel machine. We rented it for years until the company finally allowed us to buy it. Thirty years ago, we changed our system of making bagels. It's now easier." Now the bagels are boiled for about twenty seconds until they float to the top of the cauldron, then baked to a golden hue. These rolls are chewy without being tough; these are bagels you can slice open, add a *schmear* (dollop of cream cheese), and call it a meal.

Ronnie next summed up why he is still in the bakery business. "There's a lot of satisfaction in seeing your labors come to fruition every day, every twenty-four hours. What we do today is different from what we did ninety-six years ago, but it's the same. We, as a provider of our product, *won't* make an inferior product. We only have an 'A' line. The people who buy from us want our product. We can change—and we do—but we don't compromise on our product."

From the crush at the Pratzel retail store inside Simon Kohn's Kosher Market in Creve Coeur, it seems all of St. Louis, and not just Jewish-St. Louis either, wants their product. Hoards of shoppers press against the counter to pick up orders or select fresh-baked kosher, *pareve* goodies. They dash out clasping big loaves of *challah* to their chests, dangling two or three bakery bags full of sweets from their arms, juggling car keys, eager to get home—to start eating. At week's end, the big rush is to get there before the shop closes because Pratzel's is a *Shomer Shabbos* operation, observing the commandment to keep holy the Sabbath, locking the doors an hour before sunset on Friday. It is tradition.

The horse knew the way. In this case, "the way" was the established home delivery route for Meyer Teitelbaum's Imperial Bakery customers in Chicago. Louis Dworkin, recently arrived from Druya, near Vilnius, Lithuania, in 1912, began working for his Uncle Meyer. After a stint as "pan-washer," he was promoted to "driver," without knowing much more English than how to read numbers. Although the horse stopped at every customer's door out of habit, Louis quickly learned their names, and, also, how to bake the goods they ordered. A few years afterward, he, his wife, and his brother, Jack, incorporated the Imperial Baking Company. Imperial grew its customer base through word of mouth. Their rye bread was legendary in the city. Braverman's Delicatessen on Chicago's Near West Side proudly served its sandwiches only on "Imperial Famous Rye." In 1976, Rosen's Bakery, Inc., another long-established company in the city, merged with Imperial to better serve their respective customers. Yet, only a few years later, Arnold Dworkin, Louis's son, who had retained the legal rights to the Imperial name, purchased Kaufman's Bakery and Delicatessen in Skokie, and started working again. The bakery business was in his blood.

It was in this small store on a commercial street replete with other storefronts, block-long strip malls, and old-time synagogues, where we learned a bit about today's bakery and delicatessen business from Bette and Judy Dworkin, Arnold's daughter and wife, and how preserving old-fashioned quality means taking no short-cuts. Innovations in terms of adding or substituting some ingredients here or there, sure, but no short-cuts. Bette advised, "We do not use bread mixes. Mom's strudel evolved here, [and also] the cherry and raisin roll." There is no skimping at Kaufman's, and they ship to customers in "Wisconsin, Indiana, Michigan, and other places," as Bette told us. She further advised:

> We make Lithuanian rye, Polish rye, Russian rye, a vegetable rye and a sauerkraut rye. We use caraway seeds, put dill in. They're all different. We make onion rye and onion pumpernickel, [also] Pumpernickel with dark raisins, [and] Russian pumpernickel with light raisins, or dark raisins and walnuts. And there is a significant difference in the process, from the amount of sour that's used to the type of rye that's used. Crusts have changed, with the advent of crusty Italian breads, what you call artisan breads. In Bohemian rye, there's a one-quarter-inch crust.
>
> We've found, especially on the bakery side, that there are certain things that we get from Europe that we can't get here. The Pistachio compound—it's from Italy—and the jams, the good jams, that we use in certain items—those are all from Switzerland and from France. . . . People comment a lot of times on the *mandel* toast [a twice-baked German-Jewish cookie, usually with almonds]. They say, "Oh, that's just like *biscotti* [a twice-baked Italian cookie]." And *biscotti*, historically, has always had anise, and you almost never find anise or fennel in any Jewish cooking that we do.

Bette mentioned that there were not too many places like her delicatessen around anymore because "it's a tough business." And she is correct, especially since kosher markets, along with Wal-Mart, K-Mart, chain groceries, and buying clubs, have opened delicatessens and bakeries inside more than a few of their stores, some of these latter kosher, some not. As a consequence, stand-alone delis and bakeries have had to become "destination stops," offering items that are "a cut above" in order to survive. Aharon Morgan, owner of the Good Morgan Fish Market and the Morgan Harbor Grill in Chicago, advised us that "Delis are hard to find anymore. The eating trend has been changed. But, that doesn't mean delis aren't popular anymore. You have kosher supermarkets that have deli departments in them, but as far as a kosher deli-restaurant is concerned, they don't exist [in Chicago] anymore. Well, the [kosher] deli store where you walk in, get your sliced meat, your corned beef, your pickles, your schmaltz herring, and all those things, they're gone."[10]

Braverman's, once a fixture on Chicago's West Side, known for artery-clogging corned beef sandwiches on good Jewish (Imperial Bakery) rye, closed in the 1980s, victim, most likely, to changing neighborhood demographics and rising food costs. But Manny's Cafeteria and Delicatessen survives. Manny's operates down near Roosevelt Road, essentially the same as when it opened in 1942, except for the addition of more recent "trendy" items to its menu, like sliced Turkey on Focaccia and a Vegetarian sandwich on whole wheat bread. Steam tables, one after another, separated from the patrons by protective glass, hold huge slabs of corned beef ("because Chicago is more of a corned beef town"), pastrami, roast beef, pickled tongue, gigantic stacks of *latkes* (potato pancakes), trays of *matzo*-balls, stuffed green peppers, *knishes* (stuffed fried or baked dumplings), *kishke* (stuffed derma), kettles of soups, pans of fried liver, sauerkraut for Reuben sandwiches, and who can say what else. You had better know exactly what you want before you even step inside the place, because the line permits no indecision. Take your tray, and move along; "cutting" is allowed. Then, there is the dining room seating about three hundred, dotted with small Formica tables and pull-up chairs—probably the original ones, too—Mid-Century modern, now all the rage. No one stands on formality here. If you see an open seat, better grab it. In the old days, Manny's patrons were the Jewish merchants along Roosevelt Road, South Water Market, and Maxwell Street, politicians from City Hall, folk back on a nostalgic taste-trip to the "old neighborhood," and curious tourists. It was a coffee shop, a cafeteria, *the* neighborhood meeting spot, a cool place to congregate during Chicago's hot summer months. Sitting there was almost like seeing a movie with an ever-changing cast of characters, only with food instead of popcorn. Deals were brokered; big money contracts sealed with handshakes; news and rumors passed along. The "City that Works" ran on Manny's version of "fast food." You always met someone you knew, or had seen in the papers. Nowadays, patrons are more likely to be University of Illinois students and faculty, along with the owners of the area's upscale condominiums. Few of the old-time Jewish merchants from surrounding streets stop in for lunch anymore. They are gone, urban-renewed away.

Kaufman's, on the other hand, may be smaller, but it is also busy, busy, busy. Open one door and you enter the bakery; open the other and you go into the deli. The marvelous aromas emanating from both sections recognize no separation. In the deli, tall shelving with all kinds of different mustards and other condiments cover one end of an upright freezer. Bette confided, "We use the deli mustard and the spicy brown mustard, but I am of the opinion that if there's one thing that a deli should have it's a good mustard. I find that I buy mustard all over. On a whim, I bought a Pomeroy (whole grain French mustard). It's a mustard that has Armagnac [in it], but instead of just putting a deli mustard or a spicy mustard [on a sandwich], it's the whole, you know, mustard-aspect of the sandwich that's changed [when you use the Pomeroy]." In the jam-packed freezer, as Bette told us, you find "soups—we have mushroom barley, split pea, [and] vegetable soup. The new ones are Cheddar-Corn Chowder—you might as well bathe in it, Vegetarian Black Bean—with Tuscan beans, Vegetable-Beef, *Kreplach*, Chicken, Mushroom-Barley, Mish-Mosh (chicken, rice, noodles, *matzo*-balls and *kreplach*)," kosher-style *knishes*, Sweet and Sour Cabbage, Chicken *Paprikash*, *Kasha* (toasted buckwheat groats) and *Varnishkas* (bow-tie noodles), Sweet and Sour Meatballs in a light tomato sauce, *Holishkes* (Stuffed Cabbage), Stuffed Peppers, Hungarian Goulash, Lamb Stew, *Tzimmes*, *Cholent*, Corned Beef Hash, and other makings for an old-fashioned Jewish meal, all homemade with no preservatives, but just not in your home. Like "Mother used to make," only better, especially because you do not have to *patchke* (fuss, bother) with the cooking aspect.

Behind the counter, strung like outdoor lights, hang the salamis. One, two, and three pounders. Hard? Summer? Garlic? On the counter, dill pickles in huge glass jars swim in clear brine. Pick one and it will be bagged up for you. Eat it now? Or save it for later? In the refrigerator cases stretching along the walls sit cheeses, homemade blintzes of all persuasions, olives, salads (coleslaw and potato), sablefish, smoked chubs, and lox. Judy stated, "Our inventory is due less to cost, and more to trying to maintain the old recipes."

About that inventory, Bette told us, "Philosophically, I'm a firm believer that when there's a recession, when it gets tough, you ratchet up the quality. You don't start cutting your corners and getting cheaper ingredients in. We have to pay attention to what the core things of this business are: that's the corned beef; that's the lox. You know we have certain things—the sable, for example, is $32 a pound! That's a lot of money! And [yet] they buy it. They buy it. They don't buy much, but they buy it."

Then, there's the corned beef brisket. You can have it sliced "deckle, regular, lean, or super-trim," warmed up or not. Betty said, "You can order the deckle, which is just that top piece. [It's] so fat laden that you might as well just stop your heart; then you have 'regular'; then you have the 'lean' which normally has a one-sixteenth to three-eighths of an inch of fat across the top, which my people know if they trim, I'm gonna take their hands off. And then we have what we call 'super trim,' where every bit of fat that we can see on the top and on the bottom of the brisket, we cut off. . . . We sell a lot of it." So, order warm corned beef piled up on toothsome bread as a sandwich, or get a pound of brisket to take home. Chopped liver, too, with a hint of sweetness, no garlic, and a texture like silk—maybe on top of the corned beef? The deli goes "through about one hundred pounds a week of chicken livers alone, not just on holidays." Why not nosh on your sandwich over on the bakery side at the counter where you can watch the cars go by and the customers pour in? You get a free cookie, maybe even an old-fashioned "Sprinkle" one like you remember from when you were a kid.

Nostalgia or tradition? Both, Bette believes. "It's important to keep traditions alive. Traditions are passed down generation to generation—the holidays—Friday night dinners. When the world is uncomfortable, the tendency is to reach back into comfort food."

Jake's Deli in Milwaukee, Wisconsin, is just such a "comfort food," tradition-keeping destination spot. In a city where beer, brats, and burgers are found on almost every restaurant menu, Jake's features the uncommon—corned beef, pastrami, salami, hot dogs, and homemade matzo-ball soup. When we read that they serve "over 600 pounds of slow-cooked corned beef hand-carved [there] each day. Jake's Reuben is piled six inches tall . . . pastrami can be carved to order. Great chicken matzo-ball soup . . . just as good as grandma used to make," we began to salivate.[11]

We travel for nostalgia, and we also travel for really good food, especially when something promises to be "like grandma used to make." So, we drove to Jake's. It is an easy ride from Chicago, less than two hours, in fact, and well worth a trip three times that long!

Stepping through Jake's restaurant door is like entering a time-warp or a living museum. The dark wooden booths with narrow seats and upright backs, the beige Formica countertop tables edged with gleaming chrome, the original soda fountain complete with tall, round free-standing pedestal stools, terra-cotta wall tiles, Eames-era wavy glass, and pendant-drop light fixtures were all installed during the 1950s, when the deli sat in the midst of downtown Milwaukee's thriving Jewish community. The owners are committed to keeping the space exactly

Figure 7. Jake's Deli, Milwaukee, Wisconsin, 2009

the same as it was when Jake Levin operated it, not for its "kitsch" value, but because the physical environment is such a critical part of what makes Jake's special to so many people. "It's a 360 degree experience," according to Brian Miller, one of three partners in the operation, who also owns a famous commercial bakery that bears his name in Milwaukee. Another is Alan H. "Bud" Selig, the commissioner of Major League Baseball. The third, Gary Plassmeyer, is Jake's on-site manager. Miller told us they are all "partners in tradition," sharing the desire "to do this for infinity, really—in perpetuity, in some capacity."[12] Of course, expansion that might involve selling corned beef sandwiches at kiosks in Miller Park or other local sports venues is not out of the question.

Jake's patrons represent a real cross section of American society—neighborhood residents who are mostly African-American, federal and state officials, politicians, students, educators, factory workers, celebrities, tourists who could have read about Jake's on the Internet, at Chowhound.com or Jane and Michael Stern's Roadfood.com, or who have heard about it from one of their friends, and folk returning to their old haunts because they yearn for the taste of Jake's specialties. Although the décor is the same, other things besides the community's makeup have changed. In all truth, the category of "delicatessen" really does not fit anymore. Jake's no longer sells the smoked fish or other staples characteristic of the old-fashioned deli trade, nor does it serve three meals a day. Instead, the owners focus on what they do best. And what they do best is pile hand-cut, made-on-premises, melt-in-your-mouth, fresh-never-frozen corned beef and smoked pastrami onto slices of Miller Bakery Company's famous caraway seed rye bread—food you can watch being prepared for you—from the moment the doors open at 10 a.m. until they close at 3 p.m., six days a week. Every sandwich is a "special presentation," with accompaniments that include "artisan-type" dill pickles and sauerkraut, and Uncle Phil's special mustard from Berlin, Wisconsin. It is a "fast-casual" kind of place, as opposed to a "fast-food" establishment.[13]

Over a heaping plate of corned beef and pastrami, accompanied by a bowl of clear chicken soup in which a truly fluffy *matzo*-ball swam, we spoke with Brian about the business. He told us:

> We all know that the world has changed; fast-paced lifestyles are the norm. That said, it's comforting for people who grew up on Jake's to know that the same experience awaits, thirty, forty, or even fifty years later.
>
> We could veer from that path to create faster service, but it wouldn't be as authentic an experience. How could it compare to having the person who calls your number make the food before you, to your specifications? Is this the most efficient way of doing things? No, but it's part of the experience of coming to Jake's . . . to have a sandwich, prepared the old-school way.
>
> We fill a void for people who crave the comfort food and ambiance of their youth. And, also, for people in this community where Jake's is the only non-fast food option. But the challenge is getting people under the age of forty in here—people are busier, and don't have time to go out of their way for lunch. Of course, tastes and eating habits have changed as well. Unfortunately, my generation seems to value the "quick-fix" more than the food itself or the associated experience.
>
> I suppose I see myself in dual roles. First, is as a caretaker of this great Jewish deli tradition built by the guys who came before me. Second, is to translate that legacy into an experience that appeals to a much broader audience—anyone who enjoys classic deli food, made to order. We simply couldn't do it any other way.[14]

Eli's cheesecake. If you mention those two words together to any Chicagoan, eyes will glaze, and you'll hear, "Yum!" We trooped over to Eli's Cheesecake factory on Forest Preserve Drive to talk to Marc Schulman, president of Eli's and Eli Schulman's son, about the company, its history, and, of course, to sample the products that *Bon Appétit* magazine once characterized as "cheesecakes for the purists."[15]

Figure 8. L-R: Marc and Eli Schulman with Eli's Cheesecakes, Chicago, Illinois, circa 1980s

The building was easy to identify, emblazoned as it is, with "Eli's Cheese-cake," and "Eli's Cheesecake World" in huge letters. Around noon, the parking lot was filled. The factory has been voted one of Chicago's Top Tourist stops. It is also a good place to grab a quick lunch. The small café serves soup with marble-sized *matzo*-balls, healthy salads, artisan bread sandwiches, freshly made muffins, and, of course, slices of delectable, rich, decadent cheesecakes with all-butter shortbread cookie crusts. Dessert-lovers will find the packed refrigerator cases an irresistible lure. Choose from among the Classic Plain, Nut, Fruit, Chocolate Chip, Turtle, *Tira Mi Su*, and no-sugar-added cheese-cakes, or try a sampler of different varieties, but be assured you will absolutely love whatever one (or more) you pick!

What would a visit to any factory be without peeping in to see how things are done? You can peer at row after row of machines from a window, or take a behind-the-scenes tour for a fascinating explanation of how this kosher-certified factory works, but first you have to cover all your hair with a hairnet, and agree to your picture appearing on Eli's website within a few days!

Eli Schulman, who grew up on Chicago's Jewish West Side, began his career in the restaurant business. He started small. In a 1978 *Chicago Tribune* article, he told Anita Gold that he purchased his favorite coffee shop/restaurant when it was in foreclosure, then renamed it "Eli's Ogden Huddle." He claimed, "At the time [1940] I didn't even know how to break open an egg—I thought running a restaurant simply meant greeting the people as they came in."[16] Eli found out quickly there was much, much more involved, including teaching himself how to cook after he fired the drunken chef. Success brought expansion. First, there was another "Huddle" on the North side, followed by a move to a more upscale neighborhood with "Eli's Stage Delicatessen" on Oak Street. Then, in 1966, Eli opened a "white tablecloth" kind of restaurant on Chicago Avenue in the Streeterville section of Chicago's Gold Coast. We recall his early advertising campaign: "Eli's, *The* Place for Steak." After all, Chicago is a beef town, more than anything else. Along with tenderloin, sirloin, filet mignon, New York strip, and who knows how many other cuts of steak, the restaurant also served "Calves Liver Eli, bite-size pieces sauteed with onions, green peppers, and mushrooms."[17] We found a copy of that entrée recipe in a *Chicago Tribune* article from years back.

Sauteed Liver

(*From Eli's The Place For Steak*)
Four servings
Preparation time: 20 minutes
Cooking time: 10 minutes

1 pound fresh calf liver
4 tablespoons vegetable oil, about
¾ large onion, coarsely chopped
1 green pepper, cored, cut into 1/2-inch strips
¼ pound fresh mushrooms, quartered
Flour
Paprika
Salt

1. Skin liver and remove veins. Slice into ¼-inch thick slices.
2. Heat 1 tablespoon of the vegetable oil in large saute pan over high heat until a drop of water sizzles in the pan. Add onion, green

pepper and mushrooms. Cook over high heat until crisp-tender, about 5 minutes. Remove vegetables from pan with slotted spoon and keep warm.

3. Dip liver in flour. Shake off excess. Add remaining oil to pan. Heat oil over high heat until very hot. Add liver. Saute, turning once, until the pink color just disappears from the inside meat and outside is very crisp, about 2 minutes. Add vegetables back to pan. Cook just to reheat vegetables. Drain away excess oil. Sprinkle with paprika and salt. Serve immediately.[18]

Then Marc sent us an archival recipe for Eli's famous "Chopped Liver" suitable as an appetizer or for hors d'oeuvres.

Eli's Famous Chopped Liver

1 large Spanish onion, finely chopped
4 tablespoons vegetable or mild olive oil
1 pound chicken livers, trimmed and patted dry
6 hard-boiled eggs, peeled
Salt and pepper to taste

Sautee onions in 2 tablespoons oil in a heavy skillet over medium heat, stirring occasionally, until golden brown; transfer to a bowl. Sear chicken livers in remaining heated oil over medium high heat, turning once. Reduce heat and continue to cook until firm, about 7 minutes. Sprinkle with salt and pepper to taste. Transfer livers to a plate and cool to room temperature.

Place eggs and onion in food processor bowl; pulse turn on and off to blend and finely chop. Transfer mixture to a mixing bowl.

Add cooked livers to the same food processor bowl; pulse on and off until finely chopped. Stir into onion mixture until combined and season with salt and pepper to taste. If mixture is crumbly, you may add 1–2 tablespoons of water.

Serve with crackers, bread, and a relish tray.

Eli's legendary cheesecake was born right in his kitchen on Chicago Avenue, making its public debut in 1980 at the first Taste of Chicago event, where it was an overwhelming success. Rich in cultured sour cream and/or cream cheese, combined with imported ingredients, such as Saigon cinnamon, Belgian chocolate, and Madagascar Bourbon vanilla, then slow-baked in small batches, you can taste-travel the world in a single bite.

We asked Marc, "Why cheesecake?" He replied, "As a restaurateur at Eli's the Place for Steak, my dad was longing for a great dessert to go with his famous steak and house specialties. After years of experimenting in the kitchen, he came up with a cheesecake recipe so 'rich and creamy' that his customers proclaimed it 'Chicago's Finest.' Without that first Taste of Chicago [event], Eli's Cheesecake may have remained a delicacy just for customers at the restaurant."[19] Then, Marc shared two recipes with us for "Eli's-Style" Cheesecakes, since the actual recipes are a closely guarded secret. "Eli's-Style" notwithstanding, they *are* a real "Taste of Chicago."

Eli's-Style Original Cheesecake

Preparation time: 20 minutes
Cooking time: 45 minutes
Chilling time: 8 hours or overnight
Yield: 12 slices

Ingredients:
4 packages (8 ounces each) cream cheese, softened
1 cup sugar
2 tablespoons all-purpose flour
2 large eggs
1 egg yolk
6 tablespoons sour cream
½ teaspoon vanilla
Graham cracker or cookie crust for 9-inch spring form pan

Preparation:
Heat oven to 350 degrees. Beat cream cheese, sugar and flour in mixing bowl of an electric mixer until light and creamy. Add eggs and yolk, one at a time, scraping down sides of bowl until completely incorporated. Add sour cream and vanilla. Beat mixture, scraping down sides of bowl, until smooth.

Pour mixture into prepared crust in ungreased 9-inch spring form pan; place on cookie sheet. Bake until cake is firm around edge and center barely jiggles when tapped, about 45 minutes. Refrigerate at least 8 hours or overnight to completely set up before serving.

Crumb Crust

1½ cups vanilla wafers (ground)
½ cup powder sugar
¾ cup melted butter

Mix all ingredients in medium bowl using your fingertips until mixture is well moistened.

Graham Crust

1½ cups graham meal
½ cup brown sugar
¾ cup melted butter
½ tsp. cinnamon

Mix all ingredients in medium bowl using your fingertips until mixture is well moistened.

Eli's-Style Chocolate Chip Cheesecake

Preparation time: 20 minutes
Cooking time: 45 minutes
Chilling time: 8 hours or overnight
Yield: 12 slices

Ingredients:
4 packages (8 ounces each) cream cheese, softened
1 cup sugar
2 tablespoons all-purpose flour
2 large eggs
1 egg yolk
6 tablespoons sour cream
½ teaspoon vanilla
1½ cups miniature bittersweet chocolate chips
Graham cracker or chocolate crumb crust for 9-inch spring form pan

Preparation:
Heat oven to 350 degrees. Beat cream cheese, sugar and flour in mixing bowl of an electric mixer until light and creamy. Add eggs and yolk, one at a time, scraping down sides of bowl until completely

incorporated. Add sour cream and vanilla. Beat mixture, scraping down sides of bowl, until smooth. Gently stir in chocolate chips.

Pour mixture into prepared crust in ungreased 9-inch spring form pan; place on cookie sheet. Bake until cake is firm around edge and center barely jiggles when tapped, about 45 minutes. Refrigerate at least 8 hours or overnight to completely set up before serving.

Chocolate Crumb Crust

1½ cups chocolate wafers (ground)
½ cup powder sugar
¾ cup melted butter

Mix all ingredients in medium bowl using your fingertips until mixture is well moistened. Press into bottom and 1 inch up the sides of a 9" spring form pan.

Graham Crust

1½ cups graham meal
½ cup brown sugar
¾ cup melted butter
½ tsp. cinnamon

Mix all ingredients in medium bowl using your fingertips until mixture is well moistened. Press into bottom and 1 inch up the sides of a 9" spring form pan.

Time was when the circus rolled into town, everyone—kids and kids-at-heart—rushed to experience the lavish pageant, the glittering, kaleidoscopic show, to ride the merry-go-round, to devour creamy, rich, custardy ice-cream, to gobble up hot dogs slathered with sweet relish and yellow American-style mustard, to point, to gape, to gawk, to revel in being part of the whirling, swirling perpetual-motion event. The circus was a place for wonder, a place to marvel, a place of splendiferous, stupendous enchantment. So, short of traveling to Baraboo's Circus World, or waiting for a mobile tent-show to set up where you live, you can visit Madison, Wisconsin's own in-town version: Ella's Deli and Ice Cream Parlor.

"Culinary tourists," people who travel to particular destinations because of the food or for unique food-related experiences, along with locals looking for a fun place to take the family, or, as the dessert menu states, "for a *bar mitzvah*," fill the tables at Ella's, primarily during the summer months.[20] Sure, they come to sample the kosher-style fare served for breakfast, lunch, and dinner, and to devour the luscious homemade desserts, but they also want to soak up the special excitement, the carnival atmosphere, that is produced by hundreds of whirring, buzzing, twirling, flying, dazzling, animated displays.

In the 1960s, Ella Hirschfeld opened a small restaurant, delicatessen, and grocery on State Street in Madison catering to the city's Jewish population and university students. She eventually sold the establishment to the Balkins, whose son, Ken, moved the restaurant to its present locale in 1976. Ken and his wife, Judy, kept *matzo*-balls, sweet and sour cabbage, and borscht soups, corned beef, pastrami, lox, tongue, chopped liver, sour dill green tomatoes, bagels, and blintzes on the menu, but expanded their offerings to include garden-fresh salads, stuffed potatoes, southern fried dill pickles, Chicago Franks, Aloha burgers, Reuben sandwiches, Philly Cheese Steak Hoagies, and other items with cross-cultural, multi-regional appeal into a twenty-one-page adult bill of fare, with a two-page children's special menu.

Another draw for Madisonians and culinary tourists has to be the desserts—tantalizingly described in twelve pages of gustatory fantasy! Rich, smooth custard churned up in seventy-year-old machines, creamy cheesecakes, apple pie, and chocolate cake, like the rest of the food, except the bagels, are all made in Ella's bustling kitchen. We joined the throngs, ordering what *Madison Magazine* in February 2005 called an icon: "Ella's Number One Sundae," the three-scoop homemade vanilla custard hot fudge sundae topped with whipped cream over a slice of lightly grilled pound cake. Despite an ever-growing passion for decorating Ella's with mechanical toys and displays, Ken Balkin firmly believes, "Our food and service are what the focus should be in a restaurant."[21] But, then, there *is* that 1927 Parker carousel out front . . .

What about the mustard that goes on your corned beef and pastrami sandwiches, and, quite honestly, with other delectables as well? For that, you need to visit Massachusetts-transplant Barry Levenson's Mustard Museum and shop, near Madison, Wisconsin. We happened to arrive on National Mustard Day, held the first weekend in August every year. What a festival! We saw the Oscar Mayer Wienermobile, that strange vehicle shaped like a giant hotdog atop a car-chassis "bun," which we remember cruising Chicago streets when we were small, a gigantic walking bottle of French's Mustard, an accordion band, a blow-up cheese maze for kids, and a "hot wheels" contest open only to mustard-colored cars. We interviewed three students from Beloit College, in Beloit, Wisconsin, who advised that they had read about this gala celebration on the Internet, and that they had spent their vacation from school traveling from local food fest to food fest. They were excitedly anticipating another day of tastings. This is Middle America during the summer.

From history, it seems that mustard experienced a resurgence in the twentieth century, after being on some home economists' lists of shunned condiments for many years. In the United States, its widespread acceptance actually followed Francis French's introduction of the now well-known mild, and certifiably pure, version that still bears the family name, at the 1904 St. Louis World's Fair.[22] Nowadays, the variety of mustards seems endless—for some, the hotter, the better. Does any one even remember John Harvey Kellogg's 1894 admonition?

More than 100,000 tourists walk through the doors of the Mustard Museum every year. They watch a video on the history of this sassy sauce, view Barry's collection of mustard-related materials and ephemera, and stop to shop at the adjacent Gourmet Foods Emporium. So much to learn about mustard. So much to see! Who knew?

There are racks and stacks, rows and shelves of mustards arranged by states and countries, plus mustards organized by "style" and ingredients: creamy, garlic, dill, chocolate, Roquefort, fruit, and coarse-ground, even kosher mustard from Silver Spring Foods in Eau Claire, Wisconsin, that also makes kosher and kosher-for-Passover horseradish sauce, and little stick pretzels to dip into sampling bowls filled with unusual varieties like sweet Root Beer. Store merchandise includes reusable mustard-colored "green" bags; logo T-shirts; silk hot dog ties, with mustard squiggles, of course; Black Widow "Leave No Survivors" hot sauce, along with pure maple syrup in old-fashioned molded glass jars. The choices seem endless and quite enticing, even if one is not a mustard enthusiast.

Barry confided that he had been distracted of late what with the museum's upcoming move to larger quarters in nearby Middleton, a venue change fraught with logistical problems, and now rain was threatening to dampen the Mustard Day festivities. But the clouds cleared, and outdoor grills began to sputter with hot dogs; streams of tourists wandered around talking, laughing, pointing, snapping photos, and the band began to play. Barry worked the crowd, posing for pictures, cracking jokes—a Borscht-Belt comedian playing in the rolling hills of Wisconsin.

We listened to the accordion ensemble; sang "Roll Out the Mustard" to the tune of the "Beer Barrel Polka"; avoided further embarrassing ourselves with mustard bottle bowling; eschewed sampling Culver's Mustard Custard (it was 10 A.M., after all, and a bit early for sweets of any variety, even ones whose names entertained our ears and reminded us of Ogden Nash), and left with smiles on our faces, along with a variety of different mustards to slather on just about anything once we returned home, an elegant silk hot dog tie, and a copy of Barry's hilarious book, *Habeas Codfish: Reflections on Food and Law* (2001), inscribed, "Condimentally Yours."[23]

In sum, then, after interviewing all the people at Kaufman's Bakery and Delicatessen, Pratzel's Bakery, Jake's Deli, Eli's Cheesecake Factory, Ella's Deli and Ice Cream Parlor, the Mustard Museum, and Morgan's Grill and Fish Market, we found that every one expressed incredible pride in what he or she does. And what they do goes beyond slavishly preserving Jewish food traditions, to innovating taste treats by adapting recipes, and, in many instances, adding new, exciting, items and experiences to their product lines. Not only that, but we discovered they really enjoy making quality foodstuffs for their customers, who, now more than ever before, include almost everyone.[24]

8

Trends in the Heartland

Authentic, and healthy. Traditional, plus tasty. We heard those phrases over and over when we asked about today's Jewish foods. Etheldoris Grais and Joseph Israel gave us examples of dishes, both Ashkenazic-based and Sephardic-inspired, meeting those criteria. The recipes they shared use Midwestern ingredients; they are also versatile, and grounded in Jewish food traditions, insofar as "Jewish foods" are often simply foods Jews eat wherever they live.[1]

Etheldoris learned to cook from her mother and an Italian friend in Hibbing, and while she was traversing the world taking cooking classes. She told us that her recipe for "Clear Wild Rice Soup" builds on techniques for cooking that specialty crop learned from the Chippewa when she was young. We believe this recipe demonstrates her enthusiasm for experimenting with the foodstuffs of other cultures, and her willingness to incorporate local ingredients, in this case, Minnesota wild rice, into her culinary repertoire. This recipe includes goodly amounts of fiber, often only minimally present in Jewish dishes.

Clear Wild Rice Soup

¼ cup uncooked wild rice
2 (10¾ ounce cans) of chicken broth
1½ cups water
4 green onions, thinly sliced (about ¼ cup)
⅛ teaspoon white pepper
½ cup very thin julienne strips of carrots
½ cup very thin julienne strips of zucchini

Cook rice. Simmer chicken broth, water, wild rice, green onion, and pepper 10 minutes. Stir in carrots. Simmer 5 minutes. Stir in zucchini. Simmer 2 minutes. Serve immediately.

Joseph says his "'Zucchini Soup' is a delicious and versatile soup that can be modified to many tastes; it starts humbly with few zucchinis and can be transformed from *pareve* to dairy or meat. Its history starts with Matilde, and we have been enjoying it for quite some time. It is usually eaten hot, but cold will also do, with pita chips or crusty baguette. I can go on and on about this simple and magnificent soup. This is a truly versatile and filling soup." Low in calories, high in vitamins, especially vitamin A, this soup makes good use of an inexpensive summer squash easily grown in Midwestern home gardens. It also fits neatly into the Sephardic foodways tradition. Like most of those dishes, it would not be foreign to anyone eating the currently popular heart-healthy "Mediterranean diet."

Zucchini Soup

Ingredients:
3–4 fresh, firm zucchinis
1 good size sweet Vidalia onion
1 small potato
Bouquet of thyme for taste—bunch a few stalks and tie
3–4 sprigs of parsley
Sea salt
Fresh ground black pepper
Vegetable kosher cube (Telma, or Osem brands)

Preparation:
Wash vegetables well, cut and discard zucchinis ends and random chop the vegetables into medium chunks and place in a large pot.
Coarse chop the onion and add to pot.
Add the thyme bouquet and parsley sprigs, add water 3–3½ quarts, to make a large pot of soup, and finally crumble and add the vegetable flavoring cube.
Season to taste.
Bring to a boil until zucchinis and potato are soft
Remove thyme bouquet and discard. Very important step, if it is left it will overwhelm the taste.

Use an immersion mixer/blender to purée until liquid with some chunks.

And that's it. Soup can be served as is with a mint garnish. You can also serve with pita chips, or [a] few corn chips. The star is the soup, not the chips. Side green or Israeli salads are quite appropriate. Another alternative is to diagonally cut baguette slices, sprinkle olive oil and oregano; lightly toast and serve hot.

Other serving suggestions:

Dairy: grate fresh cheese, or sprinkle shredded cheese. Add a small dollop of sour cream, not too much.

Spicy: sprinkle some hot sauce before serving for color and decoration.

Meat: use chicken or beef stock. Be sparing with the salt as prepared stocks are generally salty. You can also add chicken or beef pieces in the soup and purée all the ingredients together.

Another summer soup recipe, for days when it really is too hot to cook, or even to eat, is Etheldoris's "Cold Raspberry Cream Soup." It is made with fresh Minnesota berries, always somewhat expensive because of their perishable nature, unless you pick them yourself, bulked out with prepackaged frozen ones. Loaded with antioxidants and carotenoids, along with vitamins B and C, the soup is fragrant and sweet, yet with a tart nuance, that is absolutely perfect.

Cold Raspberry Cream Soup

Serves 6
Ingredients:
1 14 oz. bag frozen raspberries
1 pint fresh raspberries
1 cup water
1 8 oz. carton raspberry yogurt
1 banana cut into chunks
½ cup milk (or more to thin at end if needed)
¼ cup sugar
⅛–¼ teaspoon cinnamon, or to taste
½ cup Half and Half
2–3 Tablespoons of raspberry liqueur

Method:

Place the defrosted or washed fresh raspberries in a blender with water and yogurt. Blend until smooth. Add banana, milk, sugar, cinnamon, and liqueur, and blend again. Stir in Half and Half. Strain well through a fine sieve and correct seasoning. Use milk to thin soup if necessary. Let cool in refrigerator overnight.

Serve in a glass bowl with a few whole raspberries in the middle and garnish with a piece of mint (Spearmint preferred).

Since fish has always been a favorite, and sacred, component of Jewish meals, we searched for a kosher fish merchant, one who sells only fish with scales and fins, to learn what the trend toward healthier eating may have done to and for that kind of business. The Good Morgan Fish store located in Chicago's West Rogers Park neighborhood is connected to the small Morgan Harbor Grill restaurant, both under the same management. Aharon Morgan, a longtime restaurateur and graduate of the Culinary Institute of America, sat down with us to talk about his new sushi restaurant and the kosher fish business. Morgan established his Devon Avenue fish shop twenty years ago in the "heart of the Jewish community," with six or seven *shuls* within a one-mile radius. When the adjoining storefront recently became available, he opened his grill with the goal of being "a very good restaurant that just happened to be kosher." Ninety-nine percent of his customers are Jewish, including those who do not keep kosher, local Orthodox, including Chabad-Lubavitchners, and the more recent Russian immigrants, but he expects the one percent who are not Jewish to increase once word gets out that he serves a fine product. He confided:

> I was very hesitant in doing the sushi, but I had a few people in the community who said, "Do the sushi. It's very, very important." I didn't listen to them, and I didn't listen to them, until I started getting really serious, and I needed to make decisions about just what we were going to do with things here. So, I put the sushi [bar] in. And I can tell you it achieved the objective of getting people back [to Devon Avenue]. I'm getting all new customers, [along with] repeat customers. But, I'll tell you the interesting thing about those customers. I'd say the average age is maybe twenty-five to thirty years old. It's very much the younger crowd, very much in tune with the new way of eating. And they eat the traditional [kosher] way, but they also want to be imaginative, and they want to expand their horizons. . . . They are very much attuned to the new way of eating, but not much interested in cooking, only in ready to go. It's a convenience-oriented society.[2]

In terms of fish quality, Morgan is known to both his suppliers and his patrons as demanding. He only buys extremely fresh fish, ones with clear eyes, bright red gills, a sort of stiffness that makes them difficult to fillet, and a sweet smell, "like cucumbers." His suppliers must be "sustainable fishermen. We're an environmentally concerned business. And because of the locality here [in Chicago], we sell more whitefish than we do anything else. Whitefish is a local fish. And the next best seller is salmon."

Besides the usual whitefish, salmon, herring, red snapper, trout, flounder, halibut, and bass, he also sells premade huge, flat, fried salmon patties, *gefilte* fish with tiny, sweet bits of carrots mixed in, lox that is smoked on the premises, along with made-to-order fried Great Lakes whitefish and garlic pasta. Patrons can eat on the "fish market" side, where the walls are tiled in the blue and white colors of the Israeli flag, or over in the fifty-plus seat dining room next door. "What we have here," Aharon said, "[is] I'm trying to educate [my customers] on a daily basis. Not on 'eating culture' [because] they already know the importance of how to do that. But that eating *this* kind of kosher leads to health benefits for the household. Obviously, it's the omega-3 oils." We would also add the documented benefits of eating fish include a high-protein content, fewer calories than red meat, and versatility, because it can be broiled, fried, poached, stewed, baked, seared, steamed, or raw, all factors that affect modern consumer decisions to purchase and consume fish.

Etheldoris, in turn, gives the traditional Jewish steamed fish, often found on *seder* and Sabbath tables, a modern international flair with soy sauce and ginger, then provides it with a distinctively Midwestern touch by using Minnesota-caught crappies or walleye pike. We like to think of her recipe as "fusion" cuisine.

Chinese Style Steamed Fish

1½ – 2 # crappie (or walleye)
White pepper
½ teaspoon sugar (optional)
2 Tablespoons dry sherry
1 Tablespoon soy sauce
2 slices FRESH ginger
2 green onions cut into 1" pieces
2 green onions chopped fine
2–3 Tablespoons oil, peanut—Chinese favorite, or corn
Sweet pickled ginger

Have fish cleaned and scaled, but left whole. If walleye is too big, cut in half. Rinse well in cold water. Dry with paper towel and rub lightly with salt inside and out. Place in a shallow Pyrex pie plate or heatproof platter that has been lightly oiled.

Make slashes in fish every two inches and sprinkle pepper, sugar, sherry, soy sauce on fish. Lay ginger slices and large pieces of onion on top and place in steamer. Steam for 15 minutes. It will continue cooking for a few minutes when you take it out of steamer. Remove onions and ginger. Arrange finely chopped onion and sweet pickled ginger on top. Heat oil to very hot and pour over fish. Serve with boiled rice.

While we were looking through the large collection of local sisterhood cookbooks in the St. Louis Archives, we noted very few calling for lima beans, as we had found in Minnesota, but many that incorporated broccoli, a spring and fall crop for which Missouri is famous, since it grows well in a variety of soils. Broccoli seemed to be used in everything from scrambled eggs to stews and soups. Perhaps this difference is related to local taste-preferences, or maybe because broccoli is easy to grow in Missouri since it needs seventy days to mature and can be seeded directly into the soil during late May. Introduced to the American market from Italy, and popularized by the D'Arrigo brothers through radio advertising during the 1920s, this fiber-rich vegetable is now one of the best selling and most inexpensive green vegetables on the market in the United States. Eaten raw, boiled, steamed, sautéed, or baked, broccoli contains beta-carotene, folic acid, and large amounts of vitamins A and C.[3]

In the introduction to their 1994 synagogue cookbook, *Specialties of Our House*, the authors wrote that St. Louis's "Shaare Zedek Women's League members have the reputation of being excellent culinary artists. Whether you are a new bride or an expert in the kitchen, you will enjoy the traditional delectable recipes from Mama's Kosher Kitchen to the contemporary style of cooking for every changing food taste. Jewish cooking is based on the Jewish dietary laws and on dishes that are our specialties to celebrate the holidays of the Jewish calendar."[4] Their comments, along with the recipes they included in their cookbook, reinforce the trends toward lighter and healthier cooking that we are seeing across most contemporary Jewish cuisine.

Ruth Jacob published her recipe for "Broccoli Soup," in that fundraising book. She annotated this distinctively Midwest-flavored dish, with the classic expression "*B'Ta-ah-von*," which she translated as "Have a hearty appetite."[5]

Broccoli Soup

¼ c. chopped onions
1 Tablespoon margarine
1 (8 oz.) cream cheese, cubed
1 cup milk
¾ cup boiling water
1 (10 oz.) frozen or fresh broccoli, cooked and drained
1 chicken bouillon cube (parve)
½ teaspoon salt
½ teaspoon lemon juice
Dash of pepper

Saute onion in margarine. Add cream cheese and milk.
Stir over low heat until cream cheese is melted. Dissolve bouillon in boiling water. Add to cream cheese mixture. Stir in chopped broccoli, lemon juice, and seasonings. Heat! Makes 6 servings.

Curious, we asked Bette Dworkin how the emphasis on healthier eating has impacted her delicatessen business, whose products are not necessarily known as "heart-healthy." She told us, "There is a shift in the demands of the clientele—there *is* something of a shift toward healthier. On the one hand, I'd say, 'Yes, the food's getting a little more healthful,' but on the other hand, they [the customers] balance it [with a desire to eat foods they remember]. I think sometimes that's where the challenges fall. In some respects, we're fulfilling childhood dreams. 'Is it chicken liver the way Grandma used to make it?' 'Is it chicken soup the way my mother used to make it?' But because they have memories attached to them. . . . The challenge to us is to kind of keep those memories alive, but the difficulty is that it's never [exactly] the same. So, it's a balancing act." Aharon has found a similar phenomenon occurring among his customers. "I see the traditional way of eating generally comes out during Passover season and the High Holy Day holiday season when [people] want their *gefilte* fish, and they want it like their grandmother made it, and her grandmother made it, and her grandmother made it."

In *Swann's Way*, Marcel Proust wrote, "And suddenly the memory returns. The taste of that little crumb of madeleine . . . the smell and taste of things remain poised for a long time."[6] Both Aharon's and Bette's comments, coupled with Proust's famous quote, caused us to wonder whether "nostalgia" for the tastes of childhood, or for a more general *Yiddishkeit* (the Jewish *Volksgeist*), might be the driving forces behind the resurgence in kosher products' sales. Or is this burgeoning market driven by something else, something perhaps as fundamental as the lack of time to prepare food?[7] On the other hand, could the public's perception of kosher food as more sanitary be a contributing factor to its increasing popularity?

As far back as the nineteenth century, newspapers and advertisements touted kosher meat as cleaner and safer to eat than "other" meats. In 1883, the *Chicago Daily Tribune* discussed "'Kosher' Meat: Why the Orthodox Jews Get Better Meat than the Average Christian." This article provides the general public with a basic understanding of why Jews eat kosher meats ("a desire to protect the children of Israel against the many diseases that result from the consumption of the meat of unhealthy animals") to the role of the *shochet*, whose "duty [is] to kill and examine every animal intended to furnish food for orthodox Jewish stomachs. Here in Chicago, he has to practice principally on cattle, calves, sheep and domestic fowls." The conclusions were that "kosher" meant "clean" and disease-free; all meat or poultry found to be otherwise was rejected.[8] Another 1883 article from the St. Louis *Republican* informed the public that "under the law [rejected beef and poultry] must be thrown to the dogs, but the law was made, you see, out there in the wilderness where there was no one to eat them. Here in St. Louis they are dressed and sold to butchers who do not deal in kosher meat. A great many of the cattle are diseased, and it would be much better for the people of this city if the Board of Health would pay some attention to having them butchered properly and inspected."[9] By 1887, as a reassuring safeguard for Jewish clientele, kosher meats and poultry were stamped with a *hechsher* (seal of approval), along with the word "kosher" and the date the animal was killed.[10]

Twenty-two years after the passage of the 1906 Pure Food and Drug Act, Gladys Huntington Bevens reported on the expanding market for kosher food. She wrote, "A very orthodox Jewish woman said to me once, 'Did you know that Gentiles eat kosher meat? In fact, all good food is kosher, nowadays. Many of the laws of Moses were sanitary precautions that were necessary in the early days of Israel under the existing conditions of that time. Today we could be good Jews and eat as the Gentiles do.'"[11] By 1933, the word "kosher" was beginning to be applied to pickles, breads, restaurants, and recipes.[12] The "kosher" seal that appeared on food products signified that they had been prepared under rabbinical supervision, and were free from bugs and disease. To the general public, this translated into "sanitary."

A recent Mintel Food Service survey found that the "ethnic market" for kosher products, such as *matzos*, *gefilte* fish, and *borscht*, remains fairly stable from year to year. Obviously, the Jewish consumer who adheres to religious law is the constant behind those sales. We suspect that during Passover and the High Holy Days holidays, convenience and nostalgia may well factor in to non-observant Jews' decisions to buy these kinds of foodstuffs, too, thus causing a small seasonal "spike."

The study also recorded that the "mainstream and kosher" market is booming. It found Muslims, Seventh Day Adventists, vegetarians, and food-allergic people were purchasing kosher products since "the kosher labeling system provides a clear listing of the contents of a product, and identifies whether it contains dairy or meat."[13] But is this market segment's growth also because so many of the consumables that the average person buys, the mainstays of the food industry, like coffee, cookies, soft drinks, jams, jellies, yogurts, baby foods, and snack items, just happen to be kosher-certified? According to Eleanor Hanson's "FoodWatch" website, consumer food items and products that fit into the "mainstream" category are "widely available and easily adopted, comfortable and not threatening."[14] And could the public's renewed fears concerning *E. coli*, *Salmonella*, and adulterants in American foods also be behind increased sales in the "mainstream and kosher" market? After all, kosher foodstuffs are still perceived as being cleaner and more sanitary than the general run-of-the-mill commercial product.

Nineteenth-century reformers ran cooking classes to teach Eastern European Jewish women and children how to cook American foods, and prepare them hygienically, using the best, most up-to-date scientific principles. Newspapers, women's magazines, and journals printed recipes that took Jewish dishes and made them suitable for the American palate and table. Later, radio and television began hosting cooking shows that accomplished the same task. We are certain that, in some instances, the recipes showcased on those media elicited nostalgic memories for long-ago foodstuffs.

Radio shows, such as Iowa's KMA's *Radio Homemakers,* the U.S. Department of Agriculture's *Housekeeper's Chat* with Aunt Sammy's Radio Recipes, and France Lee Barton's *Cooking School of the Air,* sponsored by Battle Creek, Michigan's General Foods Corporation, were immensely popular among "stay at home" women, providing them with information about world happenings, as well as daily and weekly menu tips and ideas. Yiddish AM radio stations across the nation sometimes presented over-the-air recipes, too, as part of their programming. Most notable was WLTH in Brooklyn, for whom Victor Packer conducted his "Man on the Street" interviews. Packer's *Shtimes fun di Gas* (*Voices from the Street*) interviews took place during 1942 in Tenenbaum's Public Market. His show was sponsored by Sterling Kosher Salt, a product the interviewees took care to mention by name in hopes of receiving a few boxes at the end of the interview. Thanks to the recovery of old disks, we can once again hear women, in voices so evocative of a lost community, giving their favorite recipes in Yiddish, interspersed with English phrases here and there.

Mrs. Aidner from Warsaw told Packer's listeners that "for my husband, his favorite dish is *Galagarteh*. You know what *Galagarteh* is? Calf's Foot Jelly. I buy some feet from the butcher and have them chop them up. And I bring them home, and set them on to cook, and add some Sterling Salt—you have to have that—If you add Sterling Salt you know what you've got . . . Some garlic, a little spice, then it cooks, and I drain off the soup, and I take the meat, and chop it, and set it to jell. And that's it."[15]

At least three other women stopped to tell Packer how to make what they considered their best dishes. The informality of the recipe instructions could have been because the women were orally recalling what they did when they made their signature dishes, but they also hearken back to the kinds of manuscript recipes we found that suggest the recorder was standing at the elbow of a cook who knew her way around the kitchen while she talked her way through how to make a particular dish.

"I stuff up a good *kishke*. I take—according to the size, to the intestine lining—you take carrots, onions, a *bisl matzo* meal, a *bisl* farina, and chicken fat, and a little Sterling Salt, a little pepper—red pepper—and you mix that all through, and you stuff the *kishke*. Then you cook it for 2 hours. And, then, you roast it for about half an hour or so, until it gets brown. It truly *is* delicious."[16]

Another shared her recipe for "Hungarian Goulash" in the following dialogue with Parker conducted in Yiddish sprinkled with English expressions.

PARKER: "Do you prepare a dish that everyone enjoys?"

WOMAN: "Yes, goulash."

PARKER: "Hungarian goulash? Will you tell me how to prepare it?"

WOMAN: "Yeh, why not? Listen up. You make the meat kosher with Sterling Salt.

"You chop up an onion with a clove of garlic and fry it up with a piece of fat. Then you cut up the meat, and add it, and let it cook for 1 hour and 45 minutes. Then you add chopped-up potatoes with red pepper, and you let it cook 2 hours."

PARKER: "So, all together, that's 3 hours and 45 minutes?"

WOMAN: "No, no, no! Only a half hour for the potatoes because they're chopped up!"

PARKER: "Ah, so, 2 hours and 15 minutes."

WOMAN: "No, just 2 hours. An hour and a half, and a half hour the potatoes—so you don't burn the potatoes."

PARKER: "What kind of flame do you use?"

WOMAN: "A low flame—a low flame for 2 hours. Sterling Salt I use—yes, I always use."[17]

The recipe another woman shared for bread pudding indicated she was well aware of government sugar and butter rationing during wartime, as well as the cost of cooking gas. Her recipe includes only the natural sugars imparted by a single apple and some raisins. More than likely, it was healthier that way. Some bread pudding recipes call for it to be cooked in a butter-greased double-boiler on the top of the stove, which might take more than one hour, and for first toasting the bread under the broiler. However, this woman's recipe called for the economical use of leftover bread, and for baking the entire pudding in the oven, which could have been done in the same space, at the same time, as another dish requiring the same temperature.

"I make a very good bread pudding. Because being we have to be very economical now, we have to save every piece of bread—either brown bread or white bread. I soak it in milk, and then I take more than one, less than two, because—I mean less than three but more than one. And I separate the eggs. Then I put in an apple—raisins need to be in the middle so they don't burn, because I bake the pudding [completely] in the oven to save gas. . . . And it's very economical and I'm sure your children will like it too."[18]

In Chicago, during the 1970s, famed Hungarian chef Louis Szathmary regularly appeared on WGN TV's Jim Conway show, demonstrating "quick ways to Jewish cooking."[19] Perhaps his success was based on his marvelous personality, his exceptional reputation as a superb chef, or, maybe, because some viewers simply did not know how to fix the dishes he demonstrated and were anxious to learn.

Is this eagerness to learn what grandmothers knew, and which mothers may have never learned, behind the popularity of kosher cooking classes that we see advertised more and more frequently in the Chicago area? Obviously, there must be a "felt need" or these classes would not be taking place. Is the "need" because people want to return to, or recapture, their culinary and religious roots? Or is it a desire to adapt traditional Jewish recipes to more modern standards in terms of both health and spicing? Do these desires encompass only the foods, or the meanings invested in them, too?

We spoke with Stacey Schwartz of "Cooking for Fun," in Skokie, Illinois, who organizes and teaches cooking classes, both kosher and non-, for children ages five to fifteen. She confided that she believes that

> This generation, maybe not the grandmother generation, but my generation, is much more concerned about health, weight, and heart problems. People are developing an awareness of what they put into their mouths; they're trying to find out, and cooking classes [not just for children, but adults, too] are a great way to do that. Jewish cooking has taken a turn toward healthier. There's been a sort of evolution in the menus with more flavor coming from fresh ingredients and fresh herbs. It's slow, but it's there.
>
> These kinds of classes are in vogue because you can do this together [apply what you have learned in classes] at home. The children want to learn a skill, and in cooking, they learn nutrition, math, [and] science. When kids get a taste of it [the classes along with the foods they make], they come back for more. Children are very receptive to trying out different things, and they're so proud of what they do. You just have to pick the right things for them to cook. I've had parents tell me they're surprised that the children will eat things like "Mock Sloppy Joes" on whole grain buns, but these were a huge success.[20]

Spertus Institute of Jewish Studies in Chicago showcased Wolfgang Puck's renowned gourmet foods in its café until it closed in a budget crunch. The former executive chef, Laura Frankel, has "a longstanding passion for organic, local, sustainable, and fair trade ingredients."[21] Consequently, the food served at Spertus was fresh, seasonal, creative, and organic, along with being kosher. Frankel now conducts kosher cooking classes for adults and children. She says, "Kosher cooking often gets a bad rap, and some of this is deserved, since there are kosher cooks and companies that rely on processed foods. But artificial ingredients aren't good for you or the planet, they don't taste as good as natural food, and there is nothing about kosher laws that requires them. I don't mess around with faux foods created in laboratories, and I only feed my family, friends, and customers the very best ingredients."[22]

Frankel, then, appears to be espousing an "eco-*kashrut*" philosophy similar to that which Aharon Morgan discussed with us, earth-friendly and certified-kosher food products that fit in with contemporary environmental concerns, and enable Jews to work toward the ages-old goals of *tikkun olam* (the repair of the world) and social justice. The eco-*kashrut* idea was introduced during the 1970s by Rabbi Zalman Schachter-Shalomi, the founder of the Jewish renewal movement, and seems to have captured the attention of many progressive kosher-keeping Americans, since it also encourages eating organic products and buying locally produced meats, vegetables, and fruits.[23]

As a case in point, to meet the needs of Orthodox Jews, and certainly to fulfill the commandment to eat *matzo* on Passover, and perhaps build on desires to recapture the tastes and textures of the past, the kosher Chicago Shmura Matzoh Factory in Skokie manufactures the ultimate flat-bread—round, handmade *shmura matzos*. *Shmura* is not a special type of wheat, but a descriptive term, meaning that the flour has been monitored from harvesting through baking to prevent any contact with moisture. *Shmura matzos* are typically thinner, crispier, and airier than the more familiar square ones. When broken up, they make a marvelous crunchy breading for fried fish or chicken because they absorb less oil. More recently, to meet the demands of its "health conscious consumers," the company has branched out into making a variety of different *matzos*, "including 100% certified organic whole wheat and spelt, which are 75% lower in carbohydrates than conventional matzohs."[24] Aharon Morgan informed us, "People are now eating organic food. Organic food has become a big industry [that] is growing at about 20 percent a year. When we were buying it back years ago, it was very hard to get. Now you could get it at different places that have been organic-certified, and people are becoming very aware of what's in their food."

In terms of the kosher products market, David Rossi, vice president of marketing for R. A. B. Food Group, the parent company of Manischewitz, said they are working to keep the non-Jewish trend of buying kosher foods growing by pushing the "mainstream and kosher" segment even more. However, the company is struggling with one specific item that it makes. While Morgan found that kosher sushi sells equally well to his customers regardless of their ethnicity or religious beliefs, Manischewitz is still looking for "the breakout idea for selling gefilte fish to the non-Jewish."[25]

Appendix

Tastes of Home

Old recipes—as much fun as they are to read, before you try to actually "cook" the dishes, you are often faced with so many questions. What size eggs? What strength vinegar? Kosher or iodized salt? Does it make a difference? What do you do when few methods, fewer baking temperatures, sketchy or missing measurements, and no visual clues have been provided? We have produced more "culinary disasters" than we care to recall trying to update heritage recipes. Recipes allow for creativity, and sometimes for substitutions, but really do not lend themselves to "best guesses."

Nonetheless, we decided to rework a few of Ruth Dunie's recipes because they were fairly basic and traditional, yet had a certain flair. We tried to keep our revisions as close to the originals as possible. There were many times, however, when we were tempted to add a bit of parsley to one, a touch of wine to another, but then our palates are different today. So, we present ten of Ruth's updated recipes, in the order in which they appear in our text, as representative of early twentieth-century Ashkenazic cuisine, as characteristic of the kinds of foods that European Jews brought with them when they settled in the Heartland, adapted where necessary to include local ingredients, then served as "tastes of home."

Matzo Phon cake—(Pfannküchen)

Ingredients:

    1½ boards of matzos, unsalted (9" square)

    1 large egg, room temperature

    2 T. milk

3 T. + 1 t. matzo meal
1 t. baking powder
salt and pepper to taste
½ cup oil

Method:

In small bowl, break up matzos into small pieces, and soak in enough warm water or milk to cover. When softened, press to remove excess liquid. In separate bowl, whisk egg in milk, adding salt and pepper, if desired. Add combined baking powder and matzo meal. Stir in softened matzos. Heat oil in large skillet over medium heat until very hot. Drop tablespoonfuls of mixture carefully into skillet, flattening with back of spoon. Fry until bottom becomes golden, approximately 1½ to 2 minutes. Turn and fry until underside is golden, about 30 seconds. Remove from pan. Drain on paper towel. Serve.
Yield: About 8–10 3-inch matzo cakes

Sweet and Sour Fish*

Ingredients:

About ½ cup coarse kosher salt
3 pounds firm fish fillets (whitefish, salmon, carp, bass, or pike),
½–¾-inch thick
2 T. vegetable oil
1 large white onion, sliced
2 T. packed brown sugar
2 cups water
3 T. white vinegar (5%)
1 clove garlic, coarsely chopped
½ cup raisins
juice of ½ large lemon (about 2 T.)
pinch of ground cloves
About 5 T. flour
pepper to taste

Method:

Generously salt the fish, place in a shallow glass baking dish, cover and refrigerate for 3 hours. Rinse off salt, pat dry, and set aside. In large deep skillet, cook onion in oil until translucent; add brown sugar and continue cooking until onion browns and caramelizes. To this add water, vinegar, garlic, raisins, lemon juice, and ground cloves. Bring to a boil, reduce heat to medium, and simmer for 30 minutes to reduce mixture to about ¾ cup. Add the fish to broth and return to medium heat. Bring to boil, then reduce heat to low, cover, and simmer 10 to 15 minutes or until fish flakes easily. Remove the fish to a warm serving plate using slotted spatula. Strain the cooking liquid, measure, and return liquid to skillet. For each cup of strained cooking liquid, in a small bowl, stir together 2 tablespoons of flour and 2 tablespoons cold water. Bring liquid in skillet to boil; stir in flour and water mixture. Continue cooking, stirring constantly until thickened. Adjust seasoning, adding pepper if desired. Pour sauce over fish to serve.

Yield 6–8 servings

*This is a dish that may have had its origins in Sephardic cuisine but migrated with the Jews into Germany and other parts of Europe.

Potato Glace

Ingredients:
  4 cups potatoes, boiled, riced or grated, cooled
  2 large eggs, lightly beaten
  ½ cup sifted all-purpose flour
  2 slices white bread, cut into ½-inch cubes
  1 t. butter
  Melted butter
  salt and pepper to taste

Method:
  Combine potatoes, eggs and flour. Add salt and pepper if desired. Brown bread cubes in frying pan in 1 teaspoon of butter. Add browned bread cubes to potato mixture and form into 15 to 20 2-inch balls. Chill for ½ hour. In large pan, heat water to simmering. Cook dumplings, uncovered, 20 minutes. Drain using a slotted spoon. Put on a platter and cut in half. Serve drizzled with melted butter.

  Yield: About 15 to 20 dumplings

Pot Roast

Ingredients:
    1 3-pound rump or chuck roast*
    1 T. paprika
    1 t. ground ginger
    salt and pepper to taste
    1 large white onion, sliced
    1 clove garlic, chopped
    3 large or 6 small bay leaves
    4 T. shortening
    2 cups water, more if needed
    5 T. flour
    1 T. vinegar, if desired
    ½ 12-ounce can condensed tomato soup
    4–6 medium red potatoes, scrubbed

Method:

Rub the meat with salt, pepper, paprika, and ground ginger the night before cooking. Refrigerate overnight in a covered glass pan or container. Brown meat on all sides over medium heat in shortening in deep roasting pan or Dutch oven. Remove meat from pan and set aside.

Add onion and garlic to pan and sauté until onions are clear and garlic is light brown. Sprinkle with flour, stirring constantly. Gradually add the water, allowing the sauce to thicken. Bring to a boil and add the bay leaves. Reduce heat, and cook for 2 minutes. Return the meat to the pan, season lightly with salt and pepper, and vinegar, if desired. Cover, and cook for 3 hours over low heat turning the meat every 30 minutes. The sauce should bubble gently. If the sauce becomes too thick, add water. After 3 hours, add tomato soup and potatoes. Continue cooking approximately 1 hour more or until meat is fork-tender, and potatoes can be easily pierced with a fork.

Remove meat and potatoes from sauce. Set potatoes aside. Cool meat, then slice into ½ inch thick pieces. Skim off excess fat from the sauce. Strain. Return meat and potatoes to pan. Reheat gently, spooning sauce over meat and potatoes, to serve.

Yield: 4 to 6 servings

*Note: Rump roast is one of the leanest cuts, and hence, perhaps one of the toughest cuts, of meat. In addition, it is not a kosher cut of beef. A shoulder or chuck roast comes from the kosher-permitted beef forequarter, and contains more fat. This recipe becomes similar to German *sauerbraten* when the vinegar is added while marinating. Vinegar would also tenderize the meat if a rump roast were used.

Whole I[rish] Potato Cake

Ingredients:
    2 cups cake flour
    2 t. baking powder
    pinch of salt
    1 t. ground nutmeg
    1 t. ground cinnamon
    1 t. ground allspice
    2 cups granulated sugar
    ½ cup butter, softened
    2 large eggs
    1 cup potatoes, boiled and mashed
    ¾ cup milk
    1 cup chopped walnuts
    6 oz. (3 2" x 2" squares) bitter chocolate, melted

Method:
    Preheat oven to 325 degrees F.
    Grease and flour a 10-inch Angel food cake or Bundt® pan. In medium bowl, sift together the flour, baking powder, salt, cinnamon, nutmeg and allspice. In a large bowl, cream together the butter and sugar until light and fluffy. Beat in the eggs one at a time. Stir in potatoes. Add the flour mixture alternately with milk. Stir in nuts and chocolate. Pour batter into cake pan. Bake in preheated oven for 1½ to 2 hours, or until a toothpick inserted into the cake comes out clean. Cool.
    Yield: 1 10-inch cake
    Note: Can be frosted

Salt Water Pickles for winter

Ingredients & Supplies:

  8 lbs. pickling cucumbers (2–3" long; not waxed; blossom end removed)

  1½ gal. water

  1 lb. pickling salt

  4 cups white vinegar (5%)

  8 1-qt. canning jars with lids

Method:

  Sterilize jars and lids. Soak cucumbers 4–5 hours in cold water. Wash well; pack cucumbers into jars. In large stockpot, bring water to boil, add vinegar and salt. Stir until salt is dissolved, then pour over cucumbers to fill jars leaving ½ inch "headspace." Seal. Immerse sealed jars in warm water in very large pot and bring to boil. Boil 15 minutes. Remove, allow to cool, and test seals. Store in refrigerator or cool spot (65 to 70 degrees F).

Cheese Pie (Hennie D's)

Ingredients:

  2 cups small curd cottage cheese or 2 cups farmer's cheese, drained, and mashed

  1 cup plus 2 T. granulated sugar

  ½ cup heavy cream

  4 large eggs, separated, room temperature

  pinch of salt

  2 T. all-purpose flour

  ½ t. freshly-squeezed lemon juice

  ½ t. pure vanilla extract

  ½ t. cream of tartar

Method:

  Preheat oven to 425 degrees F.

  In large bowl, combine mashed cottage cheese, 1 cup sugar, cream, egg yolks, flour, lemon juice, and vanilla extract. Mix well. In a separate bowl, beat egg whites until soft peaks form, add salt, 2 T. sugar, and cream of tartar and continue beating until stiff peaks form.

Fold beaten egg white mixture into cheese batter until smooth. Pour into cooled 9-inch piecrust (see recipe below). Bake for 15 minutes at 425 degrees F, then reduce oven to 350 degrees F and bake for an additional 25 minutes or until knife inserted in center comes out clean. Cool on rack, then refrigerate.

Cookie Crust for Cheese Pie

Ingredients:
¼ cup butter (½ stick), softened
¼ cup granulated sugar
1 egg yolk
1 cup all-purpose flour, sifted

Method:
Preheat oven to 400 degrees F.
Combine sugar with butter and egg yolk. Gradually mix in flour until mixture is crumbly. Press mixture into bottom and up sides of a deep-dish 9-inch pie plate. Bake at 400 degrees F until very lightly browned, but no more than 10 minutes; remove and cool in the pan.
Yield: 1 9-inch deep-dish pie

Matzos Batter Cakes (Mrs. Summer D's)

Ingredients:
½ cup matzo meal
1 T. sugar
1 t. salt, if desired
3 large eggs, beaten
¾ cup milk
¼ stick butter, or ½ cup oil if preferred

Method:
Combine matzo meal, sugar and salt; stir in eggs and milk. Allow mixture to rest for 10–15 minutes. Adjust to consistency of pancake batter, if necessary. Melt butter or oil in large skillet over medium heat until very hot. Drop mixture by tablespoonfuls carefully into skillet. Cook, turning once, about 1½–2 minutes on each side until browned. Remove from pan. Drain on paper towels. Serve with cinnamon sugar, preserves, sour cream, powdered sugar, or syrup.
Yield: About 10 3-inch pancakes

Matzos Cake

Ingredients:
  6 large eggs, at room temperature, separated
  Juice of 1 large lemon (about 4 T.)
  1 T. freshly grated lemon zest
  1 cup sugar
  ¾ cup matzo cake meal, sifted*

Method:
  Preheat oven to 325 degrees F.
  Beat the egg yolks well in a bowl. Add lemon juice and zest, mixing with a wooden spoon. In a clean bowl, beat egg whites until soft peaks form. Gradually add sugar to egg whites, beating until stiff peaks form. Gently fold in egg mixture. Fold in sifted cake meal, one tablespoon at a time. Grease bottom of 10-inch angel food cake or Bundt® pan. Pour batter into cake pan. Bake 40 to 50 minutes, or until top springs back when touched lightly and a skewer inserted in the center comes out clean. Invert the cake to cool completely.
  Yield: 1 10-inch cake
  *Note: Matzo cake meal is available in larger chain grocery stores and at kosher markets.

Miss Hoffheimer's Straben

Sträuben (Funnel Cakes)
Ingredients:
  2 cups all-purpose flour
  2 T. sugar
  1 t. salt
  1½ cups milk
  4 large eggs, separated
  1 t. vanilla extract, optional
  Vegetable oil, for frying
  Powdered sugar or fruit compote, for topping, optional

Method:
  Combine flour, sugar and salt. In a separate bowl or large measuring cup, mix together milk, egg yolks and vanilla. Then add

milk mixture to flour mixture, stirring with a wire whisk until smooth and blended. Beat egg whites until stiff peaks form. Using a spatula or rubber scraper, fold egg whites into batter until blended. Batter will be thick but pourable. Heat 1–2 inches of oil in a heavy frying pan to 350 to 375 degrees F on a deep-fat thermometer. Transfer batter to a pastry bag fitted with a number 12 tip or pour into a zip-closed plastic bag. Cut a very small hole in one corner of the plastic bag and carefully pipe batter or drizzle batter using a small funnel into hot oil using a circular pinwheel motion starting at the middle of the pan. Fry until cake's surface is covered with bubbles. Using tongs or spatula, very carefully turn cake over. Continue to fry until light brown, about 1 minute. Remove cake from oil; drain on paper towels. When cool, transfer to a plate; dust with powdered sugar or top with fruit compote, if desired. Continue until all of the batter is used.

Yield: About 10 funnel cakes, depending on size of frying pan

Notes

Introduction

1. *Zion in the Valley* (1997), 58; see also Ben-Ur, *Sephardic Jews in America,* 47.

2. For millennia, the precepts of *kashrut* (dietary laws) have governed the selection, preparation, and consumption of food for the observant Jew. These rules dictated what could be eaten, when, and which animals were *kasher* (clean) or *treif* (unclean). Pigs, horses, and mules were unclean. Cattle and other animals that chewed their cud as well as domesticated chickens, geese, ducks, and turkeys were permissible, but only if killed according to established ritual rules.

3. According to Khane-Faygl Turtletaub, Ph.D., who translated Esther Schechter's recipe for Huckleberry Pie and Sauce, the recipe is actually written in English using Yiddish characters.

Chapter 1. The Early Jewish Presence in the Middle West

1. Ehrlich, *Zion in the Valley* (1997), 3–4, calls Solomon "Solomons." However, according to the 1905 *Publications of the American Jewish Historical Society*, on page 49, one Levy Solomons of Montreal was a merchant trading at Mackinac about the same time as Ezekiel Solomon. On the other hand, on page 116, Sharfman in *The Frontier Jews,* calls those same two men "Ezekiel Solomons" and "Levi Solomon."

2. Drake, *Indian captivities,* 296, 301.

3. American Jewish Historical Society (1905), 49, 55.

4. Ehrlich, *Zion in the Valley* (1997), 6.

5. See M. S. Nassaney's article: "Identity Formation at a French Colonial Outpost in the North American Interior," *International Journal of Historical Archaeology* 12 (December 2008): 297–318, for a list of edible flora and fauna found during archaeological excavations at a nearby French fort.

6. Sharfman, *The Frontier Jews,* 112–113.

7. See St. Louis Mercantile Library collection M-73: Joseph Philipson Business

Account Book, December 13, 1807, to July 31, 1809, content listed online at http://www.umsl.edu/mercantile/special_collections/slma-073.html; Ehrlich (1997), 14–15.

8. Advertisement, George L. Ward, *Alton* (Illinois) *Telegraph*, 1840. Available online: http://www.museum.state.il.us/exhibits/athome/1800/clues/1geo.htm.

9. Glazer, *The Jews of Iowa*, 177, 162; see also the Western Historical Company's *The History of Dubuque County, Iowa, Containing a History of the County, Its Cities, Town, &c.*, 838.

10. Glazer, 162.

11. Levy, "Pioneering in La Crosse," 201.

12. Ibid., 203–204.

13. Hirshheimer, "Jewish Settlers of La Crosse Prior to 1880," 78.

14. Ibid., 79; during the early nineteenth century, certain Jewish religious leaders in Central Europe began a movement to modernize Judaism. Reform Judaism spread to America with the German immigrants. By the 1880s, more than 90 percent of the Jews in the United States belonged to Reform congregations. Reform Jews could make personal decisions about whether to keep kosher (*kashrut*) or not; many chose not to keep the older, traditional dietary laws.

15. Ullmann, quoted in Schloff, *And Prairie Dogs Weren't Kosher*, [37].

16. Ullmann, "Pioneer Homemaker," 96–97.

17. Ibid., 98.

18. Ullmann, "Spring Comes to the Frontier," 195.

19. Ibid., 195, 200.

20. Berman and Schloff, *Jews in Minnesota*, 4; Mount Zion Hebrew Association was established in 1856 as an Orthodox congregation; the history of Mount Zion is available online at http://www.mzion.org/Secondary.cfm?PageID=10200.

21. In 1817, Jonas became Cincinnati's first permanent Jewish settler. See "The Jews in Ohio," *The Occident and American Jewish Advocate* 1 (February 1844).

22. Sharfman, *The Frontier Jews*, 183; "Jewish Ohioans," The Ohio Historical Society, 1–2.

23. "Only Land Free of Persecution," *Chicago Daily Tribune* (May 3, 1942), 16.

24. Cutler, *The Jews of Chicago*, 10–11.

25. American Jewish Historical Society (1908), 120.

26. Zeublin, "The Chicago Ghetto," 91.

27. American Jewish Historical Society (1908), 119.

28. Schonberg, "'Jewish Heritage of Wayne County' exhibit evokes nostalgia," 1–2.

29. Duffy, *Reid Duffy's Guide to Indiana's Favorite Restaurants*, 38.

30. A. D. R., correspondent for the *New York Tribune*, "From the Missouri to the Pacific," in San Francisco (California) *Daily Evening Bulletin* (July 28, 1865), col. A.

31. Nielsen, n.p.; "Boarding and Lodging," *Chicago Daily Tribune* (October 14, 1872), 8.

32. "Pioneers," ThinkQuest, 1999. Available on-line: http://library.thinkquest.org/6400/supply%20list.htm.

33. Fanny Brooks, Jewish Women's Archive, "JWS-Discover-In Focus: Jewish Women-Western Pioneers-Fanny Brooks."

34. Carvalho, *Incidents of Travel and Adventure*, 21.

35. Ibid., 31.

36. Ibid., 107.

37. Ibid., 113–114; horses and mules are not considered "clean" animals to eat according to Leviticus 11:2–3 because they do not have cloven hooves or chew their cud, like cows.

38. Ibid., 86–87.

39. In 1912, several men sent to Flint, Michigan, by the Industrial Removal Organization (IRO) complained that no boardinghouse in the city served kosher meals, according to Fairies and Hanflik, *Jewish Life in the Industrial Promised Land*, 29.

40. Jane Grey Swisshelm, "The Corbins and the Jews," Letter to the Editor, *Chicago Daily Tribune* (July 31, 1879), 6.

Chapter 2. Midwest City Life:
The Sephardim and the German-Jews

1. "Sephardim and Ashkenazim," *Milwaukee Sentinel* (January 8, 1899), 10; this same article is quoted in the *New York Times*, The Pall Mall Magazine section, attributed to Professor W. Z. Ripley (February 5, 1899), 21.

2. Gloria Asher, quoted in Ben-Ur, *Sephardic Jews in America*, 1–2.

3. Gail Rosenblum, "All Passovers are not alike," (Minneapolis-St. Paul) *Star Tribune* (April 16, 2008), 1–2. Available online: www.startribune.com/lifestyle/taste/17804154.html.

4. Sylvia Nahamias Cohen, "The History of the Etz Chaim Sephardic Congregation and Community of Indianapolis, Indiana," n.d. Available online: http://www.etzchaimindy.org/history.htm; see also "The Indianapolis Sephardic Jewish Congregation and Community: An Oral History Account, 2000," Collection #M 0907, CT 2016–2025, Manuscript and Visual Collections Department, William Henry Smith Memorial Library, Indiana Historical Society.

5. Emily Frankenstein, diary entry, August 20, 1911, included in Irma Rosenthal Frankenstein papers, Chicago Jewish Archives, Spertus Institute of Jewish Studies.

6. Stephanie Caraway, "Cooking With Stephanie," Etz Chaim Sephardic Congregation Newsletter 21, no. 3 (May/June 2008), n.p.

7. Cohen, "Sephardic Treats," 8.

8. Cutler, *The Jews of Chicago*, 90.

9. Zenner, *A Global Community*, 149–151.

10. "Schools for Babies," *Chicago Daily Tribune* (September 23, 1894), 33.

11. Woods and Kennedy, eds., *Handbook of Settlements*, 78.

12. Jane Eddington, "Spring Brings Delicacies for the Table: Asparagus, Artichokes, and Tender Greens," The Tribune Cook Book [column], *Chicago Daily Tribune* (March 31, 1929), F10.

13. Davis and Wood, "The Food of the Immigrant in Relation to Health," 25.

14. Joseph Israel, personal communication, June 2, 2009.

15. Joseph Israel, personal communication, June 4, 2009.

16. Joseph Israel, quoted in Tamar Fenton's article, "Sephardic Jews connect in Twin Cities," *American Jewish World News* (April 8, 2009), n.p. Available online: http://www.ajwnews.com/archives/category/news/page/2.

17. Steinberg, *Learning to Cook in 1898*, 10.

18. Ibid., 55.

19. Ferber, *A Peculiar Treasure*, 67.

20. Eliassof, "The Jews of Illinois," 283.

21. Ehrlich, *Zion in the Valley* (1997), 82.

22. "Bohemian Israelites in Wisconsin," *The Occident and American Jewish Advocate* 7 (September 1849): 330–331. Available online: http://www.jewish-history .com/Occident/volume7/sep1849/news.html.

23. Ehrlich, *Zion in the Valley* (1997), 84, 58; Ehrlich, *Zion in the Valley* (2002), 178.

24. Irma Rosenthal Frankenstein, undated diary entry, 1941, Irma Rosenthal Frankenstein papers; all Irma's recipes can be found in Steinberg, *Learning to Cook*; other recipes are as attributed or from the authors' personal collection of manuscript cookbooks.

25. See, for example, Henriette Davidis, *Praktisches Kochbuch für die Deutschen in Amerika*, compiled for the United States from the thirty-fifth German ed. (Milwaukee: C.N. Caspar [etc.], 1897). Davidis's cookbook has recently been republished as *Pickled Herring and Pumpkin Pie*, with an introduction by L. A. Pitschmann (Madison, Wisconsin: Monographs of the Max Kade Institute, 2003).

26. Brin, *Bittersweet Berries*, 20–21.

27. M. F. K. Fisher, "An Alphabet for Gourmets," *Gourmet* (April 1949), GOURMET magazine 1940s Archive, n.p. Available online: http://www.gourmet.com/ magazine/1940s/1949/04/alphabetforgourmets_k-l?printable=true.

28. Schankerman, "Cooking with Doe," 7.

29. See "Recipes" at www.sephardim.com/html/recipes.html.

30. It was not the ready availability of citrus fruits that contributed to their scarcity, per se, but their cost in Europe. The wealthy might have been able to afford to buy citrus fruits whenever they wanted if they were willing to pay the price, but the less wealthy may have had to save up to purchase them for special occasions. Lemons, with two crops per year, were grown in large numbers in California, Florida, the Middle East, Spain, and Italy, but import-export taxes were high. These tariffs eventually reached 83 percent in Germany, 53 percent in France, and 66 percent in Italy in 1931, according to Findlay and O'Rourke, *Power and Plenty*, 448. Prior to the twentieth century, import tariffs across Europe had regularly been above the 35 percent level. See also Ashley's 1904 book, *Modern Tariff History*.

31. Ehrlich, *Zion in the Valley* (1997), 83.

32. Joseph Israel, personal communication, June 4, 2009.

Chapter 3. Eastern European Jews in the Cities

1. "Cook Book of Past and Present," *Chicago Daily Tribune* (June 6, 1909), F3.

2. Rabbi Adolph Rosentreter, manuscript marriage record for Ruth Ginsburg and Isadore F. Dunie, September 21, 1913, n.p.

3. E. Atkinson, "The Art of Cooking," *Manufacturer and Builder*, 22, 1:18–19 (January 1890) and 22, 2:40–41 (February 1890); see also "A Cheap but Good Stove: The Device of Miss Alberta Thomas, and Will Do Delicious Cooking with Little Coal," *New York Times* (May 16, 1897), 14, for details about a coal-powered "copy-cat" version of the Aladdin oven that cost $5.00 to build.

4. *The Duplex Cook Book*, 4–7.

5. Carol Christian, personal communication, June 8, 2009; June 14, 2009.

6. Herbert S. Schechter, personal communication, June 29, 2009.

7. Bette Dworkin, personal communication, April 23, 2009.

8. Judy Dworkin, personal communication, April 23, 2009.

9. "Jewish Immigrants Coming," *St. Louis Globe-Democrat* (September 25, 1881), 9.

10. Schloff, *And Prairie Dogs Weren't Kosher*, 43.

11. "The Jews at Milwaukee," *Chicago Daily Tribune* (July 2, 1882), 4.

12. Mrs. Simon Kander (Lizzie Black), "Giving you a picture of the times," ca. 1920, included in Mrs. Simon Kander's papers, Writings, n.d., Wisconsin State Historical Society, Milwaukee Mss Coll DN, Box 3, Folder 6.

13. Rockaway, *Words of the Uprooted*, 6.

14. "To Settle in the United States," *Chicago Daily Tribune* (May 23, 1902), 3.

15. "Saturday Night in Chicago: How It Is Spent on the Best Known Street in the World," *Chicago Daily Tribune* (January 12, 1908), 8E.

16. For the musical score of *Bulbes*, see Edelman's *Discovering Jewish Music*, 33.

17. "The Jewish Immigration," *Chicago Daily Tribune* (January 19, 1903), 6.

18. For a discussion of food preservation through the ages, see Shephard's *Pickled, Potted, and Canned*.

19. Yitschok Levine, "Louis Raskas of St. Louis," *Jewish Press* (February 1, 2007), 1–3.

20. See Digital image ID # ppmsca .05651, Library of Congress Prints and Photographs Division, in the on-line exhibit: "From Haven to Home: 350 Years of Jewish Life in America," 2004. Available on-line: http://www.loc.gov/exhibits/haventohome/.

21. U.S. Department of Agriculture, Circular 109 (1918).

22. Jane Eddington, "Patriotic Cottage Cheese," The Tribune Cook Book [column], *Chicago Daily Tribune* (April 23, 1918), 14.

Chapter 4. Jews in Small Towns, on the Farms, and In-Between

1. *American Hebrew* (February 13, 1891), quoted in Rockaway, *Words of the Uprooted*, 6.

2. Levy, "Agriculture, a Most Effective Means to Aid Jewish Poor," n.p.

3. Witkin, Oral history (February 17, 1977), Tape 143A, Part 2.

4. Weissbach, *Jewish Life in Small-Town America*, 55.

5. Rockaway, *Words of the Uprooted*, 13.

6. Kahn, "Jewish Agricultural and Industrial Aid Society, New York," 87.

7. Etheldoris Stein Grais, personal communication, May 12, 2009.

8. "Can You See the Point?" *Chicago Defender* (December 9, 1911), 3.

9. Levy, "Agriculture, a Most Effective Means to Aid Jewish Poor," 100.

10. "Jewish Settlers in Iowa," *Iowa Pathways*, n.d., 1–2. Available online: http://www.iptv.org/iowapathways/myPath.cfm?ounid=ob_0001561; "Wisconsin Jewish history," n.p., n.d. Available online: http://www.wisconsinhistory.org/dictionary/index.asp?action=view&term_id=11484&term_type_id=1&term_type_text=People&letter=J; see also Max Rosenthal, "Agricultural Colonies in the United States," n.p., n.d. Available online: http://www.jewishencyclopedia.com/view.jsp?artid=909&letter=A; "Will Aid the Refugees," *Chicago Daily Tribune* (August 30, 1891), 6.

11. Meckler, *Papa Was a Farmer*, 45.

12. See Advertisement. Stanton's Foreign Fruits, Wines, Liquors, Fine Groceries, *Chicago Daily Tribune* (December 31, 1861), 4.

13. Advertisement for Humphreys' Homeopathic Dyspepsia Pills, *Chicago Daily Tribune* (May 24, 1859) 5; the same ad appeared in the *New York Times* on May 17, 1859, 5.

14. Ben Rosenberg, quoted in Schnapik, "Jewish Farmers of the Benton Harbor Area," 4–5.

15. Meckler, *Papa Was a Farmer*, 78–79.

16. Advertisement, Paine's Celery Compound, *Chicago Daily Tribune* (April 25, 1897), 6.

17. Mulvany, "Coal-Oil as a Medicinal Agent," 280–281; see also Bethard, *Lotions, Potions, and Deadly Elixirs*, 153.

18. See "As We Remember," by Jeanette Goldhar and Frances Nelson, *Indiana Jewish History* 28 (June 1992): 2–45, for a history of the Jews in Gary, Indiana.

19. Paula Dee, personal communication, April 13, 2009; June 24, 2009.

20. Kittredge, ed., *Housekeeping Notes*, 35.

21. Irma Rosenthal Frankenstein, diary entries, April 27, 1937; April 30, 1937; May 1, 1937, Irma Rosenthal Frankenstein papers.

22. Although the refrigerated car may have been invented earlier (around 1840) and elsewhere (see http://www.history-magazine.com/refrig.html), and could only be used during cold months because the ice melted, Dr. A. W. Bitting related this somewhat inaccurate information to a news reporter, who conveyed it in "After the meal they called in the cook to felicitate her," *Chicago Daily Tribune* (April 8, 1932), 26; see also Pillsbury's *No Foreign Foods*, 11, 89, and Kreidberg's, *Food on the Frontier*, 115–141, for data about preserving meats.

23. "Jewish Settlers in Iowa," 2.

24. Meckler, *Papa Was a Farmer*, 197.

25. Ruderman, "Memoirs of a Jewish Farmer in Indiana," 18; see also "Jewish Farmers of the Benton Harbor Area, by Ceil Pearl Schnapik, in *Michigan Jewish History* 2 (June 1983) for the history of Jewish farmers in that area.

26. Blanche Halpern Goldberg's oral history was collected in 1976. Portions of it appear in the Jewish Historical Society of the Upper Midwest's online exhibit "Unpacking on the Prairie: Jewish Women in the Upper Midwest." Available online: http://www.jhsum.org/jewishwomenexhibit/inside7.asp.

27. Ornstein-Galicia, "A Jewish Farmer in America," 44.

28. Ibid., 46.

29. Ibid., 47.

30. Weissbach, *Jewish Life in Small-Town America,* 36.

31. Myrtice Crews, quoted in Jones, *Mama Learned Us to Work,* 27.

32. Rabbi Isaac Meyer Wise, quoted in Marcus, *Memoirs of American Jews: 1775–1865,* 106–107.

33. Bernard Baum, quoted in Endelman, "Preserving Your Community History," 11.

34. Anonymous, "Pack on my back," 1.

35. Weissbach, *Jewish Life in Small-Town America,* 107.

36. Anonymous, "Pack on my back," 4–6, 9.

37. "Rapid Decrease in Number of Jewish Peddlers," *Chicago Daily Tribune* (March 31, 1901), 37.

38. Witkin, Oral interview (February 17, 1977), Tape 143A, Part 1.

39. Kraut, "The Butcher, The Baker, The Pushcart Peddler," 71.

40. "How a Jew Can Find a Jew," *Chicago Daily Tribune* (November 15, 1891), 33.

41. "Our Russian Exiles," *Chicago Daily Tribune* (July 19, 1891), 26.

42. "Key to the Maps," *Chicago Daily Tribune* (May 20, 1900), 45.

43. Bear, *A Mile Square of Chicago,* 328.

44. "Popcorn," *Chicago Daily Tribune* (December 2, 1883), 16; see also Grace R. Clarke, "Brass Band Draws Worshippers to Church Service on Lawn," *Chicago Daily Tribune* (August 28, 1910), B6, for mention of a Jewish popcorn peddler.

45. "Peanuts and Oranges," *Chicago Daily Tribune* (March 29, 1869), 0_4.

46. "Pretzels Made By Hand," *Atchison* (Kansas) *Daily Champion* (October 18, 1889), 3.

47. Elias Tobenkin, "At the Penny Soda Fountains Where the Poor Children of the Ghetto Refresh Themselves," *Chicago Daily Tribune* (August 2, 1908), D1.

48. Esbel and Schatz, *Jewish Maxwell Street Stories,* 91.

49. Kraig, *Hot Dog,* 23, 41.

50. See Carolyn Eastwood's *Chicago's Jewish Street Peddlers* (Chicago: Chicago Jewish Historical Society, 1991).

Chapter 5. How to Cook . . .

1. Krug, "The Yiddish Schools in Chicago," 277.

2. Ibid., 278.

3. "Soup for the Poor," *Chicago Daily Tribune* (November 5, 1893), 14; "Soup for a Penny," *Morning Oregonian* (November 8, 1893), 4.

4. "The Young Men's Hebrew Association of Cincinnati," *Daily Picayune* (November 26, 1890), 4.

5. Ehrlich, *Zion in the Valley* (2002), 58.

6. "Ghetto Tires of Invasion," *Chicago Daily Tribune* (June 18, 1906), 11.

7. "City's Social Settlement," *Chicago Daily Tribune* (November 23, 1910), A8; see also "Solving the Problem," *Chicago Daily Tribune* (November 1, 1891), 33.

8. "Racial Customs Declared Cause of Sick Babies," *Chicago Daily Tribune* (February 10, 1919), 9.

9. W. O. Atwater, quoted in "Diet of Chicago Poor," *Chicago Daily Tribune* (January 7, 1899), 1.

10. "Cook Book of Past and Present," *Chicago Daily Tribune* (June 6, 1909), F3.

11. "Women Being Taught How to Cook," *Chicago Daily Tribune* (January 3, 1895), 9; "Teaching Ghetto Children to Keep House," *Chicago Daily Tribune* (December 7, 1902); "Menu of Four Dishes," *Chicago Daily Tribune* (March 15, 1895), 3.

12. Mrs. Simon Kander (Lizzie Black), "The Settlement President's Report," March 27, 1900–March 27, 1901, included in Mrs. Simon Kander (Lizzie Black) papers, Wisconsin State Historical Society, Milwaukee Mss Coll DN, Settlement House Papers, 1900–1915, Box 3, Folder 5, 2–3.

13. "Defer to the Jewish Laws," *Chicago Daily Tribune* (April 19, 1904), 3; a prominent Chicago gynecologist connected with the Lying-In Maternity Hospital and the Chicago Public Schools Management Committee, E. C. Dudley often expressed opinions quoted in the *Chicago Daily Tribune*; these ranged from his fears that bicycle riding might be injurious to young women to interpreting school laws and public policies.

14. Cooley, *Teaching Homes Economics*, 254.

15. Kathleen McLaughlin, "Build Cakes and Character in Domestic Art Courses," *Chicago Daily Tribune* (November 13, 1931), 25.

16. "Jewish Girls' Mission," *Milwaukee Sentinel* (June 13, 1897), 1E.

17. "Only Kosher Cooking School in West," *Milwaukee Sentinel* (February 5, 1899), 8.

18. Mrs. Simon Kander (Lizzie Black), "Cooking lesson book-1898, Kosher Cooking School," manuscript notebook, included in the Mrs. Simon Kander (Lizzie Black) papers, Wisconsin State Historical Society, Milwaukee Mss DN Box 1, Folder 10.

19. Fritz, "Lizzie Black Kander & Culinary Reform in Milwaukee," 43.

20. Ibid.

21. Myrtle Baer, Transcript, oral interview, February 14, 1963, included in Myrtle Baer papers, Wisconsin Sate Historical Society, University of Wisconsin, Milwaukee, Milwaukee SC 63, 2.

22. Fritz, Abstract; see also the Wisconsin [State] Historical Society website that states "The first edition of The Settlement Cookbook appeared in 1901 and was an immediate success." Available online: www.wisconsinhistory.org/topics/kander/index.asp.

23. Kander and Schoenfeld, *The Settlement Cook Book*, 105.

24. Steinberg, *Learning to Cook in 1898*, 36–37.

25. M. F. K. Fisher, "How Victoria Set the American Table: Food: The Arts (fine and culinary) of 19th-Century America," *New York Times* (September 15, 1974), 315.

26. "A Lady" [Judith Cohen Montefiore], *The Jewish Manual*, 59.

27. Levy, *Jewish Cookery Book*, 38–39.

28. Hale, *Godey's Magazine*, 155.

29. "How to Make Mushroom Catsup," *Chicago Daily Tribune* (September 28, 1895), 16.

30. Davidis, *Pickled Herring and Pumpkin Pie*, 112.

31. Ibid., 98–99.

32. Farmer, *The Boston Cooking-School Cook Book*, 197.

33. Meeker, "Recipe," 515.

34. Moritz and Kahn, *The Twentieth Century Cook Book*, 119.

35. Saint-Évremond, quoted in "Philosophy of the Table," *New York Times* (August 17, 1879), 4.

36. Advertisement, Dr. Price's Delicious Flavoring Extracts, "The Wolf in Sheep's Clothing," *Chicago Daily Tribune* (September 24, 1891), 6.

37. Crumpacker, *The Old-Time Brand-Name Cookbook*, xvi.

38. See Bertha Wood's *Foods of the Foreign Born in Relation to Health* (Boston: Whitcomb & Barrow, 1922).

39. Addams, *Twenty Years at Hull-House with Autobiographical Notes*, 131.

40. Lincoln, "Extracts from Cookery," 141–142.

41. Ellen H. Richards, quoted in "Talks on Pure Food," *Chicago Daily Tribune* (October 21, 1893), 9; Richards, 11, 134–139.

42. Crumpacker, xvii.

43. Sinclair, "What Life Means to Me," 594.

44. Goodwin, *The Pure Food, Drink, and Drug Crusaders, 1879–1914*, 15.

45. *The Cambrian*, 287.

46. *The Iowa Citizen* (November 13, 1891), 3.

47. Haber, *From Hardtack to Home Fries*, 67.

48. John Harvey Kellogg, quoted in "Change Is Needed," *Chicago Daily Tribune* (February 12, 1894), 8.

49. Kellogg, *Science in the Kitchen*, 29.

50. Raymond, *The Social Settlement Movement in Chicago*, 90.

51. See display advertisements for the Battle Creek Sanitarium Health Food Company, *Chicago Daily Tribune* (May 7, 1899), 31; (May 14, 1899), 12.

52. William J. Gibson, testimony in front of the 1913 Tariff Schedule Hearings.

53. Mrs. Branton, "The Survival of the Best," speech or essay, ca. May 1918, Mrs. Simon Kander (Lizzie Black) Papers, 1873–1960, Wisconsin State Historical Society, Milwaukee Mss DN, Box 3, Folder 5, 3–4.

54. "How Domestic Science Is Prolonging the Life of Man," *Chicago Daily Tribune* (April 5, 1903), A5.

55. "Proscribing Sweets and Sweetmeats," *New York Times* (August 20, 1877), 8.

56. C. M. W. "Adulterated Spices," *Chicago Daily Tribune* (October 14, 1876), 11.

57. Hoodless, *Public School Domestic Science*, 50.

58. Julia Child, quoted on the Culinary Trust website: http://theculinarytrust.org/programs/endangered-treasures/.

Chapter 6. When to Cook . . .

1. The six items traditionally placed on the *Seder* plate are two kinds of bitter herbs, symbolizing the harshness of the Israelites' life under Egyptian slavery; *haroset*, a sweet mix of apples, nuts, cinnamon, and wine, symbolizing the mortar the Hebrews used to bond bricks while captive in Egypt; a vegetable other than bitter herbs that is dipped into salt; a lamb shank or chicken neck or wing that symbolizes the Passover sacrifice; and a hard-boiled, roasted and browned egg that symbolizes the sacrifices made at the Temple in Jerusalem.

2. Karen Silverstein, film, *Gefilte Fish.*

3. Etheldoris Stein Grais, personal communication, May 12, 2009.

4. Judy Dworkin, personal communication, May 20, 2009.

5. Sokolov, *Fading Feast*, 56–61.

6. Jane Eddington, "Tempting Meals for the Week," *Chicago Daily Tribune* (December 19, 1926), E6; Jane Eddington, "The Goose as a Bird," The Tribune Cook Book [column], *Chicago Daily Tribune* (September 25, 1927), 14.

7. Rose Mass, "Cholent," in *From Generation to Generation III*, n.p.

8. Corrine Keslin, "Pot Roast," *Kosher Cooking*, n.p., archived in the Eloise and Elliot Kaplan Family Jewish History Center collections, Minneapolis.

9. Betty Husney, "Syrian Spinach Souffle," in *Adath Caters to You*, 92.

10. Marilyn Feder, "Carrot Tzimmes," in *Kosher Cooking*, n.p.

11. Anonymous, "Mock Strudel," manuscript recipe included with *Kosher Cooking.*

12. Jane Eddington, "Apples Galore," *Chicago Daily Tribune* (August 11, 1911), 8.

13. Jane Eddington, "Fruit Combinations," *Chicago Daily Tribune* (August 14, 1914), 8.

14. "The Randalia News: Notes of Interest," *Oelwein* (Iowa) *Daily Register* (April 25, 1916), 4.

15. "Household Hints," Madison, Wisconsin's *Capital Times* (December 22, 1920), 5.

16. Mrs. A. C. R. "Well-Known Candle Salad," Letter to Sally Lunn, Editor, "Household Discoveries," *Chicago Daily Tribune* (September 27, 1929), 33; Mary Meade, "Adventures in Salads," *Chicago Daily Tribune* (August 20, 1933), D3; Joanne Will. "Food Customs That Proclaim a 2,200-Year-Old Miracle," *Chicago Tribune* (December 13, 1979), D2; Mary Pickett, "Jews Around the World Celebrate Hanukkah," *Post Standard* (December 3, 1980), 29; see also Shapiro, *Perfection Salad*, 90–96.

17. Joseph Israel, personal communication, June 16, 2009.

18. Annabel Cohen, "Sephardic Treats," 8. Reproduced with permission.

19. Herbert S. Schechter, personal communication, June 30, 2009.

20. Herbert S. Schechter, personal communication, June 29, 2009.

21. Esther Schechter, "Huckleberry Pie [and Sauce for Pie]." The Nathan and Theresa Berman Upper Midwest Jewish Archives. Cookbooks [collection]. DO1 S 14CA (114c). Manuscript, n.d., 67.

22. Translator's note reads: "In Yiddish transliteration the 'kh' is pronounced like the gutteral 'ch' in Loch Lomond."

23. Translator's note reads: "This word is written in 2 places with the word 'sweet' and the number '10' after it"; somewhat similar instances we located were in Brenda Weisberg Meckler's *Papa Was a Farmer*, on page 254, where she reports her mother had once asked an English-speaking neighbor how to make doughnuts; her mother replied, "She told me very slowly, and I wrote it down in Yiddish," however, this implies that Meckler's mother transliterated the English instructions into Yiddish, then wrote the recipe using Hebrew/Yiddish characters, whereas Schechter's recipe was written in English using Yiddish characters, and a comment by William L. Bernstein in *A Splendid Exchange: How Trade Shaped the World*, on page 5, that medieval traders/peddlers' records, called the Geniza Papers, found in Cairo were written in Arabic using Hebrew letters.

24. Ron Grossman, "Taste," *Chicago Tribune* (September 18, 1983), NW12.

Chapter 7. . . . And When Not to Bother

1. Herbert S. Schechter, personal communication, June 29, 2009.

2. Bette Dworkin, personal communication, April 23, 2009. All Bette's subsequent quotations were gathered on this same date.

3. "Children's Matzah Bakery Puts Focus on Jewish Soldiers," Chabad.org., Chabad-Lubavitch Media Center, n.d. Available online: http://www.chabad.org/news/photo_cdo/aid/655394/jewish/Childrens-Matzah-Bakery-Puts-Focus-on-Jewish-Soldiers.htm.

4. Joseph Israel, personal communication, July 6, 2009.

5. "Making Matzos," *Cleveland Herald* (March 25, 1884), 4.

6. "How Matzos Are Made," *Milwaukee Sentinel* (April 6, 1884), 7.

7. For the story of Manichewitz, see Nathan, *Jewish Cooking in America*, 107.

8. Jill Silverstein-Newman, in *Gefilte Fish*.

9. Elaine and Ronnie Pratzel, personal communication, May 27, 2009. All subsequent quotes attributed to them are from that same interview.

10. Aharon Morgan, personal communication, July 8, 2009.

11. "Jakes Deli," on www.citysearch.com. Available online: http://www.sortuv.com/49501-Details-Jakes-Delicatessen-Milwaukee-WI.aspx.

12. Brian Miller, personal communication, July 6, 2009.

13. Paul Barron coined the term "fast casual" in the late 1990s defining a restaurant where one could watch food being prepared, then bring it or have it brought to a table, but which did not offer "full table service."

14. Brian Miller, personal communication, July 9, 2009.

15. *Bon Appétit*, quoted in *The Eli's Cheesecake Company* commercial catalogue, [4].

16. Anita Gold, "Openers," *Chicago Tribune* (April 9, 1978), H8; Anita Gold's article quotes Eli as saying he bought his first restaurant in 1941, but Marc Schulman, Eli's son, stated it was 1940.

17. Ibid.

18. Patricia Tennison, "The Foods You Love to Hate—7 Deadly Sinners Turned Into Sure Winners," *Chicago Tribune* (June 18, 1987), Food Guide, 1.

19. Debbie Littmann Marchok, personal communication, June 30, 2009; Marc Schulman, personal communication, July 29, 2009; Marc also provided us with Eli's "Close but Not Quite" recipes for cheesecakes, chopped liver, as well as photographs of his father and himself, along with permission to reproduce them all.

20. The term, "culinary tourism" was coined by folklorist Lucy M. Long in 1998, in "Culinary Tourism: A Folkloristic Perspective on Eating and Otherness," *Southern Folklore* 55 (1998):181–204.

21. Ken Blakin, quoted in Seip, "Pure Imagination," 3.

22. For a history of French's mustards, see: www.frenchs.com/products/History .php.

23. Ogden Nash wrote a short poem titled "Mustard," in *Everyone but Thee and Me* (New York: Little, Brown, 1962), "I'm mad about mustard even on custard"; Culver Custard Company is known for creating unusual, whimsical custard tastes and even more whimsical names for those creations.

24. Brian Miller stated that Jake's food is "accessible to everyone of all races and socioeconomic groups," in Andy Tarnoff's article, "New Owner of Jake's doesn't change a thing . . . and that's why it's great," in OnMilwaukee.com (March 20, 2007), 3. Available online: www.onmilwaukee.com/dining/articles/jakes.html; from what we observed in the delis and bakeries we visited, and from what the owners told us, expanding their patron base beyond the "ethnic" market, is a goal shared by every one.

Chapter 8. Trends in the Heartland

1. Goldstein, "Will Matzoh Go Mainstream? Jewish Food in America," 2.

2. Aharon Morgan, personal communication, July 8, 2009. All subsequent quotations attributed to him were collected on the same date.

3. "History of the D'Arrigo Bros. Company." Available online: www.darrigony.com/ company_history.html; radio frequency FCC license assigned to D'Arrigo Brother California call letters: WQEW968. Available online: http://www.radioreference .com/apps/db/?action=fle&stid=6&en=D%20ARRIGO%20BROS%20OF%20 CALIFORNIA.

4. Introduction. *Specialties of Our House*, [1].

5. Ruth Jacob, "Broccoli Soup." Ibid., n.p.

6. Proust, *Swann's Way*, 65.

7. Sherri Day, "Forget Rye Bread, You Don't Have to Be Jewish to Eat Kosher," *New York Times* (June 28, 2003), C1.

8. "'Kosher' Meat: Why the Orthodox Jews Get Better Meat than the Average Christian," *Chicago Daily Tribune* (July 8, 1883), 9.

9. "Diseased Beef," article reprinted from the St. Louis *Republican*, *Chicago Daily Tribune* (June 4, 1883), 7.

10. "For the Jewish Table," *Chicago Daily Tribune* (November 13, 1887), 26; see

also the archival materials for the kosher-certification body, Vaad Hoeir of St. Louis, Boxes Box 10 f. 8–10. f.12, St. Louis Jewish Archives.

11. Gladys Huntington Bevans, "Common Sense and Knowledge Oppose Old Superstitions," *Chicago Daily Tribune* (April 14, 1928), 19.

12. Dorothy Masters, "Kosher Changes Meaning; Turned to Broader Use," *Chicago Daily Tribune* (October 20, 1933), 20.

13. "Kosher Products," Abstract, Mintel Food Service Market Report (June 2005). Available online: http://reports.mintel.com/sinatra/reports/display/id=121162.

14. "Mainstream," FoodWatch Trends, Home Page. Available online: http://www .foodwatchtrends.com.

15. Mrs. Aidner. "Calf's Foot Jelly." Interview and recipe. WLTH Yiddish Radio, "Voices of the Street," 1942. Translation provided by Yiddish Radio Project. Available online: http://www.yiddishradioproject.org/exhibits/packer/?pg=2.

16. Anonymous, "*Kishke.*" Interview and recipe. Ibid.

17. Anonymous, "Hungarian Goulash." Interview and recipe. Ibid.

18. Anonymous, "Bread Pudding." Interview and recipe. Ibid.

19. WGN Television listings for June 9, 1970, in *Chicago Tribune* (June 6, 1970), A12.

20. Stacey Schwartz, personal communication, July 29, 2009.

21. "Spertus Expands Kosher Catering Beyond Its Walls." Press Release (April 23, 2009), 2. Available online: http://74.125.95.132/search?q=cache:uohnzrWDK90J:www .spertus.

22. Ibid.

23. Waskow, *Down to Earth Judaism*, 118–129; see also Michael Y. Park, "Regulatory Food News and Trends-Kosher," in Food Services of America, 1–3. Available online: http://www.fsafood.com/; see Alan Cooperman's *Washington Post* article (July 7, 2007), "Eco-Kosher Movement Aims to Heed Tradition, Conscience," A01.

24. "Kosher Food Industry," *Kosher Today* (April 11, 2005). Available online: http://www.koshertoday.com/news/archive.asp?ItemID=3202&pcid=174&cid= 175&archive=yes.

25. David Rossi, vice president of marketing, R.A.B. Food Group, parent company of Manischewitz, quoted in Park, ibid., 3.

Bibliography

Manuscript Collections

The Nathan and Theresa Berman Upper Midwest Jewish Archives. Cookbooks. Collection D01 S 14CA (114c).

Irma Rosenthal Frankenstein. Papers. Chicago Jewish Archives, Spertus Institute of Jewish Studies. Collection No. 262, Accession No. 2004-5.

The Eloise and Elliot Kaplan Family Jewish History Center Collections, Minneapolis, Minnesota.

The Library of Congress. American Life Histories: Manuscripts from the Federal Writers' Project, 1936–1940.

Rabbi Adolph Rosentreter. Marriage Records 1911–1930, Book II; the Vaad Hoeir of St. Louis, Boxes Box 10 f. 8–10. f.12, St. Louis Jewish Archives. St. Louis, Missouri.

Louis Witkin. Wisconsin State Historical Society. Madison, Wisconsin. Oral history interview with Witkin, Louis. Call # Tape 143A. Shelf location MAD; sound Tape 143A Parts 1 and 2.

Myrtle Baer. Wisconsin State Historical Society. Milwaukee, Wisconsin. Baer, Myrtle. Papers, Milwaukee SC 63.

Mrs. Simon Kander (Lizzie Black). Papers, 1873–1960, Wisconsin State Historical Society, Milwaukee Mss Coll DN, Boxes 1, 3; Box 1, Folder 10; Box 3, Folder 5, 6.

Mrs. Branton. "The Survival of the Best," speech or essay, ca. May, 1918, in Mrs. Simon Kander (Lizzie Black) Papers, 1873–1960. Wisconsin State Historical Society, Milwaukee Mss DN, Box 3, Folder 5.

Published Sources

Addams, Jane. *Twenty Years at Hull-House with Autobiographical Notes*. New York: The Macmillan Company, 1912.

American Jewish Historical Society. *Publications of the American Jewish Historical Society* 13. Baltimore, Maryland: The Lord Baltimore Press, 1905.

———. *Publications of the American Jewish Historical Society* 11. Baltimore, Maryland: The Lord Baltimore Press, 1908.

Ashley, Percy. *Modern Tariff History: Germany-United States-France.* London: A. Murray. 1904.

"Aunt Babette" (Bertha F. Kramer). *Aunt Babette's Cook Book: Foreign and Domestic Receipts for the Household. (1889).* Chicago and Cincinnati: Bloch Publishing Company, circa 1889.

Baer, Myrtle. Papers. Oral interview February 14, 1963. Wisconsin State Historical Society. University of Wisconsin, Milwaukee. Milwaukee SC 63.

Bear, Marjorie Warville. *A Mile Square of Chicago.* Maywood, Illinois: TIPRAC, 2008.

Ben-Ur, Aviva. *Sephardic Jews in America: A Diasporic History.* New York and London: New York University Press, 2009.

Berman, Hyman, and Linda Mack Schloff. *Jews in Minnesota.* St. Paul: Minnesota Historical Society Press, 2002.

Bernstein, William J. *A Splendid Exchange: How Trade Shaped the World.* New York: Grove Press, 2008.

Bethard, Wayne. *Lotions, Potions, and Deadly Elixirs: Frontier Medicine in America.* Lanham, New York, Toronto, and Oxford: Taylor Trade Publishing, 2004.

Brin, Ruth F. *Bittersweet Berries: Growing Up Jewish in Minnesota.* Duluth, Minnesota: Holy Cow! Press, 1999.

Cambrian, The. Utica, New York: Thomas J. Griffiths Publisher, 1900.

Carvalho, Solomon Nunes. *Incidents of Travel and Adventure in the Far West with Colonel Frémont's Last Expedition.* New York: Derby & Jackson, 1860.

Cohen, Annabel, "Sephardic Treats." *Michigan Jewish History,* Jewish Historical Society of Michigan 33 (Winter 1992).

Cooley, Anna M. *Teaching Home Economics.* New York: Macmillan Company, 1919.

Crumpacker, Bunny. *The Old-Time Brand-Name Cookbook.* New York: Smithmark, 1998.

Cutler, Irving. *The Jews of Chicago: From Shtetl to Suburb.* Urbana and Chicago: University of Illinois Press, 1996.

Davidis, Henriette. *Pickled Herring and Pumpkin Pie,* with an introduction by Louis A. Pitschmann, translation of *Praktisches Kochbuch für die Deutschen in Amerika.* Madison, Wisconsin: The Max Kade Institute for German American Studies, 2003.

Davis, Michael B., Jr., and Bertha M. Wood. "The Food of the Immigrant in Relation to Health." *The Journal of Home Economics* 13 (1921).

Drake, Samuel Gardner. *Indian captivities, being a collection of the most remarkable narratives of persons taken captive by the North American Indians . . . to which are added, notes, historical, biographical, &c.* Boston: Antiquarian Bookstore and Institute, 1839.

Duffy, Reid. *Reid Duffy's Guide to Indiana's Favorite Restaurants: With a Recipe Sampler.* Bloomington: Indiana University Press, 2001.

Duplex Cook Book. Muncie, Indiana: The Duplex Mfg. Co., n.d. [circa 1910].

Edelman, Marsha Bryan. *Discovering Jewish Music.* Philadelphia: Jewish Publication Society, 2003.

Ehrlich, Walter. *Zion in the Valley: The Jewish Community of St. Louis (1807–1907)*. Vol. I. Columbia and London: University of Missouri Press, 1997.

———. *Zion in the Valley: The Jewish Community of St. Louis (The Twentieth Century)*, Vol. II. Columbia and London: University of Missouri Press, 2002.

Eli's Cheesecake Company, The. Commercial catalogue. *The Eli's Cheesecake Company*. Chicago: The Eli's Cheesecake Company, 2008.

Eliassof, Hermann. "The Jews of Illinois: Their religious and civic life, their charity and industry, their patriotism and loyalty to American institutions, from their earliest settlement in the State unto the present time." *Reform Advocate* (May 4, 1901), 283.

Endelman, Judith E. "Preserving Your Community History." *Indiana Jewish Historical Society* 19 (May 1985): 1–15.

Esbel, Shuli, and Roger Schatz. *Jewish Maxwell Street Stories*. Charleston, South Carolina: Arcadia Publishing, 2004.

Fairies, Nora, and Nancy Hanflik. *Jewish Life in the Industrial Promised Land, 1855–2005*. East Lansing: Michigan State University Press, 2005.

Farmer, Fannie Merritt. *The Boston Cooking-School Cook Book*, facsimile of 1896 edition. New York: Random House, 1997.

Ferber, Edna. *A Peculiar Treasure*. New York: Doubleday, Doran & Company, 1938.

Findlay, Ronald, and Kevin H. O'Rourke. *Power and Plenty: Trade, War, and the World Economy in the Second Millennium*. Princeton, New Jersey: Princeton University Press, 2007.

Frankenstein, Emily. Unpublished manuscript diaries, Chicago Jewish Archives, Spertus Institute of Jewish Studies, (August 11, 1911). Irma Rosenthal Frankenstein. Papers. Chicago Jewish Archives, Spertus Institute of Jewish Studies. Collection No. 262, Accession No. 2004-5.

Frankenstin, Irma. Diary entries, May 1, 1930; April 27, 1937; April 30, 1937; undated entry, 1941, Irma Rosenthal Frankenstein. Papers. Chicago Jewish Archives, Spertus Institute of Jewish Studies. Collection No. 262, Accession No. 2004-5.

Fritz, Angela. "Lizzie Black Kander & Culinary Reform in Milwaukee, 1880–1920." *Wisconsin Magazine of History* (Spring 2004): 36–49.

From Generation to Generation III. Congregation B'nai Amoona Sisterhood Cookbook. Kitchen-tested Kosher recipes. Kearney, Nebraska: Morris Press Cookbooks, 2008.

Glazer, Simon. *The Jews of Iowa: A Complete History and Accurate Account of Their Religion, Social, Economic and Educational Progress in this State . . .* Des Moines: Koch Brothers Printing, 1904.

Goldstein, Darra. "Will Matzoh Go Mainstream? Jewish Food in America." In *The Jewish Role in American Life: An Annual Review*, Vol. 4. Eds. Barry Glassner and Jeremy Schoenberg, 1–35. Los Angeles: USC Casden Center for the Study of Jewish Life in America, 2005. Available on-line: www.darragoldstein.com/matzoh.html.

Goodwin, Lorraine Swainston. *The Pure Food, Drink, and Drug Crusaders, 1879–1914*. Jefferson, North Carolina: McFarland & Company, Inc., 1999.

Grais, Etheldoris, and Maurine Shink, eds. *Adath Caters to You—All You Can Eat*. St. Paul: Adath Jerusalem Synagogue Sisterhood of AJS, 1983.

Haber, Barbara. *From Hardtack to Home Fries: An Uncommon History of American Cooks and Meals*. New York: The Free Press, 2002.

Hale, Sarah Josepha Buell, ed. "Catsups." *Godey's Magazine* 20–21 (1840): 155.

Hirshheimer, H. J. "Jewish Settlers of La Crosse Prior to 1880." *La Crosse County Historical Sketches*, series 2. La Crosse Historical Society (1935), 78–82.

Hoodless, Adelaide (Mrs. J.). *Public School Domestic Science*. Toronto: Copp, Clark Company, 1898.

Jewish Women's Archive. "JWS—Discover—In Focus: Jewish Women—Western Pioneers—Fanny Brooks." Available on-line: http://wja.org/discover/infocus/westernpioneers/fannybrooks.html.

Jones, Lu Ann. *Mama Learned Us to Work: Farm Women in the New South*. Chapel Hill: University of North Carolina Press, 2002.

Kahn, W. "Jewish Agricultural and Industrial Aid Society, New York." *Proceedings of the Second Annual National Conference of Jewish Charities*. Detroit: C. J. Krehbiel & Co.; Jewish Communal Service Association of North America, 1902, 83–96.

Kander, Mrs. Simon (Lizzie Black). "Cooking lesson book—1898, Kosher Cooking School." Papers, 1873–1960. Wisconsin State Historical Society, Milwaukee, Wisconsin, Milw Mss Coll DN, Box 1, Folder 10.

Kander, Mrs. Simon (Lizzie Black). "'The Settlement President's Report,' March 27, 1900-March 27, 1901." Papers, 1873–1960. "The Settlement," "Report of the Cooking Committee," Wisconsin State Historical Society, Milwaukee, Wisconsin, Milw Mss Coll DN, Box 3, Folder 5.

Kander, Mrs. Simon (Lizzie Black). Writings, undated, ca. 1920. "Giving you a picture of the times," Wisconsin State Historical Society, Milwaukee, Wisconsin, Milw Mss Coll DN, Box 3, Folder 6.

Kander, Mrs. Simon (Lizzie Black), and Mrs. Harry Schoenfeld. *The Settlement Cook Book: The Way to A Man's Heart*. Reprint. New York: Gramercy Publishing Company, 1903.

Kellogg, Ella Eaton. *Science in the Kitchen*. Chicago: Modern Medicine Publishing Co., 1893.

Kittredge, Mabel Hyde, ed. *Housekeeping Notes: How to Furnish and Keep House in a Tenement Flat*. Boston: Whitcomb & Barrows, 1911.

Kosher Cooking. Minneapolis, Minnesota: Women's League of B'nai Abraham Synagogue, 1962. The Eloise and Elliot Kaplan Family Jewish History Center Collections, Minneapolis, Minnesota.

Kraig, Bruce. *Hot Dog: A Global History*. London: Reaktion Press, 2009.

Kraut, Alan M. "The Butcher, The Baker, The Pushcart Peddler: Jewish Foodways and Entrepreneurial Opportunity in the East European Immigrant Community, 1880–1940." *Journal of American Culture* 6 (1983): 71–83.

Kreidberg, Marjorie. *Food on the Frontier: Minnesota Cooking from 1850 to 1900*. St. Paul: Minnesota Historical Society Press, 1975.

Krug, Mark M. "The Yiddish Schools in Chicago." In *Yivo Annual of Jewish Social Science*, IX, Ed. Koppel S. Pinson, 276–307. New York: Yiddish Scientific Institute—Yivo, 1954.

Levy, A. R. "Agriculture, A Most Effective Means to Aid Jewish Poor." In *Proceedings of the Second Annual National Conference of Jewish Charities*. Detroit: C. J. Krehbiel & Co; Jewish Communal Service Association of North America, 1902, 97–107.

———. "Jewish Farmers in America." *Reform Advocate* 28 (1904), n.p.

Levy, Esther. *Jewish Cookery Book, on Principles of Economy, adapted for Jewish Housekeepers*. Facsimile of 1871 edition. Garden Grove, California: Pholiota Press, Inc., 1982.

Levy, Fredericka Augusta. "Pioneering in La Crosse: Recollections of a Pioneer Woman of La Crosse." In *Washington Pioneering*. State Historical Society of Wisconsin (1912), n.p. Available online: Murphy Library University of Wisconsin at La Crosse: http://murphylibrary.uwlax.edu/digital/lacrosse/LevyWHS/217.htm.

Lincoln, Mary J. B. [Mrs. D. A.]. "Extracts from Cookery, or Art and Science versus Drudgery and Luck." In *The Congress of Women, Held in the Women's Building, World's Columbian Exposition, Chicago, U. S. A., 1893*, ed. MKO Eagle, 138–42. Chicago: Monarch, 1894.

Marcus, Jacob Rader. *Memoirs of American Jews: 1775–1865*. Vol. 2. Philadelphia: Jewish Publication Society of America, 1955.

Meckler, Brenda Weisberg. *Papa Was a Farmer: The Story of an Immigrant Jewish Family's Life in America's Heartland*. Chapel Hill, North Carolina: Algonquin Books of Chapel Hill, 1988.

Meeker, Mary. "Stewed Beefsteak." In *The Chicago Record Cook Book*. Chicago: The Chicago Record, 1896.

"A Lady" (Montifiore, Judith Cohen). *The Jewish Manual, or Practical Information in Jewish and Modern Cookery with a Collection of Valuable Hints Relating to the Toilette*. Facsimile of 1846 edition. Coldspring, New York: NightinGale Books, 1983.

Moritz, Mrs. C. F., and Adèle Kahn. *The Twentieth Century Cook Book*. 5th edition. New York: G. W. Dillingham Company, 1896.

Mulvany, John. "Coal-Oil as a Medicinal Agent." *British Medical Journal* (March 27, 1869): 280–281.

Nassaney, Michael S. "Identity Formation at a French Colonial Outpost in the North American Interior." *International Journal of Historical Archaeology* 12 (December 2008): 297–318.

Nathan, Joan. *Jewish Cooking in America*. New York: Alfred A. Knopf, 1996.

Nielsen, Lynn. "Tips to Stagecoach Travelers." Exploration in Iowa History Project (2003), 1–2. Available online: http://www.uni.edu/iowahist/Frontier_Life/Stagecoach/Stagecoach.htm.

Ornstein-Galicia, Jacob. "A Jewish Farmer in America." *Timeline* of the Ohio Historical Society (January/February 1995), 43–53.

Philipson, Joseph. Joseph Philipson Business Account Book, December 13, 1807, to July 31, 1809 (St. Louis Mercantile Library collection M-73). Available online: http://www.umsl.edu/mercantile/special_collections/slma-073.html.

Pillsbury, Richard. *No Foreign Food: The American Diet in Time and Place*. Boulder, Colorado: Westview Press, 1998.

Proust, Marcel. *Swann's Way*, C. K. Scott Moncrieff, trans. New York: The Modern Library, Inc., 1992.

Raymond, Josephine Hunt. *The Social Settlement Movement in Chicago*. Master's thesis. University of Wisconsin, 1897.

Richards, Ellen H. *Food Materials and Their Adulterations*. 3rd edition. Boston: Whitcomb and Barrows, 1906.

Rockaway, Robert A. *Words of the Uprooted: Jewish Immigrants in Early 20th Century America*. Ithaca and London: Cornell University Press, 1998.

Ruderman, Abe. "Memoirs of a Jewish Farmer in Indiana." *Indiana Jewish Historical Society* 19 (May 1985): 17–23.

Schankerman, Dorothy. "Cooking With Doe." Congregation Etz Chaim Newsletter 20 (May/June 2007).

Schechter, Esther. "Huckleberry Pie [and Sauce for Pie]." The Nathan and Theresa Berman Upper Midwest Jewish Archives. Minnesota Jewish Historical Society. Cookbooks [collection]. D01 S 14CA (114c). Manuscript, n.d., 67.

Schloff, Linda Mack. *And Prairie Dogs Weren't Kosher*. St. Paul: Minnesota Historical Society Press, 1996.

Schnapik, Ceil Pearl. "Jewish Farmers of the Benton Harbor Area." *Michigan Jewish History* 2 (June 1983): 3–9.

Schonberg, Marcia. "'Jewish Heritage of Wayne County' Exhibit Evokes Nostalgia." *Cleveland Jewish News* (May 1, 2003). Available online available: http://www.clevelandjewishnews.com/articles/2003/05/01/export18.

Seip, Shannon Payette. "Pure Imagination: A Look Inside the Magical Mind of Ella's Deli's Ken Balkin." *Dane County Lifestyles* (September 2008): 1–3.

Shapiro, Laura. *Perfection Salad: Women and Cooking at the Turn of the Century*. New York: The Modern Library, 2001.

Sharfman, Harold I. *The Frontier Jews: An Account of Jewish Pioneers and Settlers in Early America*. Secaucus, New Jersey: The Citadel Press, 1977; "Jewish Ohioans," The Ohio Historical Society (2009), 1–2. Available online: http://www.ohiohistorycentral.org/entry.php?rec=600&nm=Jewish-Ohioans.

Shepard, Sue. *Pickled, Potted, and Canned: How the Art and Science of Food Preserving Changed the World*. New York, London: Simon & Schuster, 2000.

Silverstein, Karen. *Gefilte Fish*. Film. (Ergo Media, Inc., Teaneck, New Jersey, 1988).

Sinclair, Upton. "What Life Means to Me." *Cosmopolitan* 41 (October 1906).

Sokolov, Raymond. *Fading Feast: A Compendium of Disappearing American Regional Foods*. Boston: David R. Godine, 1998.

Specialties of Our House. St. Louis: Shaare Zedek Women's League, 1994.

Steinberg, Ellen F. *Learning to Cook in 1898: A Chicago Culinary Memoir*. Detroit: Wayne State University Press, 2007.

"The Jews in Ohio." *The Occident and American Jewish Advocate* 1 (February 1844). Available online: http://www.jewish-history.com/Occident/volume1/feb1844/ohio.html.

Ullmann, Mrs. Joseph (Amelia). "Spring Comes to the Frontier." *Minnesota History* 33 (Spring 1953).

———. "Pioneer Homemaker." *Minnesota History* 34 (Autumn 1954).

U.S. Department of Agriculture. *Cottage Cheese Dishes.* Circular 109. Washington, D.C.: [U.S. Printing Office], 1918.

Ward, George L. *Alton* (Illinois) *Telegraph,* advertisement (1840). Available online: http://www.museum.state.il.us/ehibits/athome/1800/clues/1geo.htm.

Waskow, Arthur. *Down to Earth Judaism: Food, Money, Sex and the Rest of Life.* New York: William Morrow, 1995.

Weissbach, Lee Shai. *Jewish Life in Small-Town America: A History.* New Haven and London: Yale University Press, 2005.

Western Historical Company. *The History of Dubuque County, Iowa, Containing a History of the County, Its Cities, Town, &c.* Chicago, Illinois: Western History Company, 1880.

Witkin, Louis. Oral history interview with Louis Witkin (February 18, 1977). Wisconsin State Historical Society, Madison, Wisconsin. Tape 143A. Shelf location MAD; sound Tape 143A, Parts 1 and 2.

Woods, Robert A., and Albert J. Kennedy, eds. *Handbook of Settlements.* New York: Charities Publication Committee, 1911.

Zenner, Walter P. *A Global Community.* Detroit: Wayne State University Press, 2000.

Zeublin, Charles. "The Chicago Ghetto." In Jane Addams, *Hull-House Maps and Papers,* Chapter 5, New York: Thomas Y. Crowell & Co., 1895, 91–111. Available online: http://media.pfeiffer.edu/Iridener/DSS/Addams/hh5.html.

———. "Pack on my back." American Life Histories: Manuscripts from the Federal Writers' Project, 1936–1940, Item 46. Available online: http://memory.loc.gov/cgi- bin/query/r?ammem/wpa:@field(DOCID+@lit(wpa008010410)).

Index

ELLEN F. STEINBERG is a writer, researcher, and anthropologist as well as the author of *Learning to Cook in 1898: A Chicago Culinary Memoir*. Born and raised in Chicago, she currently lives in River Forest, Illinois.

JACK H. PROST is an associate professor of anthropology at the University of Illinois at Chicago. He has taught and written on the anthropology of cuisine and food taboos.

The University of Illinois Press
is a founding member of the
Association of American University Presses.

Designed by Jim Proefrock
Composed in 10.25/14 Minion Pro
with Archer display
by Jim Proefrock
at the University of Illinois Press
Manufactured by Sheridan Books, Inc.

University of Illinois Press
1325 South Oak Street
Champaign, IL 61820-6903
www.press.uillinois.edu